Ferrari
Road and Racing

Winston Goodfellow
and the Auto Editors of Consumer Guide®

Publications International, Ltd.

Louis Weber, CEO
Publications International, Ltd.
7373 North Cicero Avenue
Lincolnwood, Illinois 60712

Permission is never granted for commercial purposes.

Manufactured in China.

8 7 6 5 4 3 2 1

ISBN: 1-4127-1204-1

Library of Congress Control Number: 2005922657

The editors gratefully acknowledge those who supplied photography for this book:

Jan Borgfeldt; Valerie Brown and Bill Warner, Amelia Island Concours d'Elegance; Mirco DeCet; Ferrari S.p.A.; Ford Motor Company; Mitch Frumkin; The Winston Goodfellow Archives; Sam Griffith; Bill Killborn; Pete Lyons; Vince Manocchi; Doug Mitchel; Road America, Inc.; Simon Lewis Transport Books; Richard Spiegelman; Phil Toy; Nicky Wright.

The editors also express their thanks for the generous assistance of:

Steve Gordon, Vintage Auto Service; Paul Holleran, AutomobileForum.com; Brian Hoyt, Perfect Reflections; Charlie Inderbitzen Ranch; John McGovern, Epic Detail; Ed Nicholls, Laguna Seca Raceway; Patrick Ottis Company; Malcolm Page, The Mallya Collection; Julie Sebrankek, Road America, Inc.; Harold Wong, Ferrari Club Northern Califorina; Julie Yip.

CONTENTS

by Piero Ferrari

When I was in school, my father always pushed me to work on a farm or some other job. He wanted me to be in anything but motor racing.

I imagine he was saying this because, back when I was young, every year another driver died. He wanted to protect me from this fate. But then I proved to him I had a passion for cars and engines, which started with my first motorcycle at age 14. It had just 50cc, and I modified it for more horsepower.

My world changed the first time we visited the factory. We went out to a restaurant for dinner, and after that he took me over to the company. It was night, and everything was very quiet. He didn't say a word as we walked through the buildings, seeing the racing department and along the production line. I am sure my eyes were very big, looking at everything!

After that walk, I saw what I was missing—the tools! My passion was to touch them and understand them, to understand the pieces of the engine. I wanted to comprehend how they were made, designed, built, and machined.

When I look at where Ferrari is today, back then neither my father nor myself could ever imagine anything so big. It was really just a family business, and now Ferrari is a large company, an industry. The dimensions of everything are so very different.

Much of this success helped to build the myth and mystique of Ferrari, and vice-versa. I often ask myself what exactly makes Ferrari "Ferrari"? And every time I think about this, I find it such a difficult question to answer.

But some of the elements are quite clear. In the past there was endurance racing; today there is Formula 1. Even in countries where F1 isn't very popular, everyone knows about Ferrari and the cars we make. People just seem to inherently know Ferraris are desirable and exotic because each of our road cars has a strong personality. When they see a new Ferrari, a car never seen before, 99 percent of the people know it is a Ferrari and not something else. Somehow Ferraris look, and are, unique.

All this makes our history so vast and complex that I must say I cannot remember it all. So when Winston writes something, I find it worth reading. His research is thorough and insightful so it ends up an important document, one that reminds me of something or refreshes my memory on our history.

But there is much more to his words and photos, for they not just his "job," his work. They are his passion, and that may be what I appreciate most of all.

Author's Notes & Acknowledgements

This book is the result of years of research and hundreds of interviews with people involved in Ferrari, its subcontractors, and its competitors in Italy's gran turismo industry. With so much already written on Ferrari, the task was finding an approach that would appeal to both the neophyte and to the experienced collector or historian. The book was thus written so that if a first-timer was going to see a friend who owned one or more Ferraris, he or she could read just the appropriate chapter(s) and be quite knowledgeable on that car's story and background.

For the historian or experienced collector, I tried to infuse as much "primary" information as possible so they would learn something they didn't know. By quoting or using interviews from key people who actually designed, engineered or raced the cars, this gives true insight into the Ferrari story, lifting the veil of mystery on why they did what they did when they did it. It is this type of background that makes the Ferrari legend so fascinating, for it ultimately is a very human story.

The first chapter, called The Ferrari Story, is an overview of Enzo Ferrari, his character and company, much of it told by those who knew him best. This is followed by three main sections: The Road Cars, The Sports Racing Cars, and The Formula 1 Cars. These sections are organized mostly by model type, but in a few cases, the cars are grouped by appearance. This approach was used when different models so closely resemble one another they can be difficult to tell apart, or when they were a development of the previous car.

All sections are written so that by reading a section in its entirety, one will know that part of Ferrari history cold. Primary-source information and observations made this possible, as did infusing a "macroeconomic" look so one can grasp how Ferrari led or reacted to the gran turismo industry, competition circuit, and world as a whole.

I also tried to spotlight trends overlooked in other Ferrari books. For instance, in the 1970s and '80s, there was a strong belief by "old-school" Ferrari owners and enthusiasts that "real" Ferraris only had 12-cylinder engines. What caused that belief and why did it finally disappear? That and more are addressed.

Each chapter has a concise specifications table. Most of the production figures and years came from *Cavallino*, and I am indebted to the magazine for their use and for the diligence of its researchers. I also tapped a number of articles myself and others I wrote for *FORZA* to refresh my memory on facts and figures.

Regarding photography, a number of the photos I took have never been published before. A lot of people ask about my photo equipment and what may surprise many is I still use film, for no digital equipment captures the richness of colors and details like Fuji Velvia. Canon cameras and Canon "L" series lenses were used in most every photo.

Many of the pictures in *Ferrari: Road and Racing* are available as fine-art prints through my Web site, winstongoodfellow.com/ferrari.

I hope you enjoy the read and the visual tour and learn something in the process. I sure did while doing the research!

Over the past 20 years while investigating Ferrari and Italy's GT-car industry, a number of people have been extremely helpful and courteous with their time, four in particular. Carlo Felice, Bianchi Anderloni, and Sergio Pininfarina were true gentlemen, and were extremely good "instructors" in teaching me the ins-and-outs of Ferrari history, working with "The Old Man" and his company, and what it was like creating the cars. Sergio Scaglietti's memories were priceless and often humorous, while Piero Ferrari never ceased to amaze me with his grasp of his company's history. How one who has lived amongst the "trees" his entire life can step back and see the "forest" like he does is a true gift.

There are many others in the Ferrari world and exotic-car industry to thank. They often let me intrude on their lives multiple times, or interrupt them with a phone call, e-mail, or fax to make sure a certain detail was correct. They are Anna Anderloni, Nuccio Bertone, Giotto Bizzarrini, Rosanna Bizzarrini, Giuseppe Bonollo, Peter Brock, Milt Brown, Giordano Casarini, Carlo Chiti, Gian Paolo Dallara, Luca Dal Monte, Mauro Forghieri, Vladimiro Galluzzi, Marcello Gandini, Girolamo Gardini, Paolo Garella, Francesco Gavina, Franco Gavina, Dante Giacosa, Ed Gilbertson, Dario Giordano, Fabrizio Giugiaro, Giorgetto Giugiaro, Antonio Ghini, Gary Laughlin, Brandon Lawrence, Franco Lini, Richard Merritt, Maurizio Moncalesi, Francesco Martinengo, John Mecom Jr., Luca Cordero di Montezemolo, Adolfo Orsi, Lorenza Pininfarina, Enzo Prearo, Lorenzo Ramaciotti, Marella Rivolta, Piero Rivolta, Rachele Rivolta, Filippo Sapino, Simone Schedoni, Ercole Spada, Frank Stephenson, Jacques Swaters, Romolo Tavoni, Tom Tjaarda, Brenda Vernor, Count Giovanni Volpi di Misurata, Andrea Zagato, Elio Zagato, Maurizio Zanisi. I would also like to thank those who wish to remain anonymous.

All of you made the text of this book so much richer, interesting, and complete. A number of these people have since passed away, and I am so thankful their insights on Ferrari and on the history of the GT-car industry remain with us.

A handful of others need to be thanked for various tasks relating to research, acting as translators, and/or helping in general when writing a book like this. They are Silvana Appendino, Franco Bay, Matteo Bonciani, Roberto Casolari, John Clinard, Joe Corbacio, Michael Duffy, Jeff Ehoodin, Doug Freedman, Alberto Fumagalli, Elizebetta Gardini, Axel Gottschalk, Cristiano Inverni, Aaron Jenkins, Davide Klutzer, Brandon Lawrence, Marcel Massini, Glenn Mounger, Wayne Obrey, Patrick Ottis, Francesco Pagni, Simone Piatelli, Walter Pittoni, Stefano Scaglietti, Tom Shaughnessy, Bob Smith, Matt Stone, Steve Tillack, Brandon Wang.

To all the owners who have let me photograph (and drive) their cars over the past decade-plus, a special thanks is extended. If you want to truly grasp the essence of Ferrari, there is no better way than being in one at speed. Special thanks must also be given to Publications International, Ltd. and my editor, Chuck Giametta. PIL came up with the general concept of the book, then let me mold it to what I thought best. Chuck took what I thought was a good, tight manuscript and made it stellar.

If I have overlooked anyone, please forgive me for it was unintentional.

Winston Goodfellow
Monterey, California
August 2005

The
Ferrari
Story

THE MAN, THE COMPANY, THE LEGEND

In 1963, Ferrari employed approximately 450 people and made 598 cars. The American divisions of the Ford Motor Company employed 175,000 and made 2.1 million cars.

Yet, the model that Ford wanted more than anything else that fateful year was one with a Ferrari name on it. Indeed, a Ford buyout of Ferrari came very close to happening, but unraveled at the last minute, causing Ford to create its own legend: the GT40.

So why would one of America's most powerful companies, one that, as a Ford executive put it recently "lost more [cars] in rounding errors than Ferrari made in a year," want to acquire Ferrari?

The answer is simple: Mystique. In the early 1960s, no other firm so perfectly represented the concept of winning, technology, performance, and high style. And that's just as true today.

Enzo Ferrari, Modena 1930

THE MAN BEHIND THE LEGEND

The magic of the Ferrari legend starts with its founder, Enzo Ferrari. He was called an "agitator of men" by noted ex-Ferrari engineer Giotto Bizzarrini, and characterized similarly by scores of others. In his domain, Ferrari was a master psychologist who would do almost anything to extract the most from his employees.

Famed designer and coachbuilder Sergio Pininfarina was just 26 when he started working with Ferrari in 1952. He remembered visiting the factory numerous times after a sports-car win or a Formula 1 victory. Pininfarina often found Enzo in the racing department or on the production line barking orders, being as hard as ever on his men. But when the coachbuilder visited the factory after a defeat, Ferrari was complimenting his troops for giving their all.

It took Pininfarina a bit to grasp what Ferrari was doing: Enzo didn't want his subordinates to relax when it was the perfect time to do so. And he recognized when to motivate through positive reinforcement. Ferrari's employees were willing to work night and day for him, and often did.

Enzo was born in the central Italian town of Modena on February 18, 1898, the younger of two children. That Ferrari and his small firm achieved worldwide fame surprised him and his family. "We lived in a modest house in the suburbs," he wrote in his memoirs, "four rooms over my father's metalworking business....I shared one of the rooms above the workshop with my brother Alfredo and we were woken up by the hammering every morning when the men started work."

In his earliest years, Ferrari had an aversion to school and enjoyed target shooting and roller skating. Then the nascent automotive world hit his radar screen in 1908 "...when my father took me to my first automotive race. The crowds were all shouting for the No. 10 car driven by Felice Nazzaro who won the race. My father and brother were always talking about cars and I got more and more interested as I listened to their talk."

Ferrari was hooked when he saw his next race a year later. "[B]eing that close to those cars and those heroes," he wrote, "being part of the yelling crowd, that whole environment aroused my first flicker of interest in cars."

It would be 10 years before Ferrari took the first unnoticeable steps to worldwide fame. His father wanted him to be an engineer, but young Enzo was more interested in a life in opera, as a tenor, or one in journalism, as a sportswriter. By age 16, he was freelancing for several newspapers.

In 1917, Ferrari was drafted into the army. He returned home with a severe illness that left him hospitalized. His father and brother had passed away two years earlier, so after recovering, Enzo headed to Turin, some 150 miles to the north, to find work.

Turin was well on its way to becoming an industrial center in Italy, thanks in great part to Fiat. By the mid 1920s, Fiat was Italy's dominant industrial concern, and its cars actively raced around the world, often with great success.

Ferrari traveled to the bustling city to try for a job with Fiat, a letter of introduction in hand from his commanding Army officer. He was turned down, but soon found work at a small firm in Bologna that stripped trucks for their chassis, then used them for cars.

That job found Ferrari traveling to northern Italy's other economic engine. Milan was some 100 miles west of Turin, and one of Ferrari's favorite haunts was the Vittorio Emanuele bar, a well known hangout for racing drivers and others in the automotive world. Enzo may have been a bit green, but the first sprinklings of his charisma were starting to show through. He was a good talker in the social setting, and soon found himself hired on as a test driver by the Milan automaker, Costruzioni Meccaniche Nazionali.

THE ALFA ROMEO CONNECTION

CMN's roots were in the aviation business, but it turned to automobile production at the end of the war to keep its workforce busy. Ferrari graduated from tester to racing driver, and that rekindled his childhood dream of being a top competitor.

He remained with CMN for a year, then pooled resources with mechanic Guglielmo Carraroli to buy an old Isotta Fraschini Grand Prix car. But it was Ferrari's piloting of an Alfa Romeo 20/30 to second overall in 1920's grueling Targa Florio that landed him on the racing-driver map.

"I felt like I was the Lord of the Universe," he wrote of driving the Alfa. "Still, what mattered to me most was the fact it gained me an official entry into the Alfa circles, made me practi-

Enzo the racer, 1921

1914, the company was embroiled in strikes and labor discord, a matter exacerbated by insufficient operating capital. In 1915, Nicola Romeo, a successful industrialist with a background in engineering, purchased the firm; he would change the cars' name to Alfa Romeo in 1918.

Alfa was relatively flush with cash from wartime munitions and tractor production when Enzo Ferrari entered the fold. Enzo was a proficient driver, not up to the stature of teammates such as Giuseppe Campari, but still good enough to garner press coverage and the occasional victory, the first of which was at Circuito di Savio in 1923.

By then, Alfa was once again in financial difficulty, thanks to the failure of one of its largest creditors and to the era's chronic labor strife. Intervention by Prime Minister Benito Mussolini, himself an auto enthusiast, helped prevent the firm from going under.

Though Ferrari continued to race through the 1920s, by the middle of the decade, he was proving to be a power behind the scenes. Nicola Romeo sent him to Turin to lure Vittorio Jano to Alfa, and Ferrari set the wheels in motion for the noted engineer to join the company in late 1923. Ferrari traveled constantly, in contact with the era's best drivers and with numerous influential individuals, in and out of the auto industry.

By the second half of the decade, Ferrari was examining his driving career. "If you want spectacular results," he noted in his memoirs, "you have to know how to treat your car badly. Ill treatment means excessive gearshifts, pushing the car further than the engine will bear, reckless braking, all the things that got in the way of my feeling for the machinery. The fact is I don't drive simply to get from A to B. I enjoy feeling the car's reactions, becoming a part of it, forming a single unit. I couldn't inflict suffering on it."

Ferrari driving an Alfa Romeo 20/30

cally an Alfa team driver like Campari and Baldoni."

He had indeed reached the big leagues. Alfa Romeo was only 10 years old at the time, but it was, along with luxury maker Isotta Fraschini, the biggest fish in Milan's burgeoning automotive industry. Originally named A.L.F.A. (Anomica Lombardo Fabbrica Automobili), the firm produced sports and racing cars along with airplane engines and large, sturdy automobiles. Thanks to a class win in April 1911, at the 1,500 kilometer, five-stage Modena trials, competition became a core element of the company's *raison d'être*.

Alfa's jump into the winner's circle and onto the front pages of Italy's newspapers was not a smooth one. From 1912 to

Ferrari (in cap) and his Alfa mount for the 1924 Targa Florio

He thus diversified by investing in businesses in the auto industry. He became Alfa Romeo's dealer for the Emilia-Romagna region around Modena, and set up an office in Bologna.

"I found myself overwhelmed by an almost morbid desire to do something for the motor car, for this creature I was so passionately fond of," he wrote. "So although I was doing well enough to justify pursuing a driving career, I had my sights set on wider, more ambitious horizons."

SCUDERIA FERRARI

Those horizons came into focus one evening in 1929, as Ferrari dined with driver Mario Tadini and enthusiasts and fiber merchants Alfredo and Augosto Caniato. The men decided to start the Scuderia Ferrari, a company composed of driver-owners that prepared cars for competition and offered support for the owners who raced them.

The firm's favored mounts were Alfa Romeos. Ferrari remained tightly woven with engineers Jano and Luigi Bazzi, men he helped recruit to the company. This helps explain how he was able to get top-flight racing machinery for his clients.

"The original idea was to make the Scuderia a team of owner drivers, but eventually it acquired an official team of professional drivers," Ferrari explained. "Alfa Romeo never saw [it] as a competitor and there was no hint of a future rivalry. The way Alfa saw it, the Scuderia offered it a chance to enter lots of races and maintain a racing image despite no longer wanting to be directly involved."

That was clearly demonstrated in 1933, when Alfa Romeo announced its withdrawal from Grand Prix racing and Ferrari convinced the firm to let him continue racing their formidable P3 single-seater. The Scuderia subsequently won the Grand Prix of Pescara that year.

Scuderia Ferrari, Modena, 1929

Even more telling was Ferrari's success in endurance racing, a highly visible activity thanks to the backing of Mussolini's Fascist government and its desire to promote road and railroad construction. In 1930, Ferrari's Scuderia entered 22 races and scored eight victories. At 1933's Mille Miglia, Alfa Romeos swept the top 10 places, led by an 8C 2300 prepared by Ferrari.

To differentiate his Alfas from the others, Ferrari in 1932 began painting on his cars a large crest that featured a prancing

horse on a yellow background. Ferrari said he was given the crest by Countess Paolina Baracca, whose son, Francesco, had served in the same WWI flying squadron as Ferrari's brother, Alfredo. The visage of a rearing black horse (the symbol of the city of Stuttgart) was said to have come from a German fighter plane the ace Baracca had shot down. Ferrari gave it the background of yellow, the official color of Modena.

By the mid 1930s, Ferrari was a well-known name in the auto industry. "[He] had become a celebrity, something of a sensation," historian Luigi Orsini noted in *Automobile Quarterly*, "more so certainly as an organizer than he ever was as a racing river."

This was all the more remarkable, given the turmoil of the times. Hostility between nations was escalating, and the Wall Street crash of 1929 inflicted global economic pain. "You have to understand the period to [grasp] the enormity of what Ferrari accomplished," Frenchman Rene Dreyfus, a noted former Scuderia driver, told Orsini. "There had never been anything like the team he had, never anything that big and so well organized—and the problems: the interference from the Fascists, the sensitivity of relations with Alfa, the personality problems and rivalries within the team.

"Yet despite all this there was no doubt he was the 'Boss'—and the only Boss. If you raced for Mercedes or Auto Union or even the Alfa works team, you raced by committee. The Scuderia was his dream. He was the whole thing."

Ferrari tempered this air of authority with a certain charm. Sergio Scaglietti was a teenager who repaired Ferrari's Alfas by working at a small coachbuilding facility across the street from the Scuderia, and he vividly recalled Enzo's magnetism. Tall and large boned for an Italian, Ferrari was quite handsome and simply had presence.

"Even back then," Scaglietti remembered, "he had a lot of charisma and was never nasty with the people who worked for him. Having said that, I have to say none of us foresaw the success he achieved later."

FERRARI'S FIRST CAR: THE AAC 815

But that "It" factor and years of success weren't enough to prevent an acrimonious divorce with Alfa Romeo in January 1938. Things likely began their downhill slide in the summer of 1936, when Jano resigned after Alfa managing director Ugo Gobbato hired Wifredo Ricart, the talented Spanish engineer. Ferrari and Gobbato had an immediate clash of personalities, a dislike fueled by their different engineering opinions.

Gobbato was also antagonizing the situation. Backed by the German government, the racing programs of Mercedes-Benz and Auto Union were an unstoppable tidal wave. Their chain of victories was a disaster for Alfa and other competitors. With corporate and national pride at stake, Gobbato desired to have "everything planned in advance, down to the last detail," Ferrari noted in his memoirs. But Enzo believed the best way to create and campaign a racing car was with a small group working under a flexible management style that allowed it to respond quickly.

"Not many agreed with me and there were times Jano and I

1940 Auto Avio Costruzioni 815

and the drivers found ourselves muttering together like conspirators in the Alfa Romeo yard," he remembered. "In the end I was sacked, which seemed to be the only logical solution to the situation that had developed."

As a condition of the split, Ferrari signed an agreement that said he could not build a car under his own name for four years. But with ambition burning in his heart and cash doing the same in his pocket, he quickly formed a new company, Auto Avio Costruzioni. AAC remained in the same downtown Modena location as the Scuderia, and to make his new car, Enzo soon hired well-known technicians Luigi Bazzi and Federico Giberti, and engineers Vittorio Bellentani and Gioachino Colombo.

Ferrari then put in charge of the project Alberto Massimino, a talented 45-year-old engineer who had moved to Modena to work on the Alfa 158 race car. Increasing border tensions throughout Europe were causing severe materials shortages, so Ferrari had his men use a Fiat 508 C as their starting point. Fiat had made a handful of these mainstream sedans into endurance racers, so Ferrari's team reinforced the chassis but left untouched the brakes, transmission, steering, and front suspension.

No so the engine. They took two 508 C 1100cc four-cylinder engines, reduced the bore and stroke, cast a new block and cylinder heads, and joined the two engines together. The result was an inline 1496cc 8-cylinder that produced 72 horsepower at 5500 rpm.

For the car's body, Ferrari turned to Felice Bianchi Anderloni, the design head of Italy's preeminent coachbuilder, Carrozzeria Touring. Ferrari had admired Anderloni's work on a plethora of competition and street Alfa Romeos over the previous decade.

Felice's son, Carlo Biachi Anderloini, was then a 23-year-old cadet in the military, and thanks to his photographic memory, well-recalled his father speaking of Enzo's visit to Touring.

"He said Ferrari wanted something that could be recognized as a Ferrari at a glance," the younger Anderloni remembered, not aware at the time that he would hear the exact words a decade later. "Ferrari was obviously thinking of some type of production, for he wanted his car to have a touch of luxury."

Felice Anderloni made some initial sketches, then refined them through use of his "visualizers," men who turned his initial drawings and ideas into detailed renderings. A 1:10-scale model was then constructed and analyzed in a wind tunnel.

The first 815 (8-cylinders, 1.5-liters) underwent tests on public roads. Carlo Anderloni said Touring's favorite stretches were between Milan and Como and between Milan and Bergamo. "The car was covered in felt strips," he said, "then followed by a second car with a photographer onboard who took pictures. Once the photos were developed, my father looked at the felt strips to analyze the airflow."

Two 815s were built and entered in 1940's Gran Premio Brescia della Mille Miglia, a one-time substitute for the traditional Mille Miglia. They were valiant competitors. One dominated its class and ran as high as 10th overall late in the race.

Both had to retire with mechanical failures, causing Ferrari to note a bit harshly, "The experiment that started so brilliantly ended in failure, largely because the car had been built too hastily."

The 815s were the last cars Ferrari would work on for years. Italy officially entered World War II on June 10, 1940, when a general order to proceed to local Fascist headquarters swept the country. Ferrari survived the conflict by producing oil-driven grinding machines and machine tools.

Two years into the war, the government issued an order for Italy's industries to decentralize. Ferrari moved the Auto Avio Costruzioni works from Modena to Maranello, a rural suburb some 10 miles to the south, where he already owned a parcel of land. According to then-Ferrari employee Girolamo Gardini, the move happened on July 26, 1943. By September, the company was once again at work, and its labor force increased to 140 from 40 over the following two years.

Allied bombs twice hit the factory, the second raid badly damaging the facility. But these proved only temporary setbacks. "I was not unprepared for the end of the war," Ferrari noted in his memoirs. Indeed, his passion for cars and competition was evident by the two 815s illustrated at the top of AAC's wartime sales brochures.

BIRTH OF THE FERRARI COMPANY

No sooner had hostilities ended in 1945 than Ferrari was on the phone to Gioachino Colombo. The stalwart engineer was then in his early 40s, and his résumé included a number of Alfa's most famous models.

Colombo lived in Milan and welcomed the call from his friend. The engineer had been laid off from Alfa, and rumors of Fascist involvement surrounded him. "There was no unemployment compensation in my case," Colombo wrote of his bleak situation in his autobiography, *The Origins of the Ferrari Legend*. "[That phone call] was something which could obliterate in one stroke those five years of war, bombardments and sufferings, and the upsets of evacuation."

He traveled through the ruins of the Italian countryside with Enrico Nardi, a one-time Lancia test driver and future steering-wheel manufacturer. Within the first minutes of his meeting with Enzo, the engineer and Ferrari, the budding car constructor, got to the heart of the matter. Ferrari asked Colombo what he would propose for a new 1500cc engine. "Maserati has a first-class eight-cylinder, the English have the ERA six-cylinder job, and Alfa have their own eight-C," the engineer replied. "In my view you should make a 12-cylinder."

"My Dear Colombo," Ferrari responded, "you read my thoughts."

Ferrari had been eyeing such an engine configuration for nearly two decades. "In the years immediately after the war I had an opportunity of observing the new Packard 12-cylinder on the splendid vehicles belonging to high-ranking American officers," he noted in his memoirs. "I recall it was one of these 12-cylinder jobs which was purchased by Antonio Ascari in 1919, and then passed on by him to Maria Antonietta Avanzo, the first courageous woman driver of the postwar era."

Baroness Avanzo confirmed her V-12-powered car did indeed give Ferrari the inspiration. "The Packard went from owner to owner," she said in a 1969 interview with automotive journalist Valerio Moretti, "and no one managed to get any good results from it except Enzo Ferrari, who said that it had given him the inspiration for his future twelve-cylinder cars."

Colombo returned to Milan, his head filled with ideas. Using a drafting board borrowed from Anderloni at Touring, he toiled away in the bedroom of his apartment. He began by designing the cylinder heads, then worked on the balance of the car. Assisting him were Angelo Nasi, head of Alfa's industrial-vehicle chassis design, and Luciano Fochi, a young freelance designer.

Colombo worked on Ferrari's car until November 1945, when Alfa management learned of his activities and rehired him to run its sports-vehicle division. The engineer recommended as his replacement was Giuseppe Busso, a talented technician who also had roots in Alfa.

Busso jumped at the chance. "I had to be ruthless in order to pull the 125 through its childhood illnesses, which were neither few nor insignificant," he remembered in *Ferrari Tipo 166*. Giving Busso, Luigi Bazzi, and their group of young apprentices headaches were the V-12's ignition and its cylinder-head gaskets. No less of a problem was the lack of high-grade materials and the poorly machined components from suppliers.

The motivated group kept at it until September 28, 1946, when the engine underwent its first bench tests. That same year, Ferrari changed the name of his company to "Scuderia Ferrari-Auto Avio Costruzioni." Then, on March 12, 1947, Ferrari's first car—a 125 without coachwork—ran under its own power for the first time. Busso captured the moment on film, a smiling Ferrari wearing a suit seated in the rudimentary car, surrounded by proud workers in grubby overalls.

The 125's platform was simple—a tubular chassis supple-

1947 125 S

mented by leaf springs and shock absorbers. The 1496cc engine, depending upon its state of tune, produced between 72 and 118 horsepower. The five-speed gearbox was a rarity in an era when four-speed manuals were the rule for European sporting cars.

During the struggle to complete that first car, "I was beginning to be sincerely fond of Ferrari," Busso observed. "[T]he practical experience of battling successfully with theoretical and practical problems of bringing a car like the 125 was very important to me and was to prove invaluable when I [later] confronted Alfa's problems. Possibly my frequent contact with his son Dino and Signora Ferrari, even my listening to Ferrari unburdening himself about the health problems of these two and the anguish of seeing him cry many a time when talking about Dino, all may have contributed to my affection for Ferrari."

Busso and his men made two 125s. The first was completed on May 8, 1947. It had a roadster body vaguely similar to that of the 815. The second 125 was finished the following day and was a much more elementary car with a torpedo body and cycle fenders.

The 125's initial appearance was at Piacenza on May 11, and piloting the roadster was Franco Cortese, a talented driver who also was Ferrari's traveling salesman in his machine tool business. Cortese's contract was drawn up in April 1947, and stated he would earn 50,000 lire a month (around $84 at the time), with traveling expenses and incidentals covered by the company. Cortese would keep the driver's race winnings, while Ferrari kept those won by the team.

In the 30-lap, 60-mile race, Cortese's 125 S ran 27 laps before its fuel pump let go. Still, he set the fastest lap, showing his potential, and the car's. Two weeks later in Rome, that potential was fully realized. After 40 laps and some 85 miles, Cortese and the 125 S took the checkered flag with an overall victory.

And so began the Ferrari legend. Cortese scored another victory that year, plus a pair of seconds and two class wins. "We would race every Sunday to test the car," Cortese recalled in *Ferrari Tipo 166*. "I was alone [and] the others were mainly [driving] Maserati. But we were superior, the Ferrari was a more modern car, I would say exceptional for that period.

"It drove very easily [but]...it [had] a somewhat different engine. We were used to normal four- and six-cylinder motors [and] this twelve-cylinder was like an electric motor. It would 'spin' very easily, so one had to be careful."

MARKETER AND MASTER MOTIVATOR
Ferrari built one more car in 1947, modifying the coachwork and engine of each of his three machines as needed. By August, the V-12's displacement had increased to 1902cc and the model designation evolved to 159. By early 1948, Ferrari was making the 166 with its 1996cc capacity; it became the company's mainstay.

The 166 won more races than the 125 or 159, but Ferrari soon recognized he had a problem. His cars had a variety of bodies, from slab-sided torpedo shapes to cycle-fender jobs to a

1947-48 166 Sport Corsa

coupe and spider made by Carrozzeria Allemano in Turin. The Allemano coupe won 1948's Mille Miglia, but its look was completely different from any of its predecessors. This greatly troubled Ferrari's marketing instincts—how could one identify the car as "a Ferrari"?

Enzo turned to Felice Bianchi Anderloni of Touring for the solution. His talented friend gladly accepted the commission. But shortly after the project started, Anderloni became ill and died after a trip to Rome; this thrust his son Carlo into the position of design director.

Carlo Felice Bianchi Anderloni, 32 years of age, had been working full-time in the company for five years, but still felt the pressure of his new circumstance. "It was not an easy position to be in," he reflected. "We have a saying in Italy that it is best to present a good face in a bad situation, and that is what I tried to do.

"This was my first work and it was vitally important because people understood that Touring meant my father. I knew many were quietly wondering 'What will happen now? Can the son follow in his father's footsteps?'"

Enzo Ferrari had no such doubts, and let Anderloni know he had his full confidence. Carlo bit into the project with vigor, richly rewarding Ferrari's belief when Touring's 166 MM "barchetta" made its debut at the 1948 Turin Auto Show in September.

One of the postwar period's seminal designs, the Barchetta won the Mille Miglia and the Le Mans 24 Hours in 1949. Those victories and others formed the foundation for Touring's design

1950 166 MM Barchetta

and construction of a series of berlinetta and coupe 166s. All used the same design language, and Ferrari had its first "look."

As orders increased, Anderloni got a firsthand taste of Enzo's character and motivational techniques. One day, Ferrari took a rare trip to Milan to examine barchettas under construction for the Mille Miglia. Shortly after his arrival, he launched into a screaming tirade. The work was unsatisfactory. It was moving too slowly. He might cancel his order. Enzo stormed out of the Touring works and drove back to Modena.

Stunned, Anderloni remembered looking at Touring coowner Gaetano Ponzoni, who handled the administrative side of the company. After the shock of the episode wore off, the two retired to the administrative offices to come up with a game plan: Carlo would drive down and see Ferrari the following day in Modena, no short order given the disarray of Italy's postwar infrastructure.

The trip was arduous, and Anderloni arrived at Enzo's factory late in the morning. He was immediately escorted into Ferrari's office and invited to sit down. "What brings you here?" Ferrari asked. "This is a wonderful surprise."

"Yesterday's blowup had us a bit distressed," Anderloni replied. "What can we do to help the situation?"

"Yesterday?" Ferrari responded, dismissing the entire episode with a wave of the hand and shrug of the shoulders. "Shall we go get an early lunch?"

THE DRIVER'S CHASSIS OF CHOICE

By the early 1950s, Ferrari was constructing a car every 10 days to two weeks. A string of endurance-racing victories at the hands of factory drivers and privateers were fueling orders for the road cars. Many found their way to the racetrack, often driven by wealthy sportsmen and privateers, such as Italy's Marzotto brothers.

"I met Enzo Ferrari in 1949," Paolo Marzotto recalled in *Ferrari 1947-1997*. "Vittorio, Umberto, Giannino and myself had gone to Modena, to the firm's old headquarters. That is where the 'Commendatore' met customers. Maranello only housed the workshops.

"We had gone to buy a couple of cars and to ask to drive another two for the Scuderia in the Italian Sport Championship the following year.... [W]ith his subtle astounding eloquence, [Ferrari] convinced us to buy four cars.

"And if we wanted the official cars, we just had to earn them. There was something innovative about Ferraris that other cars did not have, and the man who created them was extraordinary: pleasant, curious, biting, overpowering, and conciliatory. He exploited every opportunity with a mixture of managerial skills and missionary zeal...."

Ferrari was now competing in Grand Prix racing as well. The origins of open-wheel competition traced to 1906, and in the late 1940s, international racing's organizing body, the Paris-based Federation Internationale de l'Automobile (FIA), began planning for an annual world-championship competition for drivers. The first Formula 1 Grand Prix was held at Great Britain's historic Silverstone course on May 13, 1950.

Ferrari began building and competing in open-wheel racing in 1948, and entered the Grand Prix fray in 1950's second race, in Monaco on May 21. Since then, a Ferrari car has competed in every Formula 1 race.

Alfa Romeo drivers Nino Farina and Juan Manuel Fangio dominated the first championship, finishing 1-2 in the driver standings as Alfa won every race.

The following year was a different story. Ferrari handed Alfa its first postwar defeat, at Silverstone in July, and narrowly lost 1951's championship to Alfa in the season's last race in Spain. As if recognizing the handwriting on the wall, Alfa withdrew from Grand Prix competition.

Alfa's Silverstone defeat and its eventual withdrawal was bittersweet for Ferrari. "I still feel for our Alfa the adolescent tenderness of first love, the immaculate affection for the mamma," Enzo wrote in a letter to Alfa's managing director after beating his onetime employer.

1951 166 F2, Franco Cortese driving

Ferrari dominated Grand Prix racing in 1952 and '53, losing only one race and easily winning the championships both years. But even more important to the forming Ferrari legend was its success in sports-car competition, in the epic endurance races of the day in particular.

"In Ferrari's early years, I am sure endurance racing was more popular than Formula 1," said Piero Ferrari, Enzo's surviving son. "This was before the 1970s, when F1 started to grow through television involvement. Endurance racing was really part of the Ferrari myth, and was what built up the Ferrari myth in that age."

Indeed, in the world's most-famous long-distance road races—Le Mans, the Mille Miglia, the Carrera Panamericana, Sebring—Ferrari's sports cars were more often victorious than not. A number of these racing-winning models could be ordered as grand-touring cars, equipped with less-powerful engines and more-luxurious interiors, but with coachwork often identical to that of the race winners. This was quite a lure for customers, and it helped create an aura around the man and his company with the era's top race drivers.

"When I first met [Ferrari] he was 55 and I was 25," remembered Umberto Maglioli, winner of 1954's Carrera Panamericana in a Ferrari 375 Plus. "A good-looking big man, his hair was nearly all white, already a legend," Maglioli wrote in *Ferrari 1947-1997*. "You approached him with reverential fear, influenced because you saw everyone else treating him with great deference, careful not to irritate him, and there were no two sides about it. He lorded it over everybody, made his own rules, good and bad,"

Enzo's reverence for the machinery was evident to Maglioli. "'We are car builders,' he would say. It was an extreme attitude....But Ferrari was like that. He felt real displeasure when one of his cars had an accident, to the point that he didn't want to see pieces of it when it returned to the plant. That is one aspect of Ferrari's character that has possibly not been sufficiently emphasized."

Maglioli's observation underscored the fact that Ferrari's relationship with the men who risked their lives in his race cars was a complex one.

"At the end of 1955 I had the possibility of retiring," wrote the great Fangio in *Ferrari, The Grand Prix Cars*, "[but] decided to postpone my retirement for another year. As Mercedes-Benz had withdrawn, I returned to Europe to race with Ferrari in 1956, but I wasn't very happy about it.

"Since I first raced in Europe I had always been in a team opposing Ferrari. Now I was joining them…but he would never say who [was] the number-one driver, although the younger men told me 'Juan, you are the leader.'

"Ferrari was a hard man. His team raced in every category and his drivers drove always for him. He wanted victory primarily for his cars and this suited my attitude, because I never raced solely for myself, but the team as a whole.

"But a driver must have a good relationship with his mechanics, and I found this rather difficult to achieve with the Ferrari team. I suppose it was because I had been their opposition for so many years and now here I was as their driver."

THE COACHBUILDER'S CHASSIS OF CHOICE

Ferrari's sports-racing victories and the prestige they generated caused the industry's top coachbuilding firms to clamor for his chassis. Many of Italy's coachbuilders made it through World War II by dreaming about what they would design and produce once hostilities ended, but it took a few years for that creativity to come to the fore. Europe's second-half of the 1940s was ruled by a wartime mentality: Restraint and simply surviving were the keys to most everyone's existence.

Recovery finally took hold in the early 1950s, and as the pace of material growth quickened into what became known as the "economic miracle," the European spirit was rejuvenated, as well.

Automotive production grew exponentially, carrying along with it the gran-turismo and sports-car industry and the coachbuilders who served it.

"It was like a giant, compressed spring; when the war ended, that spring released," recalled Filippo Sapino, the designer of Ferrari's 512S showcar of 1970. Sergio Pininfarina expressed it this way: "Because people went a long time without walking, they took big steps, not little ones."

Enzo Ferrari was acutely aware of how styling impacted his company and the industry. "It was a very, very important element for him," Piero Ferrari said. "First was the engine performance, for he was an engine-oriented person. But second was the coachwork—styling was very important."

Couple that with Ferrari's ever increasing reputation as the pinnacle of speed and prestige, and it's easy to understand why coachbuilders clamored to show their work on a Ferrari chassis.

1953 250 MM and 1951 212 Inter

Touring dominated Ferrari's designs from the debut of the 166 barchetta in 1948 to the end of 1950. Stablimenti Farina would show the occasional design, as would Milan's Zagato and Sapino's future employer, Carrozzeria Ghia.

But by 1951, the most prolific coachbuilder for Ferrari was Carrozzeria Vignale. Alfredo Vignale started his firm in 1946, and produced mostly nondescript shapes until he combined his talents with the era's most formidable stylist, Giovanni Michelotti, then in his early 30s. "You could easily title his biography 'Michelotti: An Artist,'" said a Michelotti coworker.

Vignale's initial designs for Ferrari were restrained, but as 1951 turned to 1952, Michelotti's creativity was unleashed. Whether it was an endurance racer, such as the 340 Mexico, or a luxurious gran turismo, such as a 212 Inter or 375 America, the shapes were superb and startling in their originality.

Still, it was another coachbuilder who truly bewitched Ferrari. By the early 1950s, Battista "Pinin" Farina and his firm were the masters of the styling universe, their only rival being Anderloni and Carrozzeria Touring. Pinin Farina's seminal 202 Cisitalia

1952 340 Mexico

berlinetta of 1947 opened a new age of design.

"My father was very intuitive," Sergio Pininfarina remembered. "He believed Ferrari would one day become the most important name in Italy, much like Alfa Romeo prior to the war. This made him want to go to Ferrari. At the same time, Mr. Ferrari wanted to work with Pinin Farina because, in his mind, he thought Pinin Farina was the best."

Though the two men had known one another since the early 1920s, they admired the other's work from afar. "Both were prima donnas," Sergio Pininfarina explained with a chuckle. "Ferrari was a man of very strong character, and my father was much the same. Mr. Ferrari was not coming to Pinin Farina, and my father was not going to Modena. So they met halfway, in Tortona, something like Gorbachev and Reagan agreeing to meet in Iceland."

Their luncheon in Tortona altered the Ferrari universe. By 1954, it was clear who was Ferrari's favored coachbuilder. Be it a gran turismo built in limited quantities, an endurance racer, a sensational show car, or a one-off for royalty, Battista and Sergio Pininfarina's work showed extraordinary creativity, refinement, and grace.

In describing his philosophy years later, Battista's passion for timeless form was obvious. "The inter-relation between the body of a beautiful woman and that of a Farina designed car,"

he said, "is that both have a simplicity and harmony of line, so that when they are old one can still see how beautiful they were when they were young."

Also gaining Ferrari's favor was local coachbuilder Sergio Scaglietti. The humble Modenese artisan had worked on Ferrari's Alfa Romeos prior to the war. He founded Carrozzeria Scaglietti in 1951, in a building not far from the growing Ferrari works in Maranello.

Scaglietti's initial efforts on Ferrari chassis consisted of rebodies for customers. The quality of the work caught Enzo's attention, and by 1955, Scaglietti was building the majority of Ferrari's competition cars.

A DEATH IN THE FAMILY

That began a close relationship between the two men that lasted until Enzo's death in 1988. Central to the bond was that Scaglietti's carrozzeria had become a second home to Ferrari's son, Dino. Named after Enzo's father, Alfredo, and shortened to the affectionate Dino, Enzo's first son was in his early 20s as the '50s dawned, and was suffering from muscular dystrophy.

"Every day [Dino] would drive over to our workshop to see how things were going," Scaglietti remembered. "He was actively interested, saying 'We can do this, we can do that.' These visits were his main link to his father's cars.

"But you could tell he was not well. Often, he fell and then pretended like he tripped on a hammer or something else lying on the shop's floor...."

Dino had followed his father into the family business and had showed early promise as an engineer. His death in 1956 cast a

Enzo Ferrari and his son, Dino, 1940

pall over Enzo's world. He preserved Dino's desk as a memorial, visited his grave daily for many years, and wore only black neckties in his honor. "[T]he only perfect love in this world is that of a father for his son," Enzo wrote in his autobiography six years after Dino's death.

Ferrari also forever remembered the comfort Dino found in Scaglietti's presence. By the late 1950s, Scaglietti was part of Enzo's inner circle. Europe's economic miracle had treated both men well. Ferrari production had increased nearly 1,000 percent since 1950, and Scaglietti, as one of Ferrari's key subcontractors, had benefited greatly.

The coachbuilder was ready to break out and form his own company. "I needed money to make my own factory," he remembered. "Because I did not have the funds to underwrite the expansion, Ferrari called his banker and cosigned the loan for me when I bought the land. Without that type of generosity, I wouldn't have been able to do what I wanted to do."

ENGINEERING, GROWTH, AND THE PURGE

By the early 1960s, the Legend was well in place. Between 1953 and 1961, Ferrari sports-racing cars earned Maranello the Constructors World Sports Championship seven times. Mercedes-Benz and Aston Martin tied for second, with one title each.

It was a similar showing in Europe's two most important road races, the glamorous 24 Hours of Le Mans in France and the punishing 1,000-mile trek through Italy, the Mille Miglia. Between 1949 and 1961, Ferraris won Le Mans five times, a record matched only by Jaguar. Between 1948 and 1957, Ferrari was victorious in the Mille Miglia eight times; next-best was one win apiece for Mercedes, Lancia, and Alfa.

A large part of this success and the aura it generated was Enzo's unwavering belief in the V-12 engine configuration.

"The main reason for the victories," endurance ace Paul Frere noted in *Ferrari 1947-1997*, "was the superb 12-cylinder engine. [This] managed to cover up defects...such as the aerodynamics which would only let our Testa Rossa reach 260 km/h with difficulty on the straights at Le Mans. [A] few weeks after the race I asked Ferrari why he had not paid more attention to aerodynamics, he answered, 'Dear Frere, aerodynamics are for people who don't know how to build good engines!' He always had a ready answer, just as he also had all the qualities necessary to win a place in both the history and the legend of racing."

The V-12 did indeed dominate the early Ferrari engineering package; it wasn't until the late 1950s that Enzo would begin to adopt the very latest chassis, suspension, brake, and gearbox technologies. When he did, Ferrari's eye for talent, and the ability to exploit it, was beautifully illustrated in the hiring of three key engineers: Giotto Bizzarrini, Carlo Chiti, and Mauro Forghieri. It was they who brought greater sophistication to the balance of his cars' components.

Bizzarrini came from Alfa Romeo in 1957, and had in his background a one-off Fiat Topolino modified for his graduating thesis at the University of Pisa in 1953. Bizzarrini recalled Ferrari telling him years later, "The reason I hired you is I respected your courage when I saw the car you were driving."

What Bizzarrini said he appreciated about the Ferrari organization was its "very neat and clear division between the road and racing cars. Other companies such as Maserati often built them side by side, but in Ferrari, even in the competition department there was a division between Formula cars and sports cars."

Thanks to Bizzarrini, Chiti also jumped from Alfa, and was soon made Ferrari's technical director. "In practical terms," Chiti recalled, "I spent my whole time with [Enzo]. In the evening we watched TV together. We talked about racing or discussed ideas. Racing was not the only conversation; I was struck by the breadth of his knowledge, his memory and above all, his intelligence."

The after-hours time together may have been relaxing. Office hours were anything but. Chiti said he and his fellow engineers lived under a blanket of fear of making a mistake. Ferrari was unsparing of even the slightest error, something easily done in the yeasty environment of a continual stream of new projects.

The different talents of Bizzarrini and Chiti ended up having a great impact on Ferrari. Bizzarrini was a master of testing sports racers and GTs on the road, then modifying them. Chiti was fabulous on the drawing board.

"Ferrari's feudal factory in Maranello continues to make the finest sports cars in the world," *Sports Car Illustrated* observed in October 1960. "No other make or builder could even have tried to duplicate Ferrari's utter sweep of...Le Mans, a race which can be dull, hard work but still proves the solid worth of an automobile. Ferrari and his men are still masters of their craft."

In their time at Maranello, Bazzarrini, and Chiti played central roles in Ferrari's four endurance crowns, two Formula 1 titles and in the greatly improving drivability of the road cars. That makes it all the more surprising the two talented engineers were let go in a house cleaning at the end of 1961, an episode that became know as The Walkout or The Purge.

Near the center of the matter was Ferrari's wife, Laura, whom he had married around 1920. Enzo's "feudal" approach created an environment of intrigue, a situation further antagonized by

Laura Ferrari and Dino, around 1954

Laura's intrusive ways. Chiti and another walkout participant, ex team manager Romolo Tavoni, recall her being a meddlesome presence inside the company. Chiti told author Oscar Orefici in *Carlo Chiti: Sinfonia Ruggente* that "she was a woman totally devoid of any diplomatic sense...(and) had none of the characteristics needed to live alongside a man of the stature of her husband."

The flashpoint was a physical altercation at the factory involving Ferrari's powerful sales manager, Girolamo Gardini. Laura was viewed as the instigator. Loyalties were divided. Bizzarrini, Chiti, and a number of other department heads were ousted.

"A group of us tried to unify and support Gardini to have Ferrari bring him back," Bizzarrini remembered, summing up for the several participants in The Purge interviewed by this author. "But Ferrari said 'no' and fired everybody!

"I was stunned to find myself on the outside of the organization, for Ferrari was like a second father for me when I was younger. He had faith in me and the team—there was a complete feeling between us."

Mauro Forghieri had been with the company only two years. But in another display of Enzo's ability to pick talent and motivate it, he promoted the inexperienced, ambitious 27-year-old engineer to head the technical office.

"Ferrari made it very clear he was behind me 100 percent," Forghieri remembered. "He said he would look after the politics and the money if I concentrated on the technical side. This gave me the courage I needed.

"He was a tremendous man and this gave me the chance to become what I always dreamed of. Ferrari was a great place to work during that period."

GOLDEN YEARS, FORD VERSUS FERRARI; THE DINO
Ferrari didn't miss a beat following The Walkout. His cars won Le Mans in 1962, '63, '64, and '65. An onslaught of victories by his sports-racing machines and competition GTs won Ferrari various constructors world sports-car titles in 1962, '63, '64, and '65. John Surtees was F1 world champion in a Ferrari in 1964, a year in which Ferrari also won the F1 makes title.

All the while, the road cars were fortifying their standing as the world's best high-performance sports and GT automobiles. Production more than doubled over four years.

It was a luster that proved quite appealing to Ford Motor Company in the early 1960s. American's No. 2 automaker was trying to cultivate a more youthful audience, and performance was the hot ticket. Nothing symbolized speed and horsepower better than racetrack success, and in the early '60s, international racing success was spelled Ferrari.

Ferrari came into focus on Ford's radar screen in January 1963. CEO Henry Ford II and his top lieutenant, Lee Iacocca, hatched the idea of purchasing the Italian automaker to jump-start Ford's assault on America's bursting youth market.

Unbeknownst to most everyone, Ford included, was that Ferrari was already in negotiations over the sale of his company to a stalwart client: the wealthy Mecom family of Texas. The Mecoms had made a fortune in oil, but when John Mecom, Jr.,

1964 250 LM

learned of Ford's interest, he knew his pockets weren't deep enough to win that bidding war. "Once Ford entered the picture," he remembered, "I backed away."

Ford's first contact with Ferrari was in May 1963, through the American company's Italian subsidiary. According to a 1966 account in *Road & Track*, Ford Vice President and General Manager Donald Frey traveled to Italy as the front man in the talks.

Frey said the framework for a deal was settled upon fairly quickly. There were to be two companies. One, called Ford-Ferrari, would be responsible for the gran turismos Ferrari was already building. The second, Ferrari-Ford, would construct competition cars. Ford would be the majority shareholder of the road-car arm. Enzo Ferrari would be the largest shareholder in the racing company.

Ten days of intense negotiations collapsed when it became apparent Enzo wanted complete control of Ferrari-Ford. Frey returned to America disappointed but not surprised. Henry Ford II listened intently to Frey's description of the failed deal, then simply stated, "That's okay. Let's go beat them."

With that, an epic automotive David versus Goliath battle was joined. It would last the better part of five years. Dearborn's principal weapon would be the GT40 series, beautiful midengine race cars developed with the full might of the Ford organization.

But endless money didn't guarantee immediate victory. In 1964, GT40s powered by 4.7-liter Ford V-8s couldn't unseat Ferrari's proven V-12 sports prototypes. So Ford responded in a proper American hot rod way: It got a bigger engine. Armed with Ford's NASCAR-based 7-liter V-8, the GT40 Mk II appeared at Le Mans in 1965, and though it lost to another midengine V-12 Ferrari, Mk IIs came back to finish 1-2-3 in the '66 race. GT40 variants would win Le Mans in '67, '68, and '69.

Enzo Ferrari was far from idle during this period. He rallied his troops, and they responded.

"When The Old Man wanted something you didn't say no," remembered Brenda Vernor, who moved from England to Italy in the early 1960s and eventually became Ferrari's personal assistant. "Not because you didn't want to do it, but because in a strange way it was a pleasure to work for Enzo Ferrari.

"So we [often] worked all day Sunday, and Monday morning I would find a little present on my desk with a card. He didn't say 'thank you' but you knew he was in effect thanking you for your effort.

"I can recall a number of times taking food and wine to the mechanics at one or two in the morning. They too would not say 'no' to The Old Man. For these men it was also a joy to work for him."

Ferrari was the last manufacturer to win Le Mans with a front-engine car—the 330 TRI/LM in 1962—and the first to win it with a midengine car—the 250 P in 1963. Now that Ford was in the game, it was time for Ferrari to play "no substitute for cubic inches." It built a variety of sports-racing prototypes with ever-larger and more-powerful 12-cylinder engines, culminating with a 1967 endurance crown on the strength of the mighty 4-liter 330 P4 and 412 P.

Ferrari's use of the midengine configuration in racing was not lost on the company's sales force, its coachbuilders or its clien-

1969 Dino 206 GT

tele. In the mid 1960s, a conflict over a midengine road car was seething behind the scenes at Maranello.

Sergio Pininfarina had personally handled his carrozzeria's Ferrari account since his father had landed it in 1952. For much of 1965, he had locked horns with a conservative, truculent Enzo, trying to convince him to produce a road-going midengine machine.

"He kept insisting it was too dangerous," the effervescent coachbuilder said. "While he felt it was fine for racing and professional drivers, he…was afraid of the safety, of building a car that was too dangerous for customers. That's why he was preparing the front engine with rear drive, the classic layout. The idea of having all the weight in the back was upsetting to him."

Even the unprecedented hoopla generated by the 1966 unveiling of Lamborghini's avant-garde midengine Miura couldn't persuade Enzo to change his mind. "I insisted and insisted, and insisted," Pininfarina recalled. "All the salesmen were with me. We had dramatic meetings in Maranello in which the salesmen and myself were pushing for a mid-engine."

Pininfarina's barrage finally yielded some results: Ferrari approved the experimental Dino for production. This one-off prototype came from Sergio's fertile mind, and broke cover at the Paris Auto Show in 1965. A second, more-refined prototype was shown the following year at Turin.

The preproduction version appeared 12 months later and the world soon had its first road-going midengine "Ferrari," though this beautiful V-6 two-seater was manufactured in cooperation with Fiat and did not, in fact, carry a Ferrari badge.

"When Mr. Ferrari finally said yes," Pininfarina recalled, "he said 'Okay, you make it not with a Ferrari name, but as a Dino.'

1972 and 1973 365 GTB/4 Daytona Spyders

This was because the Dino was a less powerful car and in his [mind], less powerful meant less danger for the customers. I therefore had the permission to develop [it]."

UNIONS, FIAT, OIL, LAUDA, AND THE 308

The popularity of the Dino 206 and 246 GTs helped push Ferrari's sales past the 1,000 barrier for the first time in 1971. Another key was the success of the 365 GTB/4 "Daytona," Ferrari's front-engine answer to Lamborghini's midengine Miura. More than 1,300 of the 170-plus-mph Daytonas were sold before it was replaced in 1974 with Ferrari's first 12-cylinder midengine car, the 365 GT4/BB "Boxer."

But ever-increasing sales, a stream of new models, victories in endurance racing, and participation in F1 couldn't hide Enzo's misery from those close to him. His company was tight on cash and under attack from forces beyond his control. It was wearing

1975 365 GT4/BB

The Old Man down.

"It was a wonderful ten years, from 1957 to 1967," Sergio Scaglietti recalled. "The economic boom was really flabbergasting...Ferrari's company was getting bigger, as was mine. We would often work straight through the night and, in the three months prior to the Mille Miglia, we would work night and day. I used to pay the night shifts quite well, separate from the normal wages. A lot of workers prospered."

That decade-plus of continual growth instilled in all of Italy's workers expectations of better, higher-paying jobs and benefits. The unions gained tremendous strength during that stretch, and in some regions, including that around Modena, social discord and labor unrest were the norm. When workers and management couldn't resolve differences over salaries and conditions, bitter work stoppages were the result.

Scaglietti's view was typical of those in the establishment. The unions, he said, "decided the workers shouldn't do the extra hours. That spoiled everything and the workers became lazy; that was the start of the trouble. The politics were just as bad. It was always influence, influence on everything...It became hell when the unions were born."

During those "hot years," people openly questioned accepted values, and many who did were attracted to Europe's agitating socialist and communist movements. Some who sought to excel at their jobs claimed they were castigated by fellow employees. Student dissent was rampant, and protests

turned violent in March 1968. Union leaders eventually joined forces with the college firebrands, and the situation became even more volatile.

Another thorn in Ferrari's side came from across the Atlantic, where America's new safety and smog regulations were crimping automotive high performance. Add that to the union confrontations and the public's changing mentality toward extravagant sporting cars, and it was easy to see how any maker of European exotics could feel under siege.

"Ferrari was indeed having problems," Scaglietti said. "The workers were giving him hassles and headaches. He was really fed up with the whole thing."

Mauro Forghieri remembered much the same. "The strikes were one of our biggest problems," he said. Parts would arrive late. Tension was constant. Production slowed. Much of the fun had gone out of the game.

In 1969, Scaglietti discovered a way out. Enzo had worked with Fiat since the mid 1960s, supplying engines for the Fiat Dino coupe and spider, and had successfully engaged company patriarch Gianni Agnelli in a conversation to buy Ferrari itself.

Scaglietti was privy to the Ferrari-Fiat talks, so Enzo called him in the spring of 1969 with a proposition—that the two men link their companies.

When Enzo asked, "What do you think of doing something like I am doing?" Scaglietti replied, "Give me the pen! I am ready to sign."

Ferrari returned to the negotiating table in Turin. Scaglietti was now part of Ferrari, he explained, and Fiat needed to purchase both companies. On June 18, 1969, Scaglietti no longer owned his carrozzeria, and Fiat owned 40 percent of Ferrari.

"That was the best thing I ever did," Scaglietti reflected. "I have never understood one thing about the communist ideal."

With the Fiat safety net in place, Ferrari built a custom test track at Fiorano, a small town approximately a mile away from his factory. Mauro Forghieri recalled Ferrari telling him, "You won't have any more economic problems, so do your best."

Ferrari went on to win the Sports World Championship for Makes in 1972 with the 312 PB, then narrowly lost the title in '73 to Matra-Simca. But despite success at the highest levels, Ferrari was questioning the return on investment of sports racing, and at the end of 1972, it closed down its factory endurance-racing program.

"Sports car racing was really what built up the Ferrari myth in the age before the 1970s," Piero Ferrari observed. "Then Formula 1 became more important, when it started to grow with television's involvement."

It was an intelligent decision. The two types of racing were on different trajectories, and for Ferrari to truly compete at the top level in F1, it needed to focus all its resources there.

"[A] problem at Ferrari in [the 1960s] was its enormous number of activities, which led inevitably to energy being expended in different sectors," John Surtees said in *Ferrari 1947-1997*. "For example, when the cars had to be prepared for Le Mans, Formula 1 was clearly overlooked, although we could compensate in part for our disappointments by the success of the Sports prototype cars."

A hitch in the plan was that Ferrari withdrew from factory-backed endurance racing without getting its Grand Prix house in order. The F1 effort was in disarray, consumed by political intrigue, hobbled by badly designed cars. Interestingly, Forghieri was able to right the Grand Prix cars by using downforce tricks learned in endurance racing. Order was restored when Luca Cordero di Montezemolo was brought in to run the team in 1973. Born in Bologna in 1947, Montezemolo was an attorney, with experience at top firms in Rome and New York and a specialty in international commerical law. On-track performance soared when Austrian Niki Lauda was hired away from BRM to be the Maranello team's No. 1 driver.

Enzo Ferrari, meanwhile, was suffering from ill health. He traveled little and lived at the home he had built in the middle of the Fiorano track. Far removed from the true ins-and-outs of the Formula 1 scene, he relied on television coverage and on-site advisors. Unfortunately, many of these individuals were more interested in protecting their fiefdoms than in the good of the team.

Forghieri and Lauda were nonetheless diligent in developing and testing Ferrari's heavily revamped F1 mount, the 312 T. The F1 effort benefited from Montezemolo's rising career path, which soon had him named senior vice president of external relations for the Fiat Group, and from Lauda's wiles in cutting through the layers of self-interest.

"If The Old Man was absent," Richard Williams wrote in his

1984 308 GTS QV and 1979 308 GTB

excellent biography, *Enzo Ferrari*, "Lauda would walk across the road to the factory, knock on his office door, and walk in. In this way he short-circuited those who had been exerting influence without taking direct responsibility. And Montezemolo's Agnelli connections gave him a particular authority and independence within the setup, as well as guaranteeing the sympathy of the parent company.

"He was young," Lauda said of Montezemolo, "but he was good."

The results of that work were spectacular: three F1 world driving championships and four constructors titles in the second half of the 1970s.

On the road, Ferrari breathed new life into its model line with the introduction in 1974 of the 308 series. Launched as the four seat Dino 308 GT/4, these were Maranello's first Ferrari-badged

road cars without a 12-cylinder engine. Along with their successor V-8 models, they became the company's financial bread and butter.

The Dino 308 GT/4 could not have been introduced at a more appropriate time. The first oil crisis had hit in October 1973, and the entire sports-car and GT universe reeled. Now the general public viewed exotics as a waste of precious, finite resources. Some nations instituted strict speed limits; Italy and others banning driving on Sunday.

"Will exotic cars survive?" asked *Road & Track* on its March 1975 cover. It was a fair question, considering that Maserati, Lamborghini, and Aston Martin had all declared bankruptcy. Ferrari sales slumped from 1,844 in 1972 to just 1,337 in 1975,

Enzo Ferrari, Maranello, December 1981

and while that did squeeze cash flow, the Fiat safety net all but assured Ferrari's continued existence.

Then Ferrari's next generation of two-seat sports cars was introduced. The midengine V-8 308 GTB and GTS were fast and beautiful. Sales took off. In 1979, Ferrari annual production crossed the 2,000-unit threshold for the first time, with 2,221 cars built.

The following year, Turin was the site of a revolt dubbed the "March of 40,000." Led by Fiat employees, it was an open rejection of the unions' power and intrusiveness. It proved a tipping point: The unions' strength was never the same. Over the next few years, companies such as Ferrari and Fiat would once again focus their efforts on designing and manufacturing new cars, rather than on battling organized labor and on simply surviving.

TWILIGHT YEARS

In December 1981, the author attended Ferrari's annual company luncheon as a guest of former Ferrari race-team manager and prominent Italian journalist Franco Lini. Everyone was there—Fiat and Ferrari brass, Sergio Pininfarina, drivers Gilles Villeneuve and Didier Pironi, and hundreds of employees.

It quickly became clear The Old Man still had the "It" factor. Though tables had been set hours earlier and doors were open, we all milled around in the restaurant parking lot until a light-blue Fiat sedan pulled up. It stopped, the rear door opened, and out popped Ferrari, the trademark dark glasses and light-colored raincoat in place. He looked around as several employees pulled out cameras for pictures and, after a moment's hesitation, walked into the restaurant.

It was as if the Red Sea parted, all of us following in his wake. When Ferrari spoke during the lunch, the room was quiet, all gripped by his words. Even when he wasn't speaking or eating but just staring off into space, one could easily sense his mind's wheels turning at full speed.

After lunch, a group of us went over to the factory, shut down for the occasion. We walked the silent production lines, then visited the racing department. A few moments later, Ferrari F1 team driver Didier Pironi came in and, while admiring the new car for the upcoming season, handed me a body panel. This was in the early years of composite materials, and much to my amazement, I easily waved a large section of the car in the air above my head.

The following year, Ferrari won the F1 constructors title and Pironi narrowly missed the driver's crown. The team won another constructors title in 1983, then entered what was a mostly downhill slide. It would be 16 years before Ferrari won another F1 championship.

In the showrooms, it was another story. Even the second oil crisis didn't slow road-car sales, and production topped 3,000 for the first time in 1985. The go-go mid '80s also saw a Ferrari spawn a new phenonemon: the instant collectible market. Intended to return Ferrari to sports-racing competition, the limited-production 288 GTO was snapped up by a rapacious

1990 F40

breed of investors and speculators who resold production cars for considerably more than their sticker price.

In the summer of 1987, journalists assembled in Maranello for the introduction of the F40, created to celebrate the company's 40th anniversary.

"A little more than a year ago," Enzo told the gathering, "I expressed a wish to my engineers: Build a car to be the best in the world. And now that car is here."

With that, a red cover was swept aside, revealing Ferrari's first road car with a claimed top speed of more than 200 mph. The journalists broke into spontaneous applause. Ferrari production topped 4,000 for the first time in 1988. And by 1990, F40s were going for more than $1 million in the frothy secondary market.

The F40 was the last Ferrari produced on Enzo's watch. In failing health as he reached 90, Ferrari died in August 1988, of

kidney failure. At his side were his surviving son, Piero, and Piero's mother, Lina Lardi. In all respects, Enzo was a man of his time and of his station in life. Lina Lardi was his long-time inamorata, and only after the death of his wife, Laura, in 1978, did Ferrari include Piero in his public life. Presented as Piero Lardi Ferrari, he would become an intergal part of the company management team.

"You really can't compare anyone to Enzo Ferrari," said Brenda Vernor in 1995. Not only had Vernor spent years as Ferrari's personal assistant, she had worked closely with a number of F1 bosses for almost three decades.

"Ferrari was a strong man—and a weak man. He never showed his feelings. But he was a very human person because he had come from nothing, and he knew what it was like to be an ordinary mechanic who had problems and needed things.

"If any of his mechanics in the racing department—or anybody, for that matter—had a problem with a doctor or needed a specialist, they would go to The Old Man and he would pick up the phone and make an appointment. He really did have a knack for getting the most out of the people who worked for him.

"He had a very good sense of humor and would always notice things. Even if he didn't say, he saw everything. He may not have let you know, but I reckon if you went to him the day after and asked 'What was Brenda wearing yesterday?' he would have been able to tell you.

"There will never be another man like him. What you must realize is...for us Enzo Ferrari is still alive, because when you speak of Ferrari you don't think of Fiat, you think of him."

A COMPANY'S REBIRTH

After Ferrari's death, the Fiat-controlling Angelli family added another 40 percent to its 50-percent share of Ferrari; Piero Ferrari retained 10 percent.

In the half-decade that followed, the Ferrari company seemed to live on Enzo's legacy, with no definitive voice to set it on track. Alain Prost narrowly missed winning the F1 championship in 1990, then the team fell considerably off the pace.

The road cars also suffered. By the early 1990s, Ferraris no

2003 Enzo

longer were regular winners of magazine comparison tests. Quality control suffered. Rocked by worldwide recession, sales plummeted from nearly 4,600 in 1991 to less than half that in 1993.

Fortunately, Ferrari's management hadn't been deceived by those lofty late-'80s sales figures and had brought in a new captain for the ship. In late 1991, Luca Cordero di Montezemolo was named Ferrari president and CEO. He was a man with a mission. "I had just bought a 348 with my own money," he recalled 10 years after his hiring, "and, with the exception of its good looks, I was utterly disappointed."

Charismatic, driven, focused, Montezemolo transformed the company in many ways. Under his leadership, one outstanding model after another left the gates of Maranello—the 355, 360 and 430, the 550 Maranello and Enzo, to name a few. He set about righting the Formula 1 effort, triggering the Schumacher era of utter domination. He also orchestated the 1999 purchase of Maserati from Fiat and the turnaround of that former crosstown rival.

Ferrari was most certainly back, and it wasn't just sales numbers and F1 titles that proved it. When debt-laden Fiat sold 34 percent of its Ferrari holdings to several banks in 2002 for approximately $700 million, it established the worth of Ferrari/Maserati at approximately $2.1 billion, or about one-third that of Fiat. At the time, combined Ferrari and Maserati annual production was around 8,000 cars. Fiat manufactured approximately 1.7 million vehicles per year.

But Montezemolo's vision extended beyond what the public saw on the roads and at the racetrack. He wanted to create an entirely new working environment, one that, as Ferrari literature expressed it, "put people at the center of innovation."

The firm began using architecture as a source of brand identity, starting with the Renzo Piano-designed avant-garde wind tunnel that opened in 1998. Then came a new machining department, a paint shop that bordered on science fiction in its operation, a product-development center and other structures. Fabulous together, each also created a unique environment on its own. The engine assembly plant, for example, was quiet, well-lit and had several atriums inside, all in the effort to create an ideal working environment.

Profitable Ferrari not only poured money into its own facility, it did the same for Maserati. The Maserati factory was fully renovated, the product line revamped. Maserati became a highly attractive holding, and in February 2005 was repurchased by Fiat, which merged it with Alfa Romeo. Ferrari once again would concentrate on its own fortunes.

If Enzo could see what had become of his factory and of Maranello, he would recognize neither. No longer a sleepy country village, Maranello had assumed an air of sophistication. It daily attracted visitors from around the world. The factory it housed was truly a small city, with roads, intersections and sign-posts listing street names to guide guests. Inside those hallowed gates, the past blended beautifully with the present, a new entrance on the eastern side of the factory as impressive as the historic gate on the west.

"When I look at where Ferrari is today," Piero Ferrari observed in 2005, "neither my father nor myself could ever imagine anything so big. It was really just a family business. Now Ferrari is a large company, an industry. The dimensions of everything are so very different."

Ferrari S.p.A., Maranello, April 2005

The
Road
Cars

1950 166 MM Barchetta

166 MM		
1948-1953		
Number made:		
	25 Barchettas	
	11 berlinettas	
	9 spyders	
Engine:	1996cc V-12, SOHC,	
	140 hp @ 6600 rpm	
Transmission:	5-speed	
Wheelbase:	86.6 inches / 2200mm	
Weight:	1,430 lbs. (approx., Barchetta)	

1948-1953
166 MM

A "LITTLE BOAT" WITH A LARGE HEART HELPS LAUNCH THE FERRARI LEGEND

Enzo Ferrari had been producing cars for little more than a year when his marketing instincts took over. The handful of machines he had made ranged in appearance from homely to plain, at best.

The immortal 166 MM "Barchetta" changed that. The "MM" designation stood for Mille Miglia, the famed 1,000-mile Italian road race won by a Ferrari in May 1948. The "166" referenced the displacement in cubic centimeters of one the engine's cylinders.

For its seminal shape, Ferrari turned to Carrozzeria Touring, Italy's most prestigious designer and manufacturer of car bodies at the time. Ferrari knew the firm from his Alfa Romeo days, when the coachbuilder was building an incredible variety of street and race-winning competition cars. Touring also designed and constructed the body and cockpit for Ferrari's first-ever cars, a pair of open two-seaters released in 1940 as the Auto Avio Costruzioni 815.

Touring's designs were not only stunning but extremely weight efficient, thanks to the company's patented "Superleggera" coachbuilding system. Superleggera means "super light" in Italian, and that was the goal of Carrozzeria Touring—to make its bodies as svelte and aerodynamic as possible. "Weight is the enemy and wind the obstacle" was how company cofounder Felice Bianchi Anderloni summed up the firm's philosophy.

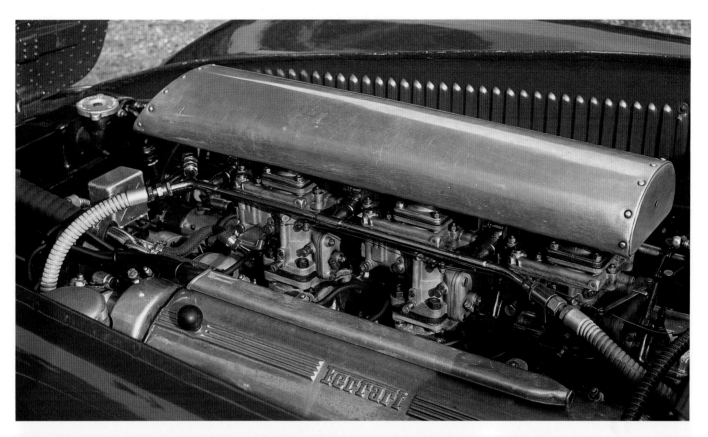

1950 166 MM berlinetta

Like all coachbuilders, Touring received a chassis from a manufacturer such as Ferrari. The carrozzeria's craftsmen would then make up a frame composed of small-diameter metal tubing that was shaped on a jig; they then gas-welded the tubing together. The frame resembled the shape of the car's body, and it was arc-welded onto the chassis. The thin aluminum body panels were formed by hand or made by mechanical hammers and welded to the supporting tube frame. The resulting package was quite rigid, durable, and very lightweight.

"Enzo Ferrari was a very clever man," remembered the man who styled Touring's 166 models, Carlo Felice Bianchi Anderloni, Touring's head of design. "He recognized he needed a sophisticated, uniform appearance so that when a number of his cars lined up at races such as the Mille Miglia, people would recognize that they were Ferraris."

Anderloni had two reasons to work exceptionally hard on the project. Ferrari was a well-known name in Italy's automotive world. And Carlo's father, Felice, had unexpectedly passed away; the industry was wondering whether the son could carry on with the same degree of creativity.

"My first impression was a car for Ferrari should not look like something already seen, for the name 'Ferrari' was new, as were the engine and chassis," Anderloni said. "This meant the body should also have a new appearance—not extravagant, but technical, something that was fresh.

"In my mind it was absolutely imperative to give Ferrari his own 'emblem'—an identity."

Anderloni met with Ferrari engineer Gioachino Colombo to brainstorm ideas. Ferrari then supplied the dimensions of the tube frame, 140-horsepower 2.0-liter V-12 engine and other mechanical components.

Even with the pressure on him, the creative process was immensely satisfying for the stylist. Carlo's mind was always working, and Ferrari had given him a blank sheet of paper. Like his father, Carlo would often wake during the night, roll over and grab the pad of paper on the bedside table, then scribble some notes.

Touring's 166 "Spyder da corsa" (racing spyder) was first seen at the Turin Auto Show in September 1948. Its arresting looks astounded all, including Italy's most-prominent automotive journalist, Giovanni Canestrini. "When he saw the open two-seater," Anderloni remembered with a smile, "he said, 'I am stunned, for that is quite unsettling. That is not a car; it is absolutely new! That is a little boat—a barchetta!'"

The name stuck, the model being forever associated with it. Not only would Barchettas go on to win many races for Ferrari, but its revolutionary looks would influence scores of sports cars, from Alfa Romeo's famed Disco Volante to Shelby's AC Cobra.

Several months later, Anderloni designed a closed coupe that also used the 166 MM's chassis. This berlinetta was primarily a competition machine, its fastback styling taking cues from the Barchetta.

The 166 MM would soldier on into 1953, and other coach-builders, such as Vignale and Zagato, made bodies for the chassis. But it was the designs from Touring that were instrumental in giving Ferrari its first "face," and they will always be most closely associated with the 166 legacy.

1950 166 Inter by Ghia

166, 195 & 212 Inter

166, 195 & 212 INTER
166 INTER 1948-1950 195 INTER 1950-1951 212 INTER 1951-1953

Number made:	
166:	37
195:	25
212:	78
Engine:	
166:	1996cc V-12, SOHC, 110 hp @ 6000 rpm
195:	2431cc V-12, SOHC, 135 hp @ 7000 rpm
212:	2562cc V-12, SOHC, 150 hp @ 6500 rpm
Transmission:	5-speed (all models)
Wheelbase:	
166:	98.4 inches / 2500mm
195:	98.4 inches / 2500mm
212:	102.3 inches / 2600mm
Weight:	
166:	2,000 lbs. (factory)
195:	n/a
212:	2,200 lbs. (factory)

GRAND TOURING: THE FIRST FERRARIS DESIGNED PRIMARILY FOR ROAD USE

The 166 Inter used the same basic mechanical setup—tubular chassis, V-12 engine, independent front suspension, rigid rear axle—as the competition-oriented 166 MM. But it was a larger, more civilized package intended for the street, not for racing.

Wheelbase was stretched 11.8 inches (300mm) for an overall span of 98.4 inches (2500mm). That provided enough additional interior space for two small rear seats, and the 2.0-liter V-12 was detuned to 110 horsepower, making it more tractable. Enzo Ferrari took a strong interest in his new four-seat model, and with good reason.

"You must remember," explained his son, Piero Ferrari, in 2001, "that my father was then 50 years old. While his name would become famous with our sports cars, he had a very strong affinity to the 2+2 because of their comfort and room."

Ferrari used "Inter" to identify cars not built specifically for competition, though many did find their way onto racetracks in the hands of private owners. This was, after all, a day in which sports cars were supposed to be capable of such dual duty.

1950 166 Inter by Ghia

The first 166 Inter was designed by Carrozzeria Touring's great styling chief, Carlo Felice Bianchi Anderloni. It took appearance cues from the 166 MM Barchetta, and Touring used its patented Superleggera coachbuilding system for the body's construction. Recognizing that Enzo Ferrari was quite tall and was fond of Lancia's cute-but-roomy Ardea sedan, Anderloni used that car's cabin dimensions for this new 2+2.

Touring's 166 Inter made its debut at the 1948 Turin Auto Show and was well-received. "Coachwork by Touring and V-12 2-litre-engined chassis by Ferrari, combined, make a high-performance car typifying the present day Italian style," said England's *The Motor.*

Always eager to maximize his cars' performance reputation on the road, and recognizing that the Inter was in fact being used in competition, Enzo took a page from the American bible of "no substitute for cubic inches" and followed the original with a more-powerful version. Introduced in 1950, the 195 Inter had a 2431cc 135-horsepower V-12, which was itself increased to 2562cc in 1951 to identify the 212 Inter.

With larger, more-powerful engines came additional race victories and prestige. That made Ferraris ever more desirable to Italy's burgeoning coachbuilding industry. Postwar raw-materiel shortages were easing, and the relationship between auto manufacturers and coachbuilders was closer than ever. There was immense pressure to introduce new models quickly. The easiest way to accomplish that was with a new body style on an established chassis, a solution made possible in great part by an abundance of inexpensive skilled labor. Coachbuilders flourished.

Adding fuel to the fire was a change in mentality of the average Italian.

"The Communist threat continued through most of 1948,"

1952 212 Inter by Pinin Farina

1952 212 Inter by Pinin Farina

1950 212 Inter by Vignale

Anderloni explained. "After they were defeated, everyone felt a tremendous release. We were all happy and wanted to amuse ourselves. This created a great desire to work, which made the concept of work very exciting."

Laborers and craftsmen flocked to Turin, Milan, and Modena—cities at the heart of Italy's expanding auto industry. Coach-builders responded with a burst of creativity and, by the early 1950s, Italy was the trendsetter in automotive design. Recalling the period, second-generation coachbuilders Sergio Pininfarina and Nuccio Bertone noted that their fathers were preoccupied during the war with what they would build when hostilities ceased. Once peace arrived, it was as if a giant spring released.

Stablimenti Farina was then in its fourth decade, and the handful of Ferraris it made were among its last before closing its doors in 1953. Many more Inter coupes and cabriolets (approximately 25) came from another Turin-based coachbuilder nearly as old, Carrozzeria Ghia.

But most prolific on the Inter chassis was Carrozzeria Vignale. This house was established in the second half of the 1940s by Alfredo Vignale, who had a homespun way of designing. "He just knew what he wanted, so he would kneel down and sketch cars on the factory floor," recalled Francesco Gavina, a Vignale worker.

1951 212 Inter by Vignale

Vignale's designs were simple until the early 1950s, when he teamed with stylist Giovanni Michelotti. Then just 30, Michelotti was an incredible talent and would be among the industry's most active designers over the next two decades. Michelotti's ideas flowed at an amazing pace, and Vignale, described by a former employee as "a magician with the hammer," would turn them into car bodies.

The variety of Vignale bodies for the Inter series was staggering. They started out fairly conservative. By the time the series ended in 1952, they evidenced remarkable creativity— and flamboyance.

Of note was one of Vignale's final 212 Inters, a red coupe encircled by a robust beltline of brightwork spearheaded by chrome front-fender "eyebrows." That didn't phase Enzo confidant and Ferrari promoter extraordinaire, Luigi Chinetti. This machine was the cover subject of the October 1953 issue of the American magazine *Auto Sport Review,* and the article quoted Chinetti pitching the 212 to its eventual buyer, one Alfred Ducato of Atherton, California. "Mr. Ducato," Chinetti said, "I am going to do something for you—I am going to see that you get the most beautiful car in the world."

1951 340 America by Touring

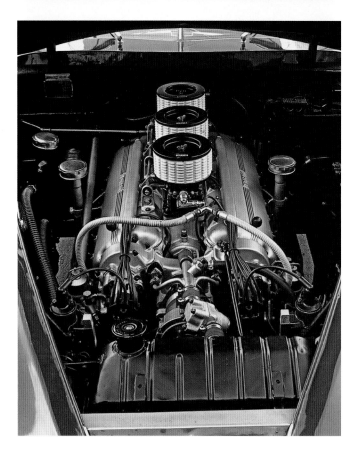

1950-1953
340 & 342 America

A LARGER ENGINE, A DASH OF AMENITIES, AND THE EMERGENCE OF FERRARI'S SIGNATURE STYLIST

In the early 1950s, Ferrari was battling Alfa Romeo for supremacy in grand prix racing. To tip the tide in his favor, Enzo turned to Aurelio Lampredi, a gifted engineer with a background in the aeronautic field. Lampredi responded by designing the "long-block" V-12, so called because the distance between adjacent cylinders was some 20mm greater than in the Colombo V-12. The long-block engine made its grand prix debut in 1950 as a 340-horsepower 4.5-liter aboard Ferrari's 375 F1 single-seater.

To civilize it for use in Ferrari's road cars, the 375's V-12's bore and stroke was decreased to produce a displacement of 4.1 liters, and its compression ratio was lowered. The result was installed in the 340 America, for which Touring, Ghia, and Vignale produced an array of open and closed body styles. These cars were used on both street and track, depending upon the commissioning client's order.

The "America" moniker belied Ferrari's keen commercial instincts and the growing importance of the U.S. market. America was a land of affluence, where everything was bigger, including the size of the client and his appetite for luxury. Thus, in 1952, the 342 America was born.

Compared to the 340 America, the 342 boasted a longer

340 & 342 AMERICA

1950-1953

Number made:
340: 23
342: 6
Engine:
340: 4101cc V-12, SOHC,
220 hp @ 6000 rpm
342: 4101cc V-12, SOHC,
200 hp @ 5000 rpm
Transmission:
340: 5-speed
342: 4-speed
Wheelbase:
340: 95.3 inches / 2420mm
342: 104.3 inches / 2650mm
Weight:
340: 2,000 lbs. (approx.)
342: n/a

1951 340 America by Ghia

1952 342 America by Pinin Farina for King Leopold of Belgium

wheelbase, wider track, a more tractable engine, and an easier-to-use gearbox with four speeds instead of five. It was also much more luxurious, as evidenced by its greater weight.

The 342 America marked the emergence of Pinin Farina as the preeminent coachbuilder on Ferrari chassis. This Turin-based carrozzeria was founded by Battista "Pinin" Farina. Pinin started in the industry when he was he was barely a teenager at his brother's carrozzeria, Stablimenti Farina. He rose through the ranks and was soon working closely with many of Stablimenti Farina's most important clients. He also traveled to America and had an audience with Henry Ford, who offered him a job.

But Pinin wanted his own firm, and in May 1930, he started S.A. Carrozzeria Pinin Farina. His first commission came from auto manufacturer Vincenzo Lancia, a friend and a confidant who had encouraged him to go independent. "You are an artist," Lancia told him, "(and) I represent the long arm of engineering."

Pinin Farina's reputation grew, and after the war, he was but a "signature car" away from recognized greatness. That car was 1947's Cisitalia 202, which basically invented the postwar berlinetta, or fastback, look. Subsequent berlinettas from Farina, Ghia, and Vignale on Ferrari and other chassis clearly derived from Pinin's seminal shape.

Enzo Ferrari watched Pinin's ascent with admiration. "I...had dealings with some of the greatest names in the business...all of them eager to build bodies for our cars," Ferrari noted in his memoirs. "What I wanted for my cars was character and I found it with the help of Giovanni Battista Pininfarina."

Pinin was just as enamored with Ferrari. "It was his character which interested me," he wrote in his autobiography *Born with the Automobile*, "as tightly closed as a walnut, disdaining the bonds the world proffered...(I)t was obvious that for some time he was looking for his 'own' coachbuilder with whom he could

1953 342 America by Pinin Farina

establish a new kind of harmony."

The two men had been acquaintances for the better part of 30 years but, thanks to strong egos, each rebuffed overtures to visit the other's factory. The dance continued for several months until they decided to meet halfway, in the town of Tortona.

Pinin assigned the Ferrari account to his son Sergio, then just in his 20s, and the first Pinin Farina body appeared in June 1952 on a handsome 212 Inter cabriolet. This was followed by a coupe that used very similar design language, and Pinin Farina went on to make a brief series of 212s, each minutely different.

Pinin's 342 Americas continued these design themes, but the 342s had a regal air with a body that appeared slightly lower and elongated than the 212s'. The first was a cabriolet ordered by King Leopold of Belgium. A second cabriolet went to Luigi Chinetti in America. Pinin then made three 342 America coupes. The last of the six 342s made was a cabriolet by Vignale.

That Pinin Farina was responsible for the majority of Ferrari's most prestigious model in 1952 was a taste of what the future held in store.

1953 375 America by Vignale

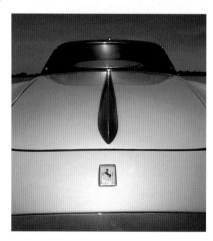

375 AMERICA

1953-1955

Number made:	14
Engine:	4523cc V-12, SOHC, 300 hp @ 6300 rpm
Transmission:	4-speed
Wheelbase:	110.2 inches / 2800mm
Weight:	2,500 lbs. (approx.)

1953-1955

375 America

A STANDARDIZED CHASSIS AND ENGINE DESIGN SET THE PATTERN FOR THINGS TO COME

In October 1953, Ferrari demonstrated he was a true constructor of motorcars by employing a technique that would become *de rigeur* in the industry much later. Platform sharing is when a manufacturer uses a chassis or "platform" to make more than one model using those components.

At the Paris Auto Show, Ferrari displayed the first 375 America. Its tubular chassis had a wheelbase of 110.2 inches (2800mm), the longest of any Ferrari to that time. The platform was identical to that used by another new model launched that year, the 250 Europa.

The 375 was aimed squarely at the American market, and half the 14 produced were sold in the United States. Part of its appeal was its 4.5-liter V-12, a Lampredi long-block with bore increased by 4mm to 84mm. Output was 300 horsepower at 6300 rpm. Depending upon the final drive ratio, this gave a quoted top speed of 144-155 mph, an astronomical figure at a time most cars struggled to reach 100.

The 375 America was the last model with Ferrari-factory-sanctioned coachwork by Vignale. Most were styled by Pinin

1955 375 America by Pinin Farina, chassis 0355 AL

Farina, and these were the versions that took the breath away.

"Beautifully clean, unbroken lines distinguish Pinin Farina's coupe body on the famous Ferrari 375 America chassis," said England's *Autocar* magazine. Indeed, Pinin Farina would use virtually identical styling on a run of 250 Europas for which it built bodies starting two months later.

These shapes helped foster a change in attitude by Enzo. Sergio Pinin Farina's work with the Ferrari account was overcoming stiff resistance from Enzo, who originally wanted only to work with Battista himself.

Pinin Farina's custom coachwork on Ferrari chassis reflected that increasing level of trust and confidence. Demand for unique automotive creations was on the rise, the stigma of showing one's success and affluence in the years after the war having given way to the "economic miracle," a decade-long expansion that swept Europe beginning in 1952.

A perfect example of the period's creativity was the last 375 America made, chassis 0355 AL. Built for Gianni Agnelli, heir to the Fiat empire and one of Italy's wealthiest men, its upright imposing front end was quite unlike anything seen on a Ferrari.

"Because only one car was made," former Pininfarina stylist Francesco Martinengo explained, "it was much easier to experiment with these type of (styling) options than it was on a production car. Owners such as Agnelli were understanding, so we only had to please one person and not a large group of customers."

Carrozzeria Scaglietti, circa 1971

Heavenly Bodies:
Italy's Coachbuilders

No high-performance sports cars can boast Ferrari's lineage of breathtakingly beautiful design, and most of the credit for that goes to the coachbuilders. For only a tiny handful of Ferrari bodies have been styled, or built, by Ferrari itself. Most are the work of peerless artisans carrying out the hallowed tradition of the carrozzeria.

In spirit, automotive coachbuilding shares much with the culture of fine custom-tailoring, and has a heritage just as long. The industry's roots in Italy can be traced to the late sixteenth century, with the construction of elegant horse-drawn carriages.

As the automobile became prevalent in the early twentieth century, the "coach" builders adapted or died, while others formed to meet the growing demand for car bodies.

By the late 1920s, carrozzerias were an integral part of the automotive industry in Italy, in much of Europe, and in America, too. In contrast to the designers responsible for the look of the millions of mass-market automobiles, coachbuilders concentrated on designing and constructing bodies for expensive, limited production cars.

"When someone wanted a car, they bought a complete running chassis at the factory," explained Carlo Felice Bianchi Anderloni, who grew up in his father's firm, Carrozzeria Touring, in Milan. "The owner then went to a carrozzeria, an

independent coachbuilder that made the body for his car. They became an important part of the production process, for they were the ones who actually finished the car."

After World War II, the carrozzerias flourished as Italy became the design center of the world.

"Most of their key people were in their early 40s to early 50s," automotive designer Tom Tjaarda reflected. "This allowed them to present mature forms, shapes without childish ideas."

Also helping was an attractive postwar labor rate of approximately 50 cents an hour. Clients from around the world sought out the coachbuilders of Italy to design and produce cars using their talented but inexpensive craftsmen.

In the 1960s, car production in Europe increased exponentially, and safety laws were initiated in numerous countries around the world. Many automakers took all design and body production in-house. Only the largest coachbuilding companies survived.

Then the oil crisis and resulting worldwide recession all but dried up demand for one-offs and *fouri serie* (limited-production) models. That killed most every small carrozzeria.

In the 1990s, auto design and engineering underwent a revolution with introduction of CAD (computer-aided design) and CAM (computer-aided modeling). These allow cars to be

Pininfarina's Grugliasco trimming plant, circa 1966

Battista "Pinin" Farina

designed on computers and in virtual-reality rooms, and the most sophisticated programs could crash-test a car. The new technology proved a boon to the coachbuilders, and a number of automakers employed such carrozzeria as Pininfarina, Ital Design, and Zagato as integral pieces of their design process.

Ferrari has a rich relationship with coachbuilders. It used numerous design houses to style and assemble its cars in the late 1940s and early 1950s before Enzo Ferrari settled on the masters at Pinin Farina and Scaglietti.

Today, Pininfarina continues to design bodies for Ferrari's road cars, while Carrozzeria Scaglietti constructs most of them. The bodies are shipped to the Ferrari factory, then painted and stored in Ferrari's huge hi-tech finishing facility, before being mated to the chassis.

1953 375 MM by Pinin Farina

1953-1955
375 MM

A COMPETITION-BRED MACHINE BRINGS HIGH SPEED AND HIGH STYLE TO THE ROAD

It was born to win races, but a handful of clients who wanted to take to the road in one of the very fastest sports cars of the day ordered a 375 MM.

With the 375 MM, Ferrari blurred the line between competition machines and road cars. Its heart was a spectacular Lampredi-designed 340-horsepower 4522cc V-12 derived from the 340 America's 4.1-liter engine. Pinin Farina in the second half of 1953, covered the 375's sturdy tubular chassis with two spectacular shapes—one a berlinetta body, the other a spyder.

Within weeks of their appearance in competition, preferred clients such as Bao Dai, the emperor of what is today Vietnam, began asking for a more comfortable version for the street. His 375 MM spyder (chassis 0450 AM) was made during the summer of 1954 and looks nearly identical to its competition brethren save a different windscreen and a more comfortable—but hardly plush—interior.

The 375 MM berlinetta was also highly prized, and was likely the fastest street car of the day. French industrialist Michel Paul-Cavallier ordered one that was nearly identical to the competition version, having a wind deflector mounted on the hood. Preferred client Enrico Wax's 375 received a more comfortable interior and different shaped fenders.

The 375 MM was the subject of two of the most spectacular Ferraris ever made.

The first was chassis 0456 AM, a berlinetta aerodinamica speciale that debuted at 1954's Paris Auto Show and would influence Pinin Farina and other manufacturers and designers for years. *Road & Track* called the one-off "the outstanding car of the show." Film director Roberto Rossellini agreed. Shortly after the show closed, he bought the Ferrari and frequently used it to drive son Roberto to school.

The second was chassis 0402 AM. This 375 started life as a Pinin Farina spyder but following an accident, owner Rossellini wanted it converted to a roadgoing coupe. Ferrari sales manager Girolamo Gardini recommended sending it to local coachbuilder Sergio Scaglietti, who created from it one of the most-beautiful Ferrari one-offs ever.

375 MM

1953-1955

Number made:	24 (includes competition cars)
Engine:	4522cc V-12, SOHC, 340 hp @ 7000 rpm
Transmission:	4-speed
Wheelbase:	102.3 inches / 2600mm
Weight:	2,400 lbs. (berlinetta) 2,000 lbs. (spyder)

1953 375 MM Berlinetta Aerodinamica by Pinin Farina, chassis 0456 AM

1954 375 MM by Scaglietti, chassis 0402 AM

1953 250 Europa

250 EUROPA & 250 EUROPA GT
250 Europa 1953-1954 250 Eurpoa GT 1954-1955

Number made:
250 Europa: 17 (16 coupes, 1 convertible)
250 Europa GT: 40 (incl. approx.10 Speciales)
Engine:
250 Europa: 2963cc V-12, SOHC,
                200 hp @ 6000 rpm
250 Europa GT: 2953cc V-12, SOHC,
                220 hp @ 7000 rpm
Transmission:
250 Europa: 4-speed
250 Europa GT: 5-speed
Wheelbase:
250 Europa: 110.2 inches / 2800mm
250 Europa GT: 102.3 inches / 2600mm
Weight:
250 Europa: 2,500 lbs. (approx.)
250 Europa GT: 2,300 lbs.

1953-1955

250 Europa & Europa GT

"GT"APPEARS IN A MODEL NAME, AND THE GOLDEN AGE OF THE FERRARI ROAD CAR BEGINS

The 250 Europa's debut at 1953's Paris Auto Show demonstrated Enzo Ferrari's determination to cost-effectively produce a greater range of cars.

Built on the robust tubular chassis of the 375 America, the Paris Show 250 Europa had spectacular Vignale coachwork and a 2963cc V-12 based on Lampredi's long-block engines. These Lampredi 250 engines were quite "square," with bore and stroke being identical at 68mm.

Though Vignale made the body for that first 250 Europa, Pinin Farina's work dominated the series, with all but two coming from Ferrari's new favorite carrozzeria. Pinin Farina also made a lovely one-off 250 Europa convertible shown at the 1954 New York Auto Show.

A year after the Europa's introduction, the Europa GT made its debut at Paris. The model was once again dominated by

1954 250 Europa GT

Pinin Farina's coachwork and was underpinned by a new chassis with a wheelbase shortened from the Europa/375 America layout by about eight inches, to 102.3 inches (2600mm). Track was widened. And starting with chassis 0387 GT, the front suspension's leaf springs were replaced with coil springs, giving the model more precise handling.

An even bigger change was under the hood. The Europa GT's V-12 measured 2953cc, 10cc less than the Europa's. But the difference was greater than the displacement indicated, for the Lampredi long-block had been replaced by a Colombo-designed V-12. Bore and stoke were the classic Ferrari 250 measurements of 73 and 58.8mm, identical to those in the race-winning 250 MM competition models.

Most Europa GTs had coachwork nearly identical to that of the 250 Europa. But starting in early 1955, Pinin Farina made a number of Speciales on the Europa GT chassis. Among the first was chassis 0385 GT, with coachwork identical to Pinin Farina's 250 and 375 MM berlinettas. Chassis 0407 had more-traditional front styling on a body quite similar to the "production" Europa GT.

That summer, Pinin Farina developed a styling theme that greatly influenced future Ferraris. Europa GT chassis 0393 GT had a striking long-nose coachwork with a fulsome sail panel, a cue carried through on chassis 0425 GT.

Pinin Farina's themes were clearly evolving. Pinin, his son Sergio, and the talented craftsmen that worked alongside them

1955 250 Europa GT, chassis 0407 GT

1955 250 Europa GT Coupe Speciale, chassis 0393 GT

1955 250 Europa GT Coupe Speciale, chassis 0425 GT

were establishing a lasting design language.

Stylist Francesco Martinengo was in the thick of things during this yeasty period. Business was rapidly expanding, so "we were often working on the razor's edge," he recalled. This led to continual experimentation and refinement of design themes. A wooden body buck would be modified slightly. Or the men might take the buck, or the resulting metal form for a certain body piece or design element, and use it on another car.

"It was really due to the panel beaters that Pinin Farina was able to make the forms that set the world on fire," Martinengo said. "Some of the areas, like where the windshield meets the hood and fender line, they were delicate sections that were hard to design. We would do it in wood and then fill it in with some material by hand, usually clay. That is how we developed some very intricate details, especially where the windshield meets the roof and where sharp curves would meet flat surfaces."

Such complexity started to become a thing of the past with chassis 0429 GT. It marked a leap forward for the design theme, one that made the coachwork easier to produce. This Europa GT's silhouette was generally the same as 0393 and 0425, but the rear roofline dropped in front of the trunklid, and the rear wheel arches were all but eliminated. Louvers by the engine compartment and on the greenhouse disappeared, and the grille was less ornate. Restrained, sleek and elegant, the car lacked the flamboyance of the earlier Europa GT Speciales. In all, Pinin Farina built five Europa GTs, the last being chassis 0447 GT.

1955 250 Europa GT

1955-1958
250 GT, 250 GT Boano & 250 GT Ellena

ARTFUL VARIATIONS ON THE THEME OF THE GRAND TOURING COUPE

Pinin Farina's work on the last five 250 Europa GTs paid dividends with Ferrari's first true production model, the 250 GT. The coachbuilder's facility was at capacity, and a new factory was under construction. So production of the 250 GT was shifted to Carrozzeria Boano.

Mario Boano and son Gian Paolo established the firm in 1954 after they left Carrozzeria Ghia. Their first Ferrari was a one-off 250 GT cabriolet in early 1956.

Their Boano 250 GT was built in 1956 and '57, the 64 examples near mirror images of Pinin Farina's 250 Europa GT prototypes.

Production was two per week when Mario Boano had an opportunity to set up and run the Fiat styling center, so he slowly wound down production and closed his firm. He passed the work to a former key employee, Ezio Ellena.

Ellena formed Carrozzeria Ellena with former Boano partner Luciano Pollo. The Turin-based firm made 49 250s, characterized by a slightly taller roofline, into mid 1958. Pinin Farina then took over 250 GT production in its new facility, introducing an all-new design.

Boano and Ellena built the lion's share of 250 GTs. But they weren't the only coachbuilders making coupes on the chassis. Milan-based Carrozzeria Zagato was well-known for its lightweight competition machines, and its run of five 250 GTs was nothing short of spectacular. Two were made in 1956, two in '57, and the last in '59; one from 1956 and one from '57 were Italian GT Championship winners.

Pinin Farina also kept active with the model. In addition to a series of beautiful cabriolets, the coachbuilder made two 250 Speciales in 1957. Both took styling cues, including covered front headlights, fender lines, and general proportions, from a seminal one-off Ferrari, Superfast 1.

They also designed a series of competition berlinettas that were manufactured by Modena's Carrozzeria Scaglietti. The styling of these 250 Competiziones had their origins in Pinin Farina's 250 Europa GT Speciales, and were an integral part in establishing the Ferrari legend.

1957 250 GT Boano

1957 250 GT Boano/Ellena

1956 250 GT by Zagato

250 GT, 250 GT BOANO & 250 GT ELLENA
1955-1958

Number made:	130 (approx.)
Engine:	2953cc V-12, SOHC, 240 hp @ 7000 rpm
Transmission:	4-speed
Wheelbase:	112.3 inches / 2600mm
Weight:	2,300 lbs.

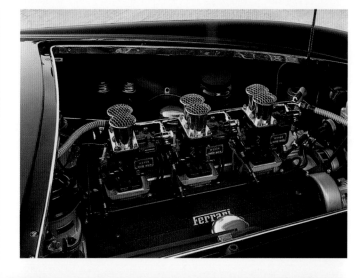

1956 410 Superamerica Series I

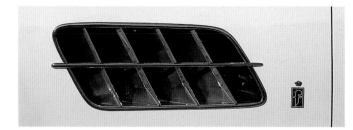

410 Superamerica

A WONDROUS RIDE FOR THE WHO'S WHO AND THE ROYALLY FLUSH

As the continent's "economic miracle" took root in the mid 1950s, Europeans were once again comfortable displaying their wealth and prosperity.

Ferrari's 250 GT was cemented as the mainstay of the company's production and as one of the world's most-prestigious sports cars. But for those who wanted more—and there were many such customers on both sides of the Atlantic—the 410 Superamerica was the ultimate in luxury and speed.

Continuing the tradition of the 375 America, the 410 SA had a 2800mm wheelbase and Lampredi long-block engine. The V-12's bore increased 4mm to 88mm, the stroke remained 68mm, boosting displacement by some 400cc to 4963cc. Horsepower increased commensurately, Ferrari quoting 340 at 6000 rpm.

The 410 SA was officially introduced at 1955's Paris Auto

410 SUPERAMERICA	
1956-1959	
Number made:	34
Engine:	4963cc V-12, SOHC,
	340 hp @ 6000 rpm
	360 hp @ 7000 rpm
	400 hp @ 7000 rpm
Transmission:	4-speed
Wheelbase:	
Series I:	110.2 inches / 2800mm
Series II & III:	102.3 inches / 2600mm
Weight:	2,800-3,000 lbs.

1956 410 Superamerica Coupé by Ghia

Show as a naked chassis. The finished car was displayed four months later at the Brussels Motor Show. Its elegant but sober body by Pinin Farina was not unlike that seen on the design house's five Europa GT prototypes.

Among other 410 SA coachbuilders, Carrozzeria Ghia created a wild one-off with large fins and styling themes echoing those of some of its mid-1950s show cars. This was Ghia's last Ferrari.

Boano made two 410s, a coupe and a convertible, that mimicked the look of its one-off 250 GT cabriolet. And Carrozzeria Scaglietti, well-known for its race-winning forms, made an ornate 410 SA.

The balance of the 410 Superamericas had Pinin Farina coachwork. Each was tailor-made to client specifications, using the same general styling themes seen on the first, chassis 0471 SA. Horsepower increased over the series run, topping out at 400 on several cars.

Chassis 0483 SA was the first 410 SA to use a shorter 102.3-inch (2600mm) wheelbase. This was the platform for Pinin Farina's Superfast 1, a seminal one-off unveiled at the 1956 Paris Auto Show. Its jet-fighter styling was arresting, and the car helped usher in a number of future-Ferrari themes, covered headlamps among them.

Production of these, the most-exclusive Ferraris of the day, continued into 1959, and the list of 410 SA owners was a Who's Who of the times—from the Shah of Iran and Emperor Bao Dai to Italian industrialist Piero Barilla.

1959 410 Superamerica Series II

1959 410 Superamerica Series III

1958 250 GT Cabriolet Series I

1957-1962
250 GT Cabriolet, Coupe & Cabriolet Series II

PININ FARINA CRYSTALLIZES ITS CLASSIC SIXTIES LOOK FOR "THE ULTIMATE IN DRIVING"

Though Boano and Ellena produced the majority of 250 GTs from 1956 to 1958, Pinin Farina also made coachwork for the chassis. In fact, it used it as the basis for one of the decade's most beautiful cars, the 250 GT Cabriolet Series I.

Pinin Farina's Cabriolet Series I used the same platform and running gear as the period's other 250s, but with stunning coachwork inspired by the designer's 410 Superamerica "Superfast I."

The first prototype (chassis 0655 GT) went to Ferrari Formula 1 driver Peter Collins. Superbly proportioned, it featured a large air intake on the hood and a dramatic cut down in the driver-side door. "The body lines are sleek and elegant," was *Autocar's* assessment.

Pinin Farina made a second 250 Cabriolet two months later. Done as a special order "café racer," it had a cut-down windshield and a fairing behind the driver seat.

1959 250 GT Coupe Speciale, chassis 1187 GT

Two other cabriolets served as the preproduction prototypes for what would become a small series; both were made in the summer of 1957. The second (0709 GT) was for Prince Aga Khan and had the definitive Series I look: smooth contours free of side air outlets, swept-back windshield, and racy wind wings.

The 250 Cabriolet Series I was produced from summer 1957 into 1959. *Motor Trend*'s summation of the model was accurate and succinct: "Mechanical perfection of the 250 Gran Turismo is augmented by smart styling and superb coachwork by Pinin Farina."

In 1958, the Series I was joined by the 250 GT. This was an extremely important car for both Ferrari and Pinin Farina. It represented the two companies' first real attempt at production standardization that would allow cars to be made in the hundreds, rather than dozens. Changes at both their factories made such large numbers possible.

In 1958-59, Ferrari set up its first formal assembly line, an elevated affair that enabled workers to construct the cars on the runway at the same time work was done underneath.

Concurrently, Pinin Farina completed its move to an all-new production facility. "(We) were convinced the only way to survive was to make more cars for our clients," Sergio Pininfarina remembered. "The old factory was too small; it did not give us the freedom we needed…(so) the workers had difficulty. There was noise, and everything was old. In the new one there was more space, better logistics, a better environment for the workers….It was a move in the right direction."

A new design direction took form with two one-off 250 GT coupes made over December 1957-January 1958. These included a Speciale on chassis 1187 GT. They had the same general proportions as the Cabriolet Series I, but with more sober lines. Both prototypes had open headlights, long hoods, airy greenhouses, and bodywork devoid of louvers and other decoration. Preproduction prototypes of these coupes were built in May 1958. The rear quarter windows of the one-offs

250 GT CABRIOLET SERIES I, 250 GT COUPE & 250 GT CABRIOLET SERIES II

CABRIOLET SERIES I 1957-1959
250 GT COUPE 1958-1960
CABRIOLET SERIES II 1959-1962

Number made:
Cabriolet Series I: 40
250 GT: 353
Cabriolet Series II: 202
Engine: 2953cc V-12, SOHC,
                                    240 hp @ 7000 rpm
Transmission: 4-speed
Wheelbase: 102.3 inches / 2600mm
Weight:
Cabriolet Series I: NA
250 GT: 2,706 lbs.
Cabriolet Series II: 2,640 lbs.

1959 250 GT Coupe

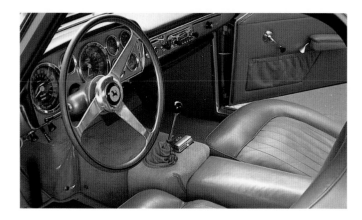

disappeared, and the roof and rear-end treatment were simpler and thus easier to produce.

This, the definitive 250 GT, was warmly greeted. Its "distinguished and racy looks sold out the first planned series of 200 cars well in advance," noted *Road & Track,* which went on to call the 250 GT "the ultimate in driving." *Sports Car Graphic* voted it 1960's "Sportscar of the Year."

Produced into 1960, the 250 GT line proved extremely popular, with more than 350 built. Most every one carried the standard coachwork, though Pinin Farina did make several one-offs for special clients.

A new convertible augmented the 250 GT for '59. The 250 GT Cabriolet Series II's looks mimicked those of the coupe, and with good reason. Not only was the Series II more comfortable and refined than the Cabriolet Series I, but Ferrari and Pinin Farina wanted to clearly differentiate it from the sportier, competition-oriented 250 Spyder California launched in 1958. That car looked much like the Cabriolet Series I.

The 250 Cabriolet Series II made its public debut at the Paris Auto Show that October and went on to great commercial success, with production that continued into 1962.

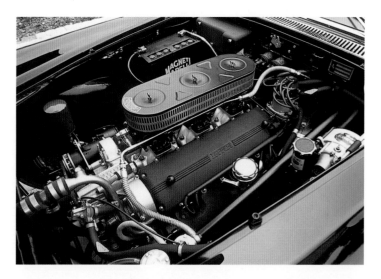

1960 250 GT Cabriolet Series II

1959 250 GT Spyder California

250 GT SPYDER CALIFORNIA		
1958-1963		
Number made:	104 (50 LWB, 54 SWB)	
Engine:	2953cc V-12, SOHC,	
	260 hp @ 7000 rpm (LWB)	
	280 hp @ 7000 rpm (SWB)	
Transmission:	4-speed	
Wheelbase:	102.3 inches/ 2600mm (LWB)	
	94.5 inches/ 2400mm (SWB)	
Weight:	2,200 lbs. (LWB)	
	2,300 lbs. (SWB)	

1958-1963

250 GT Spyder California

A "SIMPLE SPYDER" TURNS OUT SIMPLY SUBLIME

The 250 GT Spyder California's name was most appropriate, for the man ordering it was Ferrari's influential dealer in Southern California, Johnny von Neumann. "He asked us for a simple spyder," said Girolamo Gardini, Ferrari's sales manager from 1948 to 1961.

Von Neumann and the rest of the Ferrari world got that and a lot more. The Spyder California quickly became one of the ultimate "dual-purpose" cars, machines equally at home on street and track. Such versatility underscored an integral part of the Ferrari 250 legend: the firm's ability to make a range of products with the same mechanicals but divergent "personalities."

1963 250 GT Spyder California SWB

The Spyder California was available with lightweight aluminum coachwork or a steel body. Its chassis, suspension, and drivetrain came from the 250 Tour de France sports racer, which itself was nearly identical to the other 250s offered at the time. While the Spyder California looked quite similar to the Series I Cabriolet, its interior appointments were considerably more spartan, reflecting its competition orientation.

The "Cal Spyder" was launched in early 1958 and received mechanical upgrades throughout its production run, including disc brakes and more-powerful engines. Its wheelbase matched the other 250 models at 102.3 inches (2600mm), and these "long wheelbase" (LWB) Spyder Californias had both covered and open headlights—the latter in response to new Italian laws.

At 1960's Geneva Auto Show, Ferrari introduced a new version of the Spyder California with underpinnings identical to those of the 250 "Short Wheelbase" Berlinetta, which had been unveiled in late 1959.

Wheelbase now measured 94.5 inches (2400mm), and these Cal Spyders also had open and covered headlights. The engine gained 20 horsepower and, as with the LWB Spyder California, a number of owners raced their cars.

A genuine work of automotive art, the Pinin Farina-bodied 250 GT Spyder California was produced into 1963, and marked the last true open-air dual-purpose Ferrari.

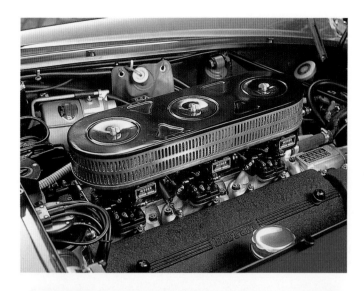

1960 250 GT SWB

1959-1962
250 GT SWB

THE DEFINITIVE DUAL-PURPOSE SPORTS CAR

If any single car can truly represent the Ferrari legend, it would be the 250 SWB. This is one of history's great "dual-purpose" machines, a car that could be driven to the racetrack, win the class or the race outright, then driven home.

The 250 SWB was the culmination of Ferrari's continual development and refinement of the 250 engine and chassis in the second half of the 1950s. It also represented Pinin Farina's ongoing experimentation with the berlinetta (fastback) theme that started with 1947's Cisitalia 202. The result was a shape so pure, so well-balanced that Sergio Pininfarina called it "the first

1961 250 GT SWB

250 GT SWB	
1959-1962	
Number made:	165 (75 with aluminum body)
Engine:	2953cc V-12, SOHC, 260-280 hp @ 7000 rpm
Transmission:	4-speed
Wheelbase:	94.5 inches / 2400mm
Weight:	2,350 lbs.

1962 250 GT SWB

of our three quantum leaps in design with Ferrari."

The model's official debut was 1959's Paris Auto Show. SWB referred to its "short wheelbase" of 94.5 inches (2400mm), some 7.8 inches (200mm) shorter than its predecessor 250 GT models. The decrease was intended to improve handling and cornering speeds, and indeed, the little two-seat coupe fashioned a storied racing career.

To demonstrate the car's dual-purpose nature, the SWB was available with a body of steel or lightweight aluminum. The engine came in various states of tune, suspensions were set up for road or track, and the interior could be fitted with luxurious leather or stripped out for competition.

The SWB's shape is an all-time Pinin Farina classic. But other coachbuilders showed their wares on the chassis, most as rebodies.

1962 250 GT SWB by Bertone, chassis 3269 GT

The only factory-sanctioned non-Pinin Farina SWBs were by Carrozzeria Bertone, Pinin Farina's sole rival in terms of size and prestige as the 1960s began. The first (chassis 1739 GT) was presented at 1960's Turin Show and had attractive but conventional styling. The second (3269 GT) appeared at 1962's Geneva show and was one of the most beautiful Ferrari one-offs, its "split-nostril" front end derived from Ferrari's fastest race cars of the period.

As the 1960s progressed, it became ever more difficult for a road car to compete at the highest levels of motorsport. From here on, Ferrari's street and racing machines would evolve along divergent paths. The fast, beautiful 250 SWB marked the passing of an era.

1959 400 Superamerica, chassis 1517 SA

1960 400 Superamerica, chassis 2207 SA

400 SUPERAMERICA	
1959-1964	
Number made:	47
Engine:	3967cc V-12, SOHC, 340 hp @ 7000 rpm
Transmission:	4-speed
Wheelbase:	95.2 inches / 2420mm 102.3 inches / 2600mm
Weight:	2,800 lbs.

400 Superamerica

AN ELEGANTLY POWERFUL FLAGSHIP AND THE LAST FERRARI AVAILABLE WITH CUSTOM COACHWORK

The 250 series of raucous racers-for-the-road was dominating Ferrari's production in the late 1950s. But Europe's most glamorous performance carmaker also attracted clients who wanted more refinement and even more exclusivity. For them, there was the 400 Superamerica.

The 400 SA was changed in numerous ways from its 410 Superamerica predecessor. The chassis was new, with a shorter wheelbase of 95.2 inches (2420mm) versus 102.3 inches (2600mm), and it had a narrower track front and rear. Most important, it had a new engine. The 410 used a Lampredi-designed V-12 with roots in Ferrari's 375 Formula 1 car. The 400's V-12, by contrast, adopted the general architecture of the first Ferrari V-12, the engine designed by Gioachino Colombo.

The bore was increased, the stroke lengthened, and updates found in the 250 GT engine, such as coil valve springs, were used. The new engine displaced 3967cc. Rounded to 4.0-liters, it meant the 400 name was the first time a Ferrari model designation reflected the overall displacement of the engine, rather than an individual cylinder in cubic centimeters. Horsepower was quoted at 340 at 7000 rpm.

The 400 SA was also the last model for which a client could order custom coachwork.

Pinin Farina did the styling for the first 400 SA (chassis 1517 SA), which made its debut at 1959's Turin show. A stout one-off for Fiat's Gianni Agnelli, it had a nearly rectangular-shaped body and quad headlamps. The next was a lovely cabriolet also from Pinin Farina; its showing at the Brussels Motor Show marked the official debut of the model.

1962 400 Superamerica

Pinin Farina built 10 cabriolets in all. Scaglietti produced a spyder and a berlinetta. But the benchmark design for the 400 SA was unveiled at the 1960 Turin Auto Show. A spectacular flowing, tapered shape, this Ferrari (chassis 2207 SA) was known as Superfast II. Aldo Brovarone, the Pinin Farina stylist who designed the car, said his inspiration was the Vanwall F1 car.

Superfast II's coachwork set the pattern for the majority of 400 SAs that followed, including the models from 1961 on, for which the wheelbase was extended to 102.3 inches (2600mm). Each 400 Superamerica was a custom-order car for its individual owner and a showpiece of the Ferrari craft.

1962 250 GTE

250 GTE & 330 AMERICA

| 250 GTE 1960-1963 |
| 330 AMERICA 1963 |

Number made:
| 250 GTE: | 954 |
| 330 America: | 50 |

Engine:
250 GTE:	2953cc V-12, SOHC, 240 hp @ 7000 rpm
330 America:	3967cc V12, SOHC, 300 hp @ 6600 rpm
Transmission:	4-speed with overdrive
Wheelbase:	102.3 inches / 2600mm
Weight:	2,900 lbs.

1960-1963

250 GTE & 330 America

ENZO'S FERRARI: A CAR FOR IL COMMENDATORE— AND A SPECIAL FRIEND OR TWO

From late-1954 to 1960, Ferrari did not produce a four-seat model. That changed with introduction of the 250 GT 2+2, commonly known as the 250 GTE.

Such a lengthy gap was surprising, given Enzo Ferrari's preference. The two-seat models "were not my father's favorite to drive," said Piero Ferrari. "He loved the 2+2…this was his personal car. My father was normally driving himself, but he always had a driver with him, and a little dog. So for him, a two-seat car wasn't enough."

The first prototype was made in the first half of 1959, its coachwork designed and built by Pinin Farina. The 250 GTE's development also marks the increasing influence of Sergio Pininfarina, for a scale model was tested in the Turin Politechnic Institute's wind tunnel.

"I was an assistant there in the aerodynamic branch before I got my degree," Sergio Pininfarina recalled. "My father gave me the task to test and develop the Ferraris, (and) aerodynamics had a tremendous importance for noise, for rigidity, for the glass. To have a glass in the right position, it is not an effort (for airflow). To have a glass in the wrong position, the strength of the air is against you. It makes an impression and then a noise."

Ferrari combined wind tunnel research, more prototypes (four) tested for more miles than ever before, and the well-proven 250 drivetrain and underpinnings to create what would become by a substantial margin its best-selling car thus far.

"A not only grand, but glorious, touring car," *Road & Track* called the 2+2 in its 1962 road test. Enzo Ferrari certainly thought so—he was one of the model's 954 owners, using it as his personal car.

A version with more power was introduced in 1963. Called the 330 America, it used a detuned edition of the 4.0-liter V-12 from the 400 Superamerica. Different carburetors dropped horsepower to an even 300. Despite the additional muscle, the only external difference from the 250 GTE was the "America" badge on the trunk of some 330 Americas.

1963 250 GT/L "Lusso"

1962-1964
250 GT/L "Lusso"

BELLA FIGURA: THE FINAL 250 ROAD CAR MAKES AN EXQUISITE STATEMENT

When the 250 GT coupe ceased production in 1960, Ferrari was left with but one enclosed two-seat 3.0-liter model, the competition-oriented 250 SWB. Ferrari needed a proper street model, and in late 1962, it filled the void with the 250 GT/L.

Popularly known as the 250 Lusso ("luxury" in Italian) and unveiled at the Paris Auto Show, this was a vastly different type of car than the 250 SWB. It was a sumptuous gran turismo with an elegant body drawn by Pininfarina. (The coachbuilder's name officially became one word in 1961.) Scaglietti manufactured the coachwork at his Modena-based carrozzeria and the Lusso was the first Ferrari to carry a "designo di Pininfarina," indicating that Pininfarina designed it but did not build it.

The body was steel; the doors, hood, and trunklid aluminum. The grille and headlights were similar to those on the SWB, but the front fenders were elongated. The rear roofline swept back gracefully, and into the tail was sculpted a small spoiler, the first street Ferrari to have the aerodynamic aid.

The car's new chassis was derived from the immortal 250 GTO, and shared that sports-racer's wheelbase of 94.5 inches (2400mm). The engine was placed several inches forward compared to other 250s, creating a roomy cockpit. Two comfortable bucket seats faced an unusual instrument panel that put the sup-

250 GT/L	
1962-1964	
Number made:	350
Engine:	2953cc V-12, SOHC, 250 hp @ 7000 rpm
Transmission:	4-speed
Wheelbase:	94.5 inches / 2400mm
Weight:	2,800 lbs.

plemental gauges in front of the driver and the speedometer and tachometer in the center of the dash, angled toward the driver.

The Lusso's V-12 demonstrated Ferrari's ability to continually develop and refine its powerplants. The block was common to all 250s, while some components, such as the valves and crankshaft, came from the 250 SWB, and others, including cylinder heads and pistons, came from the 250 GTE. The result was a very usable 250 horsepower.

Regarded by some as one of the loveliest Ferraris ever, the Lusso was the last 250 street model. It was extremely popular with Ferrari's clientele, and Battista Pininfarina was so fond of it he had one specially made. He gave it a more aerodynamic rear roofline and tail and created a memorable one-off displayed at the 1963 London Motor Show.

1963 250 GT/L for Battista Pininfarina

1964 330 GT 2+2 and Sergio Pininfarina

1964-1967
330 GT 2+2

THE FOUR-SEAT FERRARI TAKES ROOT

The success of the 250 GT 2+2 all but guaranteed that four-seat Ferraris would become prominent in Maranello's lineup. Its immediate successor, however, proved among the more controversial Cavallinos to date.

The 330 GT 2+2 was introduced in January 1964, and the focus immediately became its arrangement of quad headlamps, which gave the otherwise sleek and modern coupe a front end with a cat's-eye countenance.

Inspiration for the styling touch has been attributed to Pininfarina's Superfast IV, a modified version of the 400 SA Superfast II. But the man who designed the 330 says that's incorrect.

American stylist Tom Tjaarda started his prolific career in 1959 at Ghia. He moved to Pininfarina in 1961, and the 330 GT 2+2 was his first full design for the carrozzeria.

"The design brief was for us to make an up-to-date four-seat car, and I wanted to do something different," Tjaarda recalled. "At Ghia, there was a stillborn Renault Dauphine with a two-in-one headlight treatment similar to Superfast IV. I showed that idea to Martinengo and Pininfarina, and they approved."

Overall, the 330 had many improvements over the 250 2+2. Its new chassis had a longer wheelbase and wider track, and the roofline was slightly taller for more interior room. The dashboard and supplemental controls were more modern in appearance, comfort levels higher, and the trunk was larger.

The V-12 displaced 3967cc (330cc per cylinder, hence the

330 name), and it had considerably more horsepower than the 250 2+2's—300 versus 240. The larger displacement was Ferrari's response to a number of forces, among them impending smog regulations and the presence of 4.0-liter engines in rivals from Aston Martin, Maserati, and Lamborghini. The new car's suspension featured adjustable Koni shock absorbers. The rear leaf springs were assisted by coil springs. And a dual braking system gave front and rear brakes their own servo-assist units.

The 330 2+2 was updated during 1965, the biggest noticeable change being a move to a single headlight per side. The front fender vents were changed, too, and a five-speed gearbox replaced the four-speed. Alloy disc wheels became standard, the Borrani wires optional.

Both versions were popular—the quad-lamp version actually outselling its dual-lamp successor—and the 330 2+2 became the first Ferrari to exceed 1,000 units produced.

330 GT 2+2		
1964-1967		
Number made:		
four-headlight:	630 (approx.)	
two-headlight:	469	
Engine:	3967cc V-12; SOHC,	
	300 hp @ 6600 rpm	
Transmission:	4-speed w/overdrive	
	5-speed (two-headlight cars)	
Wheelbase:	104.3 inches / 2650mm	
Weight:	3,100 lbs.	

1964 330 GT 2+2

1965 330 GT 2+2

1964 500 Superfast

1964-1966
500 Superfast

**ARRIVEDERCI ONE-OFFS, ALTHOUGH STANDARDIZED
BODYWORK STILL DOES NOT A COMMON FERRARI MAKE**

Building on the warm reception given his ultraprestige, ultra-
performance 400 Superamerica, Ferrari in 1964 introduced a
successor. Unveiled at the Geneva Auto Show, the 500 Superfast
was even more luxurious than the 400 SA and, as the name
implied, was more powerful and delivered a higher top speed.

The car's lines derived from the 400 Superamerica "aerodi-
namico" coupes, which were kindled by 1960's groundbreaking
Superfast II. But the 500 Superfast rode a longer wheelbase
than any 400 SA, and its V-12, the largest found on a road
Ferrari to that time, was unique to the model.

Bore and stroke measured 88mm and 68mm, giving the V-12
a displacement of 4961cc. As with the 400 SA, the engine's
total displacement served as the name for the model (500 for
5.0-liters). Horsepower was rated at 400 at 6500 rpm.

The 500 Superfast also marked a watershed moment in Ferrari
series production. Unlike the custom-designed 400 SA, each 500
Superfast body was identical, save minor differences on items
such as door handles and taillights.

The custom coachwork era of the 1950s was slowly and quietly coming to a close. Clients favored sophistication and

refinement over one-off exclusivity, and standardized production was the only way to meet these expectations. Labor rates also increased, making true one-offs, as seen on the 400 SA and earlier Ferraris, dauntingly expensive.

Ferrari and Pininfarina clearly knew what interested this audience—comfort without compromise. The 500 Superfast's interior was extremely well-appointed, and the car was so exclusive a sales brochure was never printed.

The first run of 25 had a four-speed gearbox and was followed in late 1965 by a second series with a five-speed. Production concluded in summer 1966. The 500 Superfast accomplished its goal, embraced by an ownership that included captains of industry and genuine nobility. The Shah of Iran, for example, owned two.

1964 275 GTB "short nose" and Battista Pininfarina

275 GTB, 275 GTB/4 & 275 GTB/4 NART SPYDER

| GTB 1964-1966 |
| GTB/4 1966-1968 |
| GTB/4 NART SPYDER 1967-1968 |

Number made:
275 GTB: 235 "short nose"
                205 "long nose"
275 GTB/4:   330
275 GTB/4
  NART Spyder: 10
Engine:
275 GTB: 3285cc V-12, SOHC,
                280 hp @ 7600 rpm
275 GTB/4:   3285cc V-12, DOHC,
                300 hp @ 8000 rpm
275 GTB/4
  NART Spyder: 3285cc V-12, DOHC,
                300 hp @ 8000 rpm
Transmission: 5-speed
Wheelbase: 94.5 inches / 2400mm
Weight:
GTB: 2,425 lbs. (factory)
GTB/4:   2,663 lbs. (*Car and Driver*)
GTB/4
  NART Spyder: 2,455 lbs. (*Road & Track*)

1964-1968
275 GTB, 275 GTB/4 & NART Spyder

A BOLD NEW BERLINETTA SENDS THE FERRARI COUPE DOWN ITS OWN STYLING PATH

Introduction of the 275 series at 1964's Paris Auto Show marked the beginning of an entirely new lineup of Ferrari road cars. The series was comprised of open and closed body styles, but now the coupe's look was clearly separate in character from the convertible's. The closed 275 GTB had an aggressive new berlinetta body. Styling of the 275 GTS spyder was more conservative, but would enjoy a longer life span.

In both cases, these 275s were the first roadgoing Ferraris with independent rear suspension; it consisted of double wishbones, coil springs, Koni shocks, and an antiroll bar. Their five-speed gearbox was moved to the rear to become in unit with the differential for better weight distribution. And the engine was shifted slightly rearward, bringing the mass closer to the car's center for better cornering.

Their 3.3-liter V-12 was the final development of the Colombo-designed "short-block" engine. Stroke remained 58.8mm, but bore was enlarged to 77mm, increasing horsepower and giving better low-end torque. Three Weber carburetors were

1966 275 GTB "long nose"

standard, six an option for superior high-rpm acceleration.

The 275 GTB's stupendous body was designed by Pininfarina and built by Scaglietti. Sergio Pininfarina said the car's resemblance to the 250 GTO was anything but a coincidence; he and his design staff purposely looked to the all-conquering endurance racer when creating the GTB's berlinetta shape.

Ferrari followed the original 275 GTB with an updated version launched at the 1965 Paris Show. It was dubbed the "long-nose" edition for its slightly lengthened and lowered nose, a tweak designed to reduce front-end lift at high speeds. Its rear window was enlarged for better visibility, and the trunk hinges were now on the outside. (A handful of competition versions were also made, three having a radically different body.)

Rave reviews greeted the 275 GTB. America's *Sports Car Graphic* 1965 test car did 0-60 mph in 6 seconds flat, and topped out at 156 mph. "Sleek, fast and luxurious…it's strictly for the connoisseur" was the sum-up. *Autosport*'s six-carb GTB touched 160, and the editors called it "…a car so good it comes close to perfection."

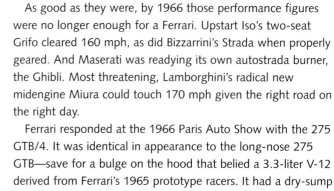

As good as they were, by 1966 those performance figures were no longer enough for a Ferrari. Upstart Iso's two-seat Grifo cleared 160 mph, as did Bizzarrini's Strada when properly geared. And Maserati was readying its own autostrada burner, the Ghibli. Most threatening, Lamborghini's radical new midengine Miura could touch 170 mph given the right road on the right day.

Ferrari responded at the 1966 Paris Auto Show with the 275 GTB/4. It was identical in appearance to the long-nose 275 GTB—save for a bulge on the hood that belied a 3.3-liter V-12 derived from Ferrari's 1965 prototype racers. It had a dry-sump lubrication system and revised cylinder heads with four camshafts that gave the car its "4" suffix. Horsepower increased by 40, to 300 at a heady 8000 rpm.

Shortly after the 275 GTB/4's October introduction, Ferrari's American importer, Luigi Chinetti, approached Enzo about making an open-air version of the car. The idea was initially struck down. But Chinetti had been dealing with Ferrari since the 1940s. He knew how to make things happen in Modena. He spoke with Sergio Scaglietti himself. An agreement was reached

1967 275 GTB/4

1967 275 GTB/4 NART Spyder

and Scaglietti went to work modifying the berlinetta to create 10 open-top versions.

The model became known as the 275 GTB/4 NART Spyder, "NART" an abbreviation for Chinetti's North American Racing Team. The first NART Spyder (chassis 09437 GT) was made in February 1967 and sent to America, where it was entered in Florida's difficult 12 Hours of Sebring race. Basically a stock car, it finished a very credible 17th overall.

The car became a celebrity of sorts. *Road & Track* tested it for a cover story in September 1967. The conclusion? It was "The most satisfying sports car in the world." Another NART Spyder had a role in 1968's *The Thomas Crown Affair* starring Steve McQueen and Faye Dunaway. Still, despite racing success, magazine coverage and a Hollywood hit, Chinetti had a hard time selling all 10 NART Spyders.

In hindsight, the NART Spyder was itself a turning point in Ferrari history. With America's emissions regulations and safety laws being enacted as 275 GTB/4 production ended, the NART Spyder would be the last Ferrari model for three decades that owed its existence to a well-connected individual's request for a special run of cars.

1964 275 GTS

1964-1969
275 GTS,
330 GTS &
365 GTS

DOLCE STIL NUOVO IS ITALIAN FOR "SWEET NEW STYLE" AND PERFECT FOR THESE TIMELESS SPYDERS

The 275 GTS made its debut alongside the 275 GTB in October 1964 at the Paris Auto Show. Like its coupe stablemate, this convertible featured all new mechanicals, including its chassis, independent rear suspension, and rear transaxle. Its 3.3-liter V-12 was new, too, and was shared with the GTB, though the spyder's was rated at 260 horsepower, the berlinetta's at 280.

Just as important was the coachwork. Designed and built by Pininfarina, the 275 GTS had softer lines than the GTB. It took the flavor of its slimmed-down rear section from the four-headlight 330 GT 2+2, and in return would give later versions of the four-seater its single headlights and grille treatment.

The GTS was much more luxurious than the 275 GTB, with

1967 330 GTS

1969 365 GTS

275 GTS, 330 GTS & 365 GTS

275 GTS 1964-1966
330 GTS 1966-1968
365 GTS 1969

Number made:
275 GTS: 200
330 GTS: 100
365 GTS: 20
Engine:
275 GTS: 3285cc V-12, SOHC,
260 hp @ 7000 rpm
330 GTS: 3967cc V-12; SOHC,
300 hp @ 7000 rpm
365 GTS: 4390cc V-12, SOHC,
320 hp @ 6600 rpm
Transmission: 5-speed
Wheelbase: 94.5 inches / 2400mm
Weight:
275 GTS: 2,960 lbs. (*Road & Track*)
330 GTS: 3,105 lbs. (*Road & Track*)
365 GTS: n/a

fully adjustable and more-comfortable bucket seats, greater luggage space, and a softer ride. The top was particularly ingenious, capable of being raised and lowered with one hand and stowing in a shallow well behind the seats.

In early 1965, the 275 GTS received a minor cosmetic update in the form of front fender louvers instead of vents. Production totaled 200 before its replacement was shown at the 1966 Paris Auto Show as the 330 GTS. This was identified primarily by its new nose, a longer tapered affair taken from the 330 GTC coupe introduced several months earlier.

The 330 GTS used a new 3967cc V-12 making 300 horsepower at 7000 rpm. The car did 0-60 mph in 6.9 seconds for *Road & Track*; the magazine's test 275 GTS had done it in 7.2. The 330 GTS reach 100 mph in 17.1 seconds (versus 18.8 for the 275 GTS), and topped out at 146 mph (versus 145).

Production of the 330 GTS stopped at 100 units, and Ferrari introduced an even more-powerful version, the 365 GTS, in January 1969. The 365 GTS was identical to the 330 GTS, save yet another change in engine-compartment vents, which moved to the hood. The 365's 4.4-liter V-12 came from the 365 California, and boasted 320 horsepower. Just 20 would be made before the model was phased out in mid 1969, and Ferrari drew the curtain on a run of timelessly classic convertibles.

1965 Dino 206 S protoype

1968-1974

Dino 206 GT, Dino 246 GT & Dino 246 GTS

1968 Dino 206 GT

ITS BADGING DIDN'T SAY FERRARI, BUT ENZO'S FIRST MIDENGINE ROAD CAR WAS A CAVALLINO IN SPIRIT

Putting the engine behind the driver was the winning trend in racing in the early 1960s. Ferrari experienced the advantages of the design first hand, winning the 1961 Grand Prix championship with the 156 F1, and, two years later fielding the first midengine car to win LeMans, the 250 P.

So it was that Sergio Pininfarina and a number of Ferrari dealers began pushing Enzo to make a midengine road car.

"He kept insisting it was too dangerous," the effervescent coachbuilder recalled. "While he felt it was fine for racing and professional drivers, he was against making midengine sports cars for customers. He was afraid of the safety, of building a car that was too dangerous."

Ferrari finally relented in 1965. "When Mr. Ferrari finally said yes, he said, 'Okay, you make it not with a Ferrari, but with a Dino,'" Pininfarina said. That meant the car would use a six-cylinder engine instead of one of Ferrari's more-powerful V-12s. "In his mind, less powerful meant less danger for the cus-

tomers," Pininfarina explained. "And therefore I had the permission to develop the Dino." The name memorialized Enzo's son, Dino, who had died in 1956.

The Dino 206 S prototype made its debut at the Paris Auto Show in October 1965. It was built on the 206 SP race-car chassis and had a longitudinally mounted 2.0-liter V-6. The car was so well-received that a year later, at the Turin Show, a second Dino 206 S prototype was displayed. Known as the Dino Berlinetta GT, it also had a longitudinal V-6, but styling was smoother and incorporated attractive covered headlights.

A final production prototype was shown at 1967's Turin Show. It looked almost identical to the Dino Berlinetta GT, but the engine was mounted transversely, directly atop the gearbox and differential, between the driver's compartment and the rear axle. Fiat in Turin built the 2.0-liter V-6, which would also be used it in its prestige model, the front-engine Dino coupe and spyder.

The 206 Dino GT went into production in 1968. It boasted a

DINO 206 GT, DINO 246 GT & DINO 246 GTS

| DINO 206 GT 1968-1969 |
| DINO 246 GT 1969-1974 |
| DINO 246 GTS 1972-1974 |

Number made:
206 GT: 152 (includes 2 prototypes)
246 GT: 2487
246 GTS: 1274

Engine:
206 GT: 1987cc V-6, DOHC,
             180 hp @ 8000 rpm
246 GT: 2418cc V-6, DOHC,
             195 hp @ 7600 rpm
246 GTS: 2418cc V-6, DOHC,
             195 hp @ 7600 rpm

Transmission: 5-speed

Wheelbase:
206 GT: 89.7 inches / 2280mm
246 GT: 92.1 inches / 2340mm
246 GTS: 92.1 inches / 2340mm

Weight:
206 GT: 2,100 lbs. (*Sports Car Graphic*)
246 GT: 2,770 lbs. (*Road & Track*)
246 GTS: 2,910 lbs. (*Road & Track*)

1972 Dino 246 GT

1972 Dino 246 GTS

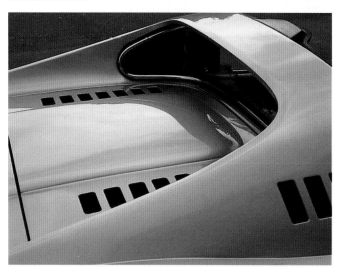

top speed over 140 mph, incredibly balanced handling, and a design among the postwar era's most beautiful. It was an instant hit with press and public alike.

"The Dino 206 GT is a wonderful car...an engineering masterpiece," said America's *Sports Car Graphic*. England's *CAR* seconded the opinion, noting "(T)he 206GT Dino stands out as one of the most advanced grand touring cars of our time."

Typical of Ferrari's almost-constant model updates—and likely also in response to Porsche increasing the size of the engine in its 911—Maranello followed the 206 GT in 1969 with the Dino 246 GT. It looked identical to the 206 save the addition of a *Cavallino rampante* on the fuel-filler door.

That it is nearly impossible to visually differentiate a 246 from a 206 is a tribute to Pininfarina and his men, for the cars had different wheelbases. To increase cabin room, wheelbase increased to 92.1 inches (2340mm) from 89.7 (2280mm). Coachwork was more durable steel in place of the 206's aluminum. And the V-6 jumped to 2.4-liters (hence the 246 name), and horsepower increased by 15 to 195.

The longer wheelbase and more-powerful engine made a good thing even better. "Of all the mid-engine cars of which I have had the experience (of testing) the Dino stands head and shoulders above the rest...," Dennis Jenkinson wrote in *Motor Sport*. "(O)nce you have experienced it, it makes all front-engined or rear-engined cars obsolete."

Minute updates and refinements created three 246 GT series: type L, type M, and type E. The 246's biggest change came with the March 1972 Geneva Auto Show introduction of the 246 GTS, which featured a one-piece removable targa top panel.

By the time assembly of the 246 GT and GTS ceased in 1974, production, including the 206 GT, totaled nearly 4,000. Ferrari's first midengine road car had become its best-selling series up to that time.

1974 Dino 246 GTS

330 GTC & 365 GTC		
330 GTC 1966-1968		
365 GTC 1968-1969		

Number made:
330 GTC:	602 (includes 4 330 Speciales)
365 GTC:	168

Engine:
330 GTC:	3967cc V-12, SOHC, 300 hp @ 7000 rpm
365 GTC:	4390cc V-12, SOHC, 320 hp @ 6600 rpm
Transmission:	5-speed
Wheelbase:	94.5 inches / 2400mm

Weight:
330 GTC:	3,160 lbs. (*Car and Driver*)
365 GTC:	3,198 lbs. (*Autocar*)

330 GTC & 365 GTC

EVERYTHING A ROADGOING FERRARI SHOULD BE

It wasn't long after the 330 GTC's introduction at 1966's Geneva Auto Show that the two-seat coupe had earned a reputation as the "best all around" Ferrari—and with good reason.

Its understated looks were classy and elegant, the steering light at most every speed, the interior commodious and comfortable, the ride superb, the engine ideal. It was truly a Ferrari one could use every day.

Pininfarina designed and built the GTC's steel body, which successfully blended the general design of the 275 GTS with the front-end treatment of the 500 Superfast. *Car and Driver's* one-word sum-up of the car's appearance: "class."

1967 330 GTC

1967 330 GTC Speciale, chassis 9439 GT

1969 365 GTC

Underneath was the 94.5-inch (2400mm) chassis found on the 275 GTB & GTS. Underhood was the 300-horsepower 4.0-liter V-12 from the larger 330 2+2, but with a redesigned block. The gearbox mounted at the rear, as on the 275 GTB, for better weight distribution. The GTC also had independent rear suspension. The model was quite popular, with almost 600 made.

In the second half of 1968, Ferrari began work on the 365 GTC. It vented the engine compartment with hood slats instead of fender louvers, but that was the only appearance change from the 330. The main difference was beneath the hood.

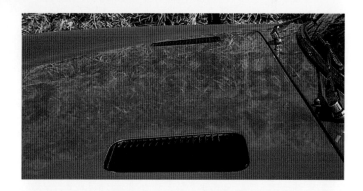

The 365 had a 320-horsepower 4.4-liter V-12, as seen in the 365 GT 2+2 introduced in late 1967. With more low-end torque, it furnished fierce acceleration while maintaining the superb road manners of the 330 GTC. The 365 GTC was built into late 1969; the last made was for Woolworth heiress Barbara Hutton.

She wasn't alone among famous women who owned a 330 or 365. Princess Lilian of Belgium was an avid enthusiast who had ordered several Ferrari one-offs. In 1966, she had Pininfarina design a new body on the 330 GTC chassis. This 330 Speciale (chassis 9439 GT) appeared in January 1967 at the Brussels Motor Show, one of three identical 330 Speciales produced. Princess Lilian owned hers until her passing in 2002.

1966 365 California

1966-1967
365 California

A CALIFORNIA OF A DIFFERENT ORDER: EXCLUSIVE, AND EXCLUSIVELY FOR THE ROAD

The 365 California was the last in a long line of Ferraris that catered to the wealthiest clientele desiring an ultraexclusive car. Unlike the 250 Spyder California—the previous model named for one of Ferrari's major markets—the 365 California was a large, luxurious grand tourer intended for street use only.

The 365 made its debut at the Geneva Show in March 1966 as successor to the 500 Superfast. Its 104.3-inch (2650mm) tubular chassis was nearly identical to that used by the 500

Superfast and the 330 GT 2+2. Underpinnings were the same, with independent front suspension and, at the rear, a rigid axle and leaf springs supplemented by coil springs and Koni shocks.

The 4390cc V-12 was derived from the one in the 365P racecars that competed in 1965 and 1966. It used the competition engine's basic dimensions (81mm bore, 71mm stroke) to produce a tractable 320 horsepower at 6600 rpm. The engine mated with a five-speed gearbox as found on the 330 2+2 and 500 Superfast.

American designer Tom Tjaarda had been with Pininfarina for four years when he was charged with creating the exclusive model's looks.

"It was strange because I did it at home during the summertime," he remembered. "They had an urgent need so I came back in September with sketches....The difficult part was making it look like a Ferrari, but different."

365 CALIFORNIA
1966-1967

Number made:	14
Engine:	4390cc V-12, SOHC, 320 hp @ 6600 rpm
Transmission:	5-speed
Wheelbase:	104.3 inches / 2650mm
Weight:	2,900 lbs. (factory)

Tjaarda recalled working long and hard with design director Francesco Martinengo to break up the long bodyside by using the door handle and scoop from 1965's Dino prototype. There were hidden fog lights on the front, and a tail indentation created only after much trial and error.

Just 14 of these flagship convertibles would be built in less than two years, each trimmed to client specification. Tjaarda himself didn't see the car until summer 1967 because he left Pininfarina for another opportunity.

"The first one I saw was in Santa Margherita on the Italian coast with some rich-looking guy driving it; everyone was turning their heads. That really surprised me because we had a running joke at Pininfarina—we thought it would be a show car only."

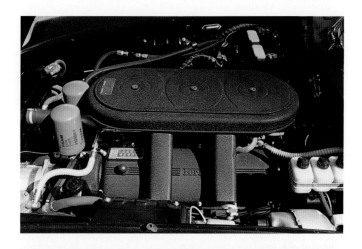

1967 365 GT 2+2

365 GT 2+2

**CIVIL BUT NEVER SERVILE, A FOUR-SEAT FERRARI HELPS
MARANELLO STAY BUOYANT IN UNCERTAIN SEAS**

By the second half of the 1960s, Ferraris were becoming ever
more sophisticated, refined, and easier to drive. This was particularly true of the 2+2s, which catered to an older audience less
inclined to compromise. It is revealing that the four-seat models
were in fact Ferrari's best-selling cars throughout the 1960s.

The decade's final 2+2 was arguably the best. It was the 365
GT 2+2, and it was introduced at the 1967 Paris Auto Show.
The attractive Pininfarina coachwork resembled the Princess
Lilian 330 Speciale shown earlier in the year, but with a longer
wheelbase and different rear roofline and tail treatment.

Its 4.4-liter V-12 was a bored-out version of the 330 GT 2+2
4.0-liter; this powerplant would also be used in the 365 GTC &
GTS. All had 320 horsepower at 6600 rpm. The chassis was
similar to that of the 330 2+2, but with a wider track for
increased interior and trunk room.

The 365 was the first Ferrari 2+2 with independent rear suspension, following the lead of the 275 GTB and GTS, then the 330 GTC. In another first for Ferrari, the 365 GT's rear wishbones, coil springs, Koni shocks, and antiroll bar were supplemented by a hydro-pneumatic self-leveling system. The Koni-developed setup was designed to compensate for the weight of rear passengers.

The 365 GT 2+2 was a superlative grand-tourer, with air conditioning, power windows, and power steering standard. England's *CAR* rightly called it "the most civilized Ferrari yet." *Car and Driver* also appreciated its easy temperament and regal nature. "It's not the same feeling you get when you handle an old Gibson or Purdey shotgun; they demand virtuosity of the user," the magazine said. "But anyone with a license can get behind the wheel of a Ferrari 365 GT 2+2 and feel almighty."

As the 1960s drew to a close, the 365 2+2 was the only Ferrari sold in America. That was attributed largely to new U.S. emissions and safety laws. At least the tightening regulations didn't have a detrimental effect on the car's performance. A 356 GT 2+2 did 0-60 mph in 7.2 seconds and cleared 150 mph for *Road & Track*. Recognizing the car's size and weight, *R&T* gave it a nickname that stuck for years: The Queen Mother of Ferraris.

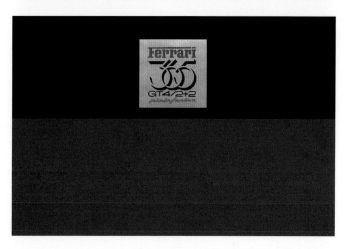

365 GT 2+2	
1967-1971	
Number made:	809
Engine:	4390cc V-12, SOHC, 320 hp @ 6600 rpm
Transmission:	5-speed
Wheelbase:	104.3 inches / 2650mm
Weight:	4,020 lbs. (*Road & Track*)

1968-1973
365 GTB/4 & GTS/4 Daytona

"THE HORSE DOES NOT PUSH THE CART, IT PULLS"
—ENZO FERRARI

That Enzo Ferrari marched to the beat of his own drum can be summed up in one word: Daytona.

The automotive world In the second half of the 1960s was awash in midengine mania, thanks in great measure to Lamborghini's 170-mph Miura, introduced in 1966. Conventional wisdom held that Ferrari would respond with a midengine 12-cylinder car.

When ever did Enzo hue to conventional wisdom?

The Daytona story begins in 1966, when Pininfarina designer Leonardo Fioravanti laid eyes on a naked 330 GTC chassis. "It struck me as something unique," he remembered. "I wanted to follow its shape and dimensions, while paying close attention to the aerodynamics."

Fioravanti put pen to paper and presented his renderings to Sergio Pininfarina, whose entreaties to Ferrari to build a midengine V-12 model had been continuously rebuffed. When Sergio saw Fioravanti's stunning proposal for a new front-engine design, he accepted it warmly.

"The fundamental objective we set for ourselves was to obtain a thin, svelte car, like a midengine design," Pininfarina

365 GTB/4 & GTS/4	
1968-1973	
Number made:	
GTB/4:	1284
GTS/4:	122
Engine:	4390cc V-12, DOHC, 352 hp @ 7500 rpm
Transmission:	5-speed
Wheelbase:	94.5 inches / 2400mm
Weight:	
GTB/4:	3,600 lbs. (*Road & Track*)
GTS/4:	n/a

1967 Daytona prototype

1968 365 GTB/4 Daytona

recalled. "The whole idea was really a search for this sense of
lightness and rake, a slender look."

Although "the 275 GTB/4's successor wasn't being discussed," Fioravanti said, Ferrari liked what he saw. So two prototypes were built in late 1967 and early '68, mostly using 275
GTB/4 mechanicals.

The cars followed Fioravanti's general lines. They employed
the front of the 275 berlinetta and the rear of what would be
the Daytona. Pininfarina then altered the nose to get a more
modern look and the "lightness and rake" he desired.

The chassis continued Ferrari's tradition of welded oval-section
tubes and a 94.5-inch (2400mm) wheelbase, but with a new,
wider track. Suspension was independent, and the disc brakes
had improved ventilation to keep them cool under hard use.

1969 365 GTS/4 Daytona

1973 365 GTB/4 Daytona

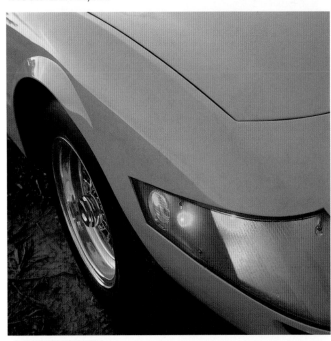

The production Daytona's V-12 displaced 4.4-liters and, like the 275 GTB/4, had four overhead cams. It was crowned by six downdraft Weber carburetors. The lubrication system featured a dry-sump oiling system. Quoted horsepower was 352 at a heady 7500 rpm.

The Daytona bowed at the 1968 Paris Auto Show. It formally was the 365 GTB/4: 365 being the size of one cylinder in cubic centimeters, 4 referring to the engine's four cams. But Ferrari also referred to the car as the Daytona, in commemoration of the marque's 1-2-3 sweep at Florida's famed 24-hour sports-car race in 1967. The 365 GTB/4 also marked another Maranello milestone: It turned out to be the last model made by Ferrari before Enzo sold his company to Fiat in June 1969.

That Ferrari's new GT did not have a midengine design was of little consequence once it was driven.

England's *Motor* called it "the anti-Miura production car." Declared *Road & Track* in its first road test: "It might as well be said right now, the Ferrari 365 GTB/4 is the best sports car in the world. Or the best GT...."

Autocar came to the same conclusion. "It is hard to capture in mere words all the excitement, sensation and sheer exhilaration of this all-time great among cars. For us it has become an important new yardstick, standing at the pinnacle of the fast car market."

And indeed it was the pinnacle as the 1970s began. The Miura S *Autocar* tested had a top speed of 172 mph; the Daytona bettered that by 2 mph. The Ferrari was quicker, too, doing the quarter-mile in 13.8 seconds, the standing kilometer in 24.3. The Lamborghini needed 14.5 and 26.1 seconds, respectively. That level of performance would also propel the Daytona to a long, storied racing career.

Fioravanti said he never envisioned a convertible Daytona when he conceived the car, but that didn't stop Sergio

Scaglietti. The coachbuilder had made Daytona bodies since the car's Paris debut, and with Sergio Pininfarina's approval, created an open-air prototype. The transformation was "an easy one," in the words of the Modenese magician, and Ferrari was soon assaulted with requests for the Daytona Spyder.

The convertible bowed at the 1969 Frankfurt Auto Show, designated the 365 GTS/4 by Ferrari. Production began in mid 1970 and just under 125 were built over three years. Almost 80 percent went to America. The Daytona Spyder proved to be the final hurrah for "old-school" Ferrari, one where Scaglietti could approach Pininfarina, then have Ferrari sign off on production.

Other changes were afoot, as well. Spyder production coincided with tightened American safety and emissions regulations. They proved so costly and complex that Ferrari would not import to the U.S. the 365 GT4/BB, the midengine supercar that in 1974 replaced the Daytona as Ferrari's flagship.

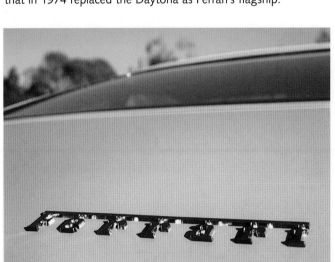

1972 365 GTC/4

365 GTC/4

TAILORED AND TERRIFIC: RATHER LIKE A HIGHLY REFINED DAYTONA IN "PLUS-2" CLOTHING

If the 330 GTC was regarded as the best all-around Ferrari in the 1960s, then a contender to that title in the 1970s was its successor, the 152-mph 365 GTC/4.

Like the 330 GTC, the "C4" was understated, refined, extremely comfortable, and easy to drive, but had an advantage of considerably more room inside. This was truly a Ferrari that could be used daily without compromise.

First seen at 1971's Geneva Motor Show, the 365 GTC/4 seemed to be a replacement for the 365 GT 2+2. The GTC/4 was a four-passenger car—technically. But its shorter wheelbase (98.4 inches/2500mm to the 365 GT 2+2's 104.3 inch-es/2650mm) and a lower, sloping roofline made its tiny rear seats token at best. Ferrari compensated by having the rear seatbacks flip down to make a practical storage tray.

Pininfarina's coachwork featured a swooping fenderline and flush-fitting glass. The V-12 had the 81m bore, 71mm stroke, double overhead cams, and 4390cc displacement of the Daytona's engine. But the C4's hood was lower because its six Weber carburetors were horizontally mounted rather than set vertically atop the engine. Horsepower was listed at 320, versus Daytona's 352.

The GTC/4 had power steering, power brakes, and self-leveling independent rear suspension. Coupled with excellent heating and ventilation, *Road & Track* believed it would be "a fine car for a cross country trip in any weather….

"Every new Ferrari model brings some noteworthy advance over previous ones," the magazine continued. "The GTC4's is mechanical refinement. Less mechanical thrash comes through from the engine room than in any previous Ferrari, and the controls are smoother and lighter than ever, making the car deliciously easy to drive well."

The 365 GTC/4 cost several thousand dollars more than a Daytona, but equaled the faster two-seater in sales while they were offered concurrently. Still, though some 500 were made, its life span was less than two years.

365 GTC/4	
1971-1972	
Number made:	500
Engine:	4390cc V-12, DOHC
	320 hp @ 6200 (USA)
	340 hp @ 6600 rpm (Europe)
Transmission:	5-speed
Wheelbase:	98.4 inches / 2500mm
Weight:	3,825 lbs. (*Road & Track*)

1973-1984
365 GT4/BB, 512 & 512i "Berlinetta Boxer"

ENZO PRESENTS A MIDENGINE 12-CYLINDER FERRARI, BUT ON HIS TERMS, OF COURSE

Enzo Ferrari wasn't blind to the success of the Dino, or to the market's yearning for a midengine 12-cylinder Ferrari. When finally he decided to make one, however, he surprised most everyone by using a "flat-12" engine rather than a V-12.

The engine design was dubbed a "boxer" because the pistons were opposed parallel to one another and moved like a boxer throwing jabs. Ferrari had used the flat-12 configuration for years. It appeared first in its Formula 1 cars in 1964 and '65, then in 1969's undefeated hillclimb champion, the 212 E Montagna. Ferrari's 1970 and '71 F1 machines also were flat-12 powered.

1968 P6 Prototype

1975 365 GT4/BB

"I very much liked the Boxer engine because of its space architecture," Sergio Pininfarina said. "For years I had to fight with a high engine and a large radiator because the engine's height automatically (dictated) the radiator's height….The boxer engine was lower, making everything easier."

This was the world's first roadgoing flat-12 engine. But the fact that it displaced the same 4.4-liters as the Daytona's V-12 allowed Ferrari to use components already in production, including pistons and connecting rods. This Ferrari engine was also the first in any high-performance sports car with camshafts driven by belts rather than by chains. That made it quieter, less costly to build, and easier to service. The transmission was off-set to the left, with the gearbox located ahead of the final drive to provide room for the engine oil sump.

The chassis was a semimonocoque design around the cabin, with tubular subframes front and rear. Suspension was independent all-around.

Pininfarina used 1968's P6 racing prototype as the design's starting point. Making the 365 GT4/BB's lower portions a different color from the top was a styling touch from the designer's 1956's Superfast I showcar. "The idea was to 'cut' the car in two to make it look slender," Pininfarina explained.

The prototype Boxer made its debut at the Turin Auto Show in 1971, its top speed listed at a heady 188 mph. But it would be two years before it entered production. And the world that

365 GT4/BB, 512 BB & 512 BBi

365 GT4/BB 1973-1976
512 BB 1976-1981
512 BBi 1981-1984

Number made:

365 GT4/BB:	387
512 BB :	929
512 BBi :	1007

Engine:

365 GT4/BB:	4391cc flat-12, DOHC, 360 hp @ 7700 rpm
512 BB :	4942cc flat-12, DOHC, 340 hp @ 6800 rpm
512 BBi :	4942cc flat-12, DOHC, 340 hp @ 6800 rpm
Transmission:	5-speed
Wheelbase:	98.4 inches / 2500mm

Weight:

365 GT4/BB:	3,420 lbs. (*Road & Track*)
512 BB:	3,615 lbs. (*Road & Track*)
512 BBi:	3,615 lbs. (*Road & Track*)

1983 512 BBi

greeted Ferrari's fastest car was far different from the one that worshipped the Daytona. The oil crisis, political strife, crippling strikes, and material shortages affected the Boxer's build quality and production process.

That may very well have affected its performance, and any performance deficit was a damage to its reputation. For while every magazine met or exceeded the Daytona's 174-mph claimed top speed, none got close to the Boxer's quoted maximum. For example, in its June 1975 road test, *Road & Track* called the Boxer "the fastest road car we've ever tested." But the 175 mph it recorded was well short of 188.

Worse, acceleration times were disappointing; *R&T* needed 7.2 seconds to hit 60, some 2 seconds off factory figures. A slipping clutch and a transmission that frequently remained in neutral when upshifting at redline certainly didn't help. And at speeds above 130, the front became light on undulating roads.

Other magazines encountered similar problems, but when a 365 BB was right, it was really right. Mel Nichols clocked 0-60 in 5.4 seconds and 0-100 in 11.3 in a *CAR* road test that lauded the Ferrari effusively.

Refinement issues were addressed in 1976, with introduction of the 512 BB. The new name signified the engine's 5.0-liters and 12 cylinders. Rear track increased 1.7 inches, and the body was 2 inches wider and 1.5 inches longer. The front end had a small chin spoiler, and NACA ducts helped rear brake cooling.

Road & Track tested a federalized 512 in March 1978. Sixty now took 5.5 seconds and 100 took 13.2. Though the editors didn't record its actual maximum speed, they marveled at its ability to keep accelerating, easily running it beyond 150 mph. "The 512 (is) the best all-around sports & GT car we have ever tested," they concluded.

At 1981's Frankfurt Show, Ferrari introduced the most refined version of the series, the fuel-injected 512 BBi. This would prove the most-popular of the BBs. It looked almost identical to its predecessor, save minor exterior details such as badging, but its flat-12 featured Bosch K-Jetronic fuel injection instead of multiple carburetors and used a Digiplex ignition system.

The close of Boxer production in 1984 represented yet another milestone in Ferrari history. "It was something special," said coachbuilder Sergio Scaglietti, whose firm made the bodies. "It was the last car where we made everything by hand."

1984 400i

1972-1989
365 GT4 2+2, 400, 400i & 412

A 2+2 PLAYS THE ANGLES TO BECOME A MARANELLO MAINSTAY AND AN AUTOMATIC SUCCESS

The elegant angular lines and airy greenhouse of the 365 GT4 2+2 marked a new design direction for Ferrari. Unveiled at 1972's Paris Auto Show, this square-cut new four-seater looked much different than the 365 GTC/4. Moreover, it was stretched over a longer wheelbase—106.3 inches (2700mm) versus 98.4 (2500)—and had a wider track, allowing it to have proper rear seats.

But otherwise, it was nearly identical to the 365 GTC/4 under the skin. Both had independent suspension front and rear with self-leveling units in back, power-assisted disc brakes, power steering, and a robust tubular chassis. The GTC/4's 4.4-liter 320 horsepower V-12 and five-speed transmission also carried over untouched. But because of America's new smog and safety regulations, the car was never imported into the United States.

A revised version appeared at Paris in 1976. Called the 400 GT, its V-12 displaced 4.8-liters. But the most important mechanical change was the gearbox: This was the first Ferrari available with a factory-installed automatic transmission. Ferrari adapted General Motors' state-of-the-art three-speed Turbo-Hydramatic for use with the V-12 and created the 400 Automatic. It was a very popular move for owners.

Externally the five-speed-manual 400 GT and the 400 Automatic were nearly identical to the 365, save taillights reduced in number from six to four and the addition of a small front spoiler. The interior, however, was substantially revised, with new seats and more leather trim, making it much more luxurious.

The 400 would soldier on into the mid 1980s. The main revision came in late 1979 with introduction of fuel injection. The 400i (for injection) was offered with both the five-speed and automatic. Fuel injection spread to the rest of the Ferrari lineup within a year.

The 412 replaced the 400i in 1985. Unveiled at the Geneva Auto Show, it was at the time the only Ferrari imported into the U.S. by the factory. Displacement grew slightly to 4.9-liters, and the body received minor detail changes, with bumpers now painted the same color as the car. The last 412s were made in 1989, a demonstration of the lasting elegance of the car's shape.

An interesting side note to the 412 story is the factory-sanctioned convertible built in 1986. It was manufactured by Scaglietti as an experiment in carbon-fiber body panels. This was Sergio Scaglietti's last design for Ferrari before retiring. Because of the outstanding performance made possible by its lightweight construction the great coachbuilder lovingly called the convertible "a bomb!"

365 GT4 2+2, 400 GT, 400 AUTOMATIC, 400i, 400i AUTOMATIC & 412

365 GT4 2+2 1972-1976
400 GT & AUTOMATIC 1976-1979
400i & AUTOMATIC 1979-1984
412 1985-1989

Number made:

365 GT4 2+2:	521
400 GT & Automatic:	521
400i & Automatic:	1308
412:	577

Engine:

365 GT4 2+2:	4390cc V-12, DOHC, 320 hp @ 6800 rpm
400 GT & Automatic:	4823cc V-12, DOHC, 340 hp @ 6500 rpm
400i & Automatic:	4823cc V-12, DOHC, 310-315 hp @ 6400 rpm
412:	4943cc V-12, DOHC, 240 hp @ 6000 rpm
Transmission:	5-speed (all models) 3-speed auto (400, 400i, 412)
Wheelbase:	106.3 inches / 2700mm

Weight:

365 GT4 2+2:	3,308 lbs. (factory)
400 GT:	n/a
400 Automatic:	3,745 lbs. (factory)
400i:	4,008 lbs. (factory)
400i Automatic:	3,999 lbs. (factory)
412:	3,982 lbs.

1986 412

1975 308 GT4

308 GT4	
1974-1980	
Number made:	2826
Engine:	2926cc V-8, DOHC,
	255 hp @ 7700 rpm
	230 hp @ 6600 rpm (post 1977)
Transmission:	5-speed
Wheelbase:	100.4 inches / 2550mm
Weight:	2,930 lbs. (*Road & Track*, 1974)
	3,405 lbs. (*Road & Track*, 1979)

1974-1980
308 GT4

FERRARI TURNS TO A TRUSTED OLD FRIEND TO BREAK BOLD NEW GROUND

The Dino unveiled at the 1973 Paris Auto Show was a stunning departure. The name had become so closely associated with Pininfarina's curvaceous 246 that this new angular shape by Bertone—which hadn't done a Ferrari body in years—was shocking in comparison.

Add to that the presence of Ferrari's first production V-8, the fact that this was the marque's first midengine 2+2, and the reality that the car didn't actually wear the Ferrari badge, and controversy reigned.

What press and public didn't realize was the four-seat Dino 308 GT4 was not the replacement for Pininfarina's two-seat Dino 246. That replacement was still two years away. This Dino pointed Ferrari in a new direction, a departure enhanced by the 308 label. It identified Ferrari's new 3.0-liter V-8, which mounted transversely behind the small rear seats.

As for Bertone's role, it had recently earned Enzo Ferrari's confidence by building bodies for Fiat's Dino 2+2, some of them assembled at the Ferrari plant. "My father gave the (308 GT4) project to Bertone because they had done the Fiat Dino 2+2," said Piero Ferrari, a fact confirmed by former Bertone man Enzo Prearo. "The result was the Dino GT4. He gave to Pininfarina the two-seat car, and that was the 308 GTB."

Bertone chief stylist Marcello Gandini remembered Enzo being actively involved in the design. "It was conceived under his initiative," Gandini said. "(W)e prepared a mockup with pedals, four seats, and an engine. (It) could be made longer or shorter using a hydraulic pump so Ferrari himself could decide on the pedal's position and the interior space."

Few observers called Bertone's styling pretty. But criticism weakened once magazines tested the car. Formula 1 champ Emerson Fittipaldi tried one for Italy's *Quattroroute.* He found the lines "beautiful for a 2+2" and said it was "one of the best GTs." Le Mans-winner-turned-journalist Paul Frere noted in his *Road & Track* test that "it only has eight cylinders…but by any other standard it is a Ferrari."

Still, the GT4 languished on dealer lots, particularly in the U.S., where it was the only model Ferrari offered at the time. In May 1976 the car finally was badged a Ferrari rather than a Dino, and when 308 GT4 production ended four years later, it was Ferrari's third-best-selling model to that time, at more than 2,800 produced.

GT4 sidelights include Bertone's targa-topped one-off Rainbow in 1976, and American importer Luigi Chinetti's Le Mans prepped version. And in response to the fuel crisis, a 208 GT4 with a 2-liter V-8 was made for the Italian market, where engine size was heavily taxed.

1975-1989
308 & 328

THE DINO'S TRUE SUCCESSOR ESTABLISHES THE PATTERN FOR AN ERA OF V-8 FERRARIS

If the Ferrari world was turned upside down by Bertone's angular 308 GT4 in 1973, things were righted when Pininfarina's beautiful two-seat 308 GTB made its debut two years later.

"Based on the 308 Dino GT4 (but) with only two seats (the GTB) is regarded by many as the more natural successor to the much-loved Dino 246," England's *Motor* summed up for many. "The styling is the best to come out of Pininfarina for a long time."

The Dino design comparison was apt.

"Like the 206/246 Dino," acknowledged Sergio Pininfarina, "the inspiration for the 308's lines came from the Dino Berlinetta Speciale we exhibited at Paris in 1965."

The 308 GTB was significant as the first non-12-cylinder Ferrari to use the coveted Ferrari name. And it was the first Ferrari with a fiberglass body. Its underpinnings were identical to the 308 GT4's, but its wheelbase was shortened about eight inches (210mm) to 92.1 inches (2340mm). As with that 2+2, horsepower was quoted at 255, and the European version used a dry-sump oiling system. Emissions regulations limited the first GTBs in America to 240 horsepower.

Road-testers fell in love. *Autosport*'s John Bolster marveled at its temperament: "The 308 GTB is a civilized car that anybody can drive."

"Dino 246 fans, cheer up!" was how Paul Frere began a March 1976 *Road & Track* review. "There is a worthy two-place successor to your favorite car. And it's even better, faster, quieter and more comfortable."

Ferrari in early 1977 phased out the fiberglass coachwork in favor of traditional steel panels. In September that year, it introduced the targa-topped 308 GTS ("S" for spyder). This had a removable center roof section covered in black vinyl and used louvered panels in place of rear quarter windows.

Horsepower of U.S. cars had diminished to 205 because of ever-tighter American emissions rules. Ferrari in 1980 responded by replacing the 3.0-liter's quartet of two-barrel Weber carburetors with Bosch K-Jetronic fuel injection. New 308 GTBi and GTSi badging marked the change. The injected engine remained at a quoted 205 horsepower in the U.S.; Euro versions had 214.

Concurrent cabin updates included revised bucket seats with better bolstering, and supplemental controls that were ergonomically superior. The steering wheel changed, and the clock and oil-temp gauge moved to the center console from just above the driver's left knee.

1984 308 GTS QV and 1979 308 GTB

308 GTB, GTS, GTBi, GTSi, GTB QV, GTS QV, 328 GTB & GTS

308 GTB 1975-1980
308 GTS 1977-1980
308 GTBi 1980-1982
308 GTSi 1980-1982
308 GTB QV 1982-1985
308 GTS QV 1982-1985
328 GTB 1985-1989
328 GTS 1985-1989

Number made:

308 GTB:	712 (fiberglass) 2185 (steel)
308 GTS:	3219
308 GTBi:	494
308 GTSi:	1749
308 GTB QV:	748
308 GTS QV:	3042
328 GTB:	1344
328 GTS:	6068

Engine:

308 GTB:	2962cc V-8, DOHC, 205-255 hp @ 6600-7700 rpm
308 GTS:	2962cc V-8, DOHC, 205-255 hp @ 6600-7700 rpm
308 GTBi:	2962cc V-8, DOHC, 205-214 hp @ 6600 rpm
308 GTSi:	2962cc V-8, DOHC, 205-214 hp @ 6600 rpm
308 GTB QV:	2962cc V-8, DOHC, 230-240 hp @ 6800-7000 rpm
308 GTS QV:	2962cc V-8, DOHC, 230-240 hp @ 6800-7000 rpm
328 GTB:	3185cc V-8, DOHC, 260-270 hp @ 7000 rpm
328 GTS:	3185cc V-8, DOHC, 260-270 hp @ 7000 rpm

Transmission:	5-speed
Wheelbase:	92.1 inches / 2340mm

Weight:

308 GTB:	3,090 lbs. (fiberglass)
308 GTS:	3,290 lbs. (*Car and Driver*)
308 GTBi:	3,280 lbs. (*Car and Driver*)
308 GTSi:	n/a
308 GTB QV:	n/a
308 GTS QV:	3,230 lbs. (*Car and Driver*)
328 GTB:	n/a
328 GTS:	3,170 lbs. (*Road & Track*)

1988 328 GTS

Though the injected engine brought smoothness and a more flexible power curve, it needed more punch. So in 1982, Ferrari introduced the 308 quattrovalvole. These "QV" V-8s still displaced 2962cc, but had 230 horsepower in U.S. trim, 240 for Europe. Credit went to their higher compression ratios and, more important, to their new four-valve-per-cylinder heads. Road tests in America and Europe found them the best performing 308s of all.

The 308 GTB QV and GTS QV were replaced in 1985 by the 328 GTB and 328 GTS. The 328 was a subtle update to the 308's stunning lines, the most obvious changes being a new grill in front, the addition of one in the rear, and form-fitting bumpers that matched the body color. New five spoke wheels with a concave shape were also standard. Inside, the dash was redone, as were the seats, supplementary controls and door panels.

The best change was in the engine compartment, where the V-8 increased some 200cc to 3185cc. Horsepower jumped to 260 in U.S.-spec cars, 270 for European versions. Performance reflected the change. *Car and Driver*'s 328 GTS hit 60 mph in 5.6 seconds, 1.8 seconds quicker than its GTS QV. Top speed rose 9 mph to 153.

Like the 308, the 328 was immensely popular. "(It) is a rare and beautiful car," England's *Motor* said in a 1986 test, "as close to a work of art as any modern car can be. That it is also faster than ever and easier to live with makes it a car you ache to own. It is, after all, a Ferrari."

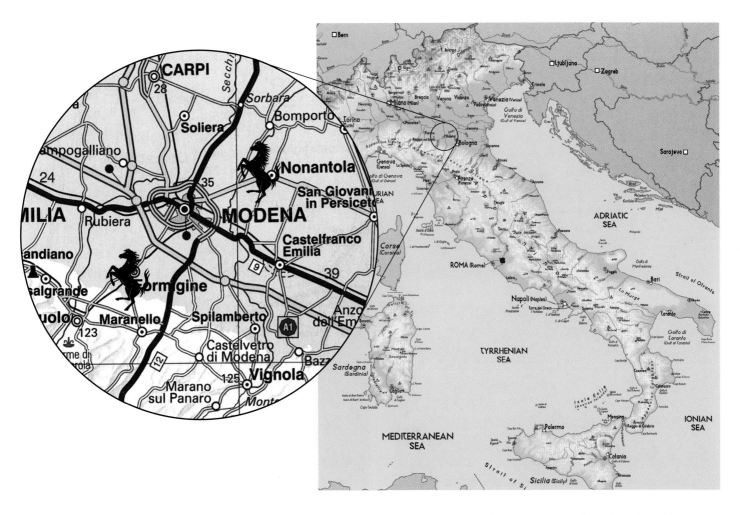

Modena:
Cradle of Speed

At the beginning of the twentieth century, the cities of Turin and Milan in northwest Italy were the industrial centers of the country and home to many of the nascent motor car industry's earliest automakers and coachbuilders. But in the 1920s and '30s, a small number of constructors and automotive-related businesses began springing up in central Italy's Reggio Emilia region, with the town of Modena the epicenter.

In hindsight, this seems surprising, for Modena, located some 150 miles south of Milan, was a small city surrounded by agriculture. Its population was hardy, robust, and mostly poor.

"We had no money, nothing," said Sergio Scaglietti, a resident of the region who was a teenager at the time. He dropped out of school to work after his carpenter father died unexpectedly. To get warm during Modena's cold, foggy winters, "I used to go to a place that had a furnace, where we would help the son of the owner. It took me five months to be able to buy a bicycle."

The region's transformation to capital of the performance-car universe started in 1933-34, when Modena native Enzo Ferrari's Scuderia Ferrari took over Alfa Romeo's racing efforts and transferred the operation to his hometown. Around the same time, Modena-based industrialist Adolfo Orsi bought Maserati, a

small constructor of competition machines based in Bologna. He moved the firm and its personnel to Modena in 1938.

The region was dedicated to war production in the early 1940s, and though Maserati returned to racing in 1946, and Ferrari did the same in '47, Modena still faced a surplus of engineering and manufacturing proficiency.

"There was a big fallout in our aircraft industry in the late 1940s," says Giordano Casarini, a talented manager for numerous firms whose lengthy career started at Ferrari. "There were many engineers and craftsmen who were incredibly skilled. Since there was no longer a need for fighter planes, they suddenly found themselves unemployed."

The auto industry was hiring, however, and in Modena, it was growing. Francesco Stanguellini was the first Fiat dealer in Modena, and continued building racing cars there after the war. The Maserati brothers formed Officine Specializate Costruzione Automobili in 1947 and their OSCA works was another local source of high-performance machines. Alessandro de Tomaso came to Europe from Argentina in 1955 to test drive OSCA sports cars, settled in Modena, and in 1959, formed De Tomaso Automobili S.p.A.

All these cars benefited from the region's heritage of aircraft technology. And for years, the likes of Juan Manuel Fangio in his Maserati 250F was among the drivers putting cars built in the area through their paces at the Modena Autodrome.

Ferrari and Maserati production increased more than 1,000 percent in the 1950s, and Modena, its constructors and their glamorous offerings jumped into the jet-set limelight. OSCA and Stanguellini disappeared in the 1960s, but industrialist Ferruccio Lamborghini came on the scene in 1963, manufacturing his Ferrari-rivaling supercars at nearby Sant'Agata Bolognese.

But Modena was not immune from the ebbs and flows of the world at large. Union disruptions and social unrest in the 1960s, oil crises in the 1970s and early '80s, and a series of crippling global recessions sent its speed merchants reeling. Ownership of Maserati, Lamborghini, even Ferrari changed hands.

Global prosperity brought a new round of growth in the late 1980s and exotic-car manufacturers Cizeta, Bugatti, and Iso Rivolta entered the picture. The recession of the early '90s cut deeply into the health of even Modena's most-established names. But Ferrari survived, and Lamborghini and Maserati eventually proved trophy acquisitions for larger, mainstream automakers.

Modena, Italy, June 1997

By the turn of the century, the region had enjoyed nearly a decade of booming economy and construction. Many residents believed the way to get ahead now was to purchase real estate and ride the stunning appreciation in property values.

Maranello, the once-sleepy Modena suburb where the Ferrari factory is located, was transformed beginning around 2000. If Disney were to start an automotive theme park, Maranello's atmosphere would be great inspiration.

It gained a sparkling new city center, and an office/hotel complex was erected across from the Ferrari factory. Monuments to Ferrari abound throughout the area. Some were obvious, such as the large "cavallino rampante" in the center of a roundabout on the way to and from Modena. Others were tucked in cubbyholes down back streets heading to the Fiorano test track.

As genuine as ever was the locals' enthusiasm for their hometown industry and its products. Ferrari flags flew everywhere and shops brimmed with its memorabilia for sale. Bakeries featured pastries decorated with a Ferrari car or the prancing horse. Photos of Ferrari history dotted restaurant walls. The Enzo Ferrari park now stood on the grounds of the Modena Autodrome.

And people still rushed to the fences surrounding the Fiorano test track whenever there was the sound of an engine. Once they got a glimpse of something or someone, they had a piece of history to tell their friends about that evening over a plate of pasta.

1988 Mondial 3.2

1980-1993
Mondial & Mondial Cabriolet

BACK IN THE FOLD: PININFARINA GETS ITS SHOT AT A MIDENGINE 2+2

In 1974, Sergio Pininfarina was disappointed his company did not have the opportunity to design the 308 GT4. In 1980, his patience was rewarded with the debut of Ferrari's new 2+2, the Mondial 8.

This was a return from Bertone's origami lines to Ferrari-traditional Pininfarina curves. The name, meanwhile, referenced Ferrari's four-cylinder mid-1950s sports-racing cars.

Underpinnings closely mirrored those of the GT4, with a sturdy tubular steel chassis, independent suspension, transversely mounted 3.0-liter V-8, and five-speed gearbox. In two notable changes, the wheelbase was lengthened some 4 inches (100mm) for better interior packaging and space, and a separate subframe carried the engine and transmission. This latter item allowed the drivetrain to be unbolted and removed more quickly for easier servicing.

Despite these advances and the more-familiar styling themes, reviews of Ferrari's latest 2+2 were mixed.

In England, *CAR* magazine said the "Mondial 8—superbly blending dynamic ability with masterful body design, clever electronics and Porsche-like build quality—is proof positive Maranello is reaching bright new heights."

In America, response was muted, mostly because of the car's performance. *Motor Trend* saw "just a tad over 130 mph" and needed 8.2 seconds to hit 60 mph. *Car and Driver*'s test example was more than a second slower to 60. "The Mondial 8 will barely get out of its own way," *C&D* lamented, adding, "It's not much fun to drive either."

Such observations echoed a rift in the Ferrari world. It started with the angular GT4, and as U.S. Ferraris got slower and slower, many established owners began to insist that a "real" Ferrari must have a 12-cylinder engine. In this view, it didn't matter that the V-8 models brought new blood to the marque. They didn't go or sound like a 12-cylinder Ferrari, and they were built of cheaper materials. Mondial 8's lackluster performance and cost-saving plastic trim only strengthened the argument and undoubtedly hurt sales; just over 700 were built in 2½ years.

Ferrari responded in August 1982 by installing its new quattrovalvole (four valve) V-8. The change injected real snap into the Mondial's performance.

Motor ran the four-valve Mondial to 60 mph in 6.4 seconds

and to 100 mph in 16.2; its two-valve test car needed 8.5 and 25 seconds, respectively. "Quattrovalvole has effected a miracle cure," the British magazine noted, "and Ferrari's mid-engine trio (of V-8s) are back running strongly in the supercar league where they belong."

Things got even better in 1984 with the unveiling of the Mondial Cabriolet, the first convertible Ferrari since the 1970s Daytona Spyder. Its open-air design and good performance had everyone smiling.

"We now feel Ferrari has a Mondial with raison d'etre," *Road & Track*'s test summed up. "(F)aster, better looking with wind-in-the-hair driving and all the attention from the sidelines you can handle…."

The Mondial 3.2 appeared in 1985, the redesignation signifying a larger, stronger V-8 (3.2-liters, 260-270 horsepower), as seen in the 328 GTB & GTS. The Mondial coupe and Cabriolet also got minor appearance updates with bumpers that matched the body color and new wheels. Antilock brakes were introduced in 1987.

Two years later came the fastest and most refined Mondial.

MONDIAL & MONDIAL CABRIOLET

MONDIAL 1980-1993
MONDIAL CABRIOLET 1983-1993

Number made:

Mondial 8:	703
Mondial QV:	1145
Mondial 3.2:	987
Mondial t:	858
Cabriolet QV:	629
Cabriolet 3.2:	810
Cabriolet t:	1017

Engine:

Mondial 8:	2926cc V-8, SOHC, 205-214 hp @ 6600 rpm
Mondial QV:	2926cc V-8, DOHC, 230-240 hp @ 7000 rpm
Mondial 3.2:	3185cc V-8, DOHC, 260-270 @ 7000 rpm
Mondial t:	3405cc V-8, DOHC, 300 hp @ 7000 rpm
Transmission:	5-speed (all models) Valeo 5-speed automatic (t)
Wheelbase:	104.3 inches / 2650mm

Weight:

Mondial 8:	3,460 lbs. (*Motor Trend*)
Mondial QV:	3,545 lbs. (*Road & Track*)
Mondial 3.2:	3,265 lbs. (*Autocar*)
Mondial t:	3,439 lbs. (*Automobile*)
Cabriolet QV:	n/a
Cabriolet 3.2:	n/a
Cabriolet t:	3,640 lbs. (factory)

Identified by a "t" suffix, its engine grew to 3.4-liters and was remounted longitudinally with the gearbox now situated transversely, hence the "t" designation. Horsepower jumped to 300. Other mechanical changes included electronically adjustable shock absorbers, power-assisted steering, and availability of Valeo automatic transmission. Visually, the "t" had cleaner air intakes, slightly different rear wings, and rectangular instead of round headlights. The interior was more luxurious and got a new dash, seats, and door panels.

Although top speed approached 160 mph, and some testers insisted it had the best-balanced chassis of any Ferrari of the day, a stigma remained with the car.

"Among the Ferrari cognoscenti," said *Road & Track* in its 1990 road test, "some see the Mondial t Cabriolet as a concession to the times, hardly worthy of the Cavallino emblem. Other Ferrari folks, however, consider it the most useful car out of Maranello, and thus the most coveted in any realistic day-in day-out sense."

1989 Mondial t Cabriolet

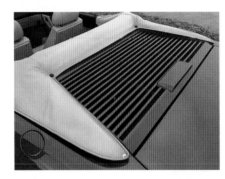

1985 288 GTO

288 GTO	
1984-1986	
Number made:	272
Engine:	2885cc twin-turbo V-8, DOHC, 400 hp @ 7000 rpm
Transmission:	5-speed
Wheelbase:	96.4 / 2450mm
Weight:	2,552 lbs. (factory)

1984-1986
288 GTO

A TURBO TERROR THAT NEVER GOT TO RACE IS A WORLD CHAMPION ON THE ROAD

The 288 GTO ushered in a new era for Ferrari and, indeed, the automotive world. Its debut was so highly anticipated, the model so coveted when it finally broke cover at Geneva in 1984, that it created the "instant collectible" market for automobiles—those rare machines that always commanded a price greater than the original sticker.

The model's name signified a fresh powertrain and honored a Ferrari immortal. 288 identified a 2.8-liter engine of eight cylinders. GTO conjured up Ferrari's 250 GTO race car of the early 1960s, and rightly so—the modern machine was a road car designed to be eligible for the increasingly popular world of rally competition.

For the beautiful body, Pininfarina design chief Leonardo Fioravanti and his crew used the 308 GTB as a starting point, then applied styling cues from the 250 GTO, most prominently the rear spoiler and the trio of rear-fender slats.

Compared to the 308 GTB, however, most every dimension (overall length and width, wheelbase, front and rear track) was increased to handle new mechanicals. The GTO's 2885cc V-8 sat longitudinally rather than transversely, and was located well forward of the rear axle for superior weight distribution. The powerplant also was mounted considerably lower than the V-8 in its 308/328 and Mondial V-8 stablemates.

The 288's V-8 itself was vastly different from the one in the 308/328 series of cars. Besides less displacement, it had two Japanese IHI turbochargers to boost power output. Other competition-oriented features included an oil cooler, dry-sump lubrication, intercoolers to reduce the turbos' inlet air temperature and an electronic injection and ignition system based on Ferrari's Formula 1 setup. The result was 400 horsepower at 7000 rpm, or 130-160 greater than a 308/328.

Suspension was independent front and rear with wishbones, coil springs over tube shocks, and antiroll bars. Braking came from huge ventilated discs. The transmission was a five-speed with a Formula 1-derived twin-plate clutch.

The 288 GTO's largest innovation was its construction. For the first time on a road car, Ferrari employed space-age composite materials in the chassis and body. This increased structural rigidity while decreasing weight. The factory quoted 2,552 pounds, more than 700 pounds lighter than its other two-seat V-8 models. It all made for stellar performance.

Automobile Revue's test car scorched the pavement, hitting 100 kilometers (62 mph) in 4.8 seconds, 100 mph in 9.7, and topping out at 288 kph (180 mph).

Road & Track's test car saw 60 in 5 seconds, reached 100 in 11 flat. That impressed the man behind the wheel, former F1 world champion Phil Hill, who had a 250 GTO on hand for comparison. Hill found the 288's cornering prowess "phenomenal, noticeably increasing with speed. One of the most delight-

ful aspects is…a light and nimble feel and not the heavy, intimidating nature of a Boxer or Lamborghini Countach.

"In total," Hill concluded, "the new GTO is miles ahead of its 22-year-old predecessor in performance, yet offers the option of air conditioning and Leoncavallo's Pagliacci in stereo….As pleased as I am to see Ferrari competing strongly in Formula One, I am delighted they will once again have gran turismo with true competition potential."

Unfortunately, the GTO never got the chance to show what it could do in the competition for which it was intended. Ferrari had constructed just five of a planned run of 20 600-horsepower 288 GTO Evoluziones when the FIA canceled the wild Group B series because of track safety issues.

That had no effect whatsoever on GTO demand. Buyers lined up, and Ferrari responded by bumping production of the road version to 272, from the planned 200. Original owners included Ferrari F1 champion Niki Lauda and Peter Livanos, a wealthy industrialist who was also part owner of England's Aston Martin.

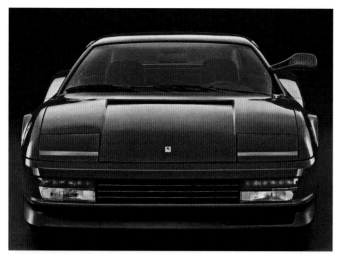
1984 Testarossa

TESTAROSSA, 512 TR & F512M	
TESTAROSSA 1984-1991 **512 TR 1992-1994** **F512M 1994-1996**	
Number made:	
Testarossa:	7177
512 TR:	2261
F512M:	501
Engine:	
Testarossa:	4942cc flat-12, DOHC, 390 hp @ 6300 rpm
512 TR:	4942cc flat-12, DOHC, 428 hp @ 6750 rpm
F512M:	4942cc flat-12, DOHC, 448 hp @ 6750 rpm
Transmission:	5-speed
Wheelbase:	100.4 inches / 2550mm
Weight:	
Testarossa:	3,660 lbs. (*Motor Trend*)
512 TR:	3,527 lbs. (*Autocar*)
F512M:	3,533 lbs. (*Autocar*)

1984-1996
Testarossa, 512 TR & F512M

A FERRARI ONCE AGAIN REFLECTS ITS TIMES, AND HELPS SHAPE THEM

Few Ferrari introductions could match the polarizing effect of the Testarossa upon its unveiling at the 1984 Paris Motor Show. A *Motor Trend* poll of automotive design chiefs elicited reactions from "I hate it" to "exciting, aggressive, and awesome."

The marketplace sided with the latter. Buyers lined up for Ferrari's 512 BBi replacement, and Testarossa-inspired bodyside strakes and outrigger mirrors soon appeared on new models from other automakers and became staples of aftermarket catalogs.

The Testarossa was named for Ferrari's famed sports-racing car of the late 1950s and early 1960s. Its groundbreaking styling was a response to engineering requirements and a backlash against the conservatism that blanketed Europe and Italy's automotive manufacturers during the most of the 1970s.

For much of that tumultuous decade, automobiles were reviled as a waste of natural resources. The continent's growing socialist and communist influences meant displays of material wealth were increasingly scorned. The goal of individual achievement at work was questioned. Terrorism became a growth industry in Italy and Germany, and the power of unions increased tremendously. Automotive design and engineering progress suffered.

That changed in Italy in the early 1980s with "The March of 40,000" when Fiat's workforce rebelled against the unions' clout. Organized labor's pull slowly diminished over time, and Italy heaved a sigh of relief. With the lid off the kettle, creativity was free to boil. The result was what Sergio Pininfarina called

1990 Testarossa

"an exaggeration in flamboyance."

That may have described the Testarossa's astonishing looks. But there was engineering and wind tunnel testing behind the ebullient shape. The track, for example, was much wider at the rear than the front for stability and handling. And the straked air intakes fed radiators efficiently located at the sides rather than in the front as on the 512 BBi.

The Testarossa was roomier, more refined, and comfortable than the 512 BBi. It retained a flat-12 engine of 4942cc, but added four-valve heads and other mechanical changes for an output of 390 horsepower on European cars, 380 for U.S.-spec versions.

The new car had particular significance for America as the first 12-cylinder Ferrari offered in the States since 1973's Daytona. Once it hit U.S. shores, it was clearly the fastest production car available.

Motor Trend's test example hit 60 mph in 5.29 seconds, 100 in 11.3. "Once you get beyond the way you expect its size and weight to feel," the magazine noted, "the Testarossa is surprisingly cooperative and unintimidating to drive—particularly in comparison to its Boxer forerunner....It's an all-around delight to drive, fast or slow, and is a hospitable grand tourer."

1995 F512M

Such friendly road manners and exposure in the trendsetting TV series *Miami Vice* helped the Testarossa become Ferrari's most-popular 12-cylinder model by a wide margin, with more than 7,000 sold.

Ferrari turned up the wick with the 512 TR, which was launched in 1992, appropriately enough, at the Los Angeles Auto Show. It looked much the same as the Testarossa, save larger wheels and a smaller, more-traditionally shaped grille. Powertrain modifications bumped horsepower to 428.

"Ferrari is back where it belongs, making the finest supercar

in production," *Autocar* declared. "This goes beyond the best engine there is, past its superb handling and massive presence and visits those places where supercars rarely venture. It's quiet, comfortable and amazingly easy to drive...."

Ferrari sold almost 2300 512 TRs in under three years. Even a decade after the original design broke cover, the modern Testarossa formula showed it was good for one final version. The F512M introduced at 1994's Paris Auto Show added its "M" for modificata. Principal areas addressed were weight, horsepower, and aesthetics. Most obvious was the last, the M honoring the Daytona and other classic Ferrari models with exposed headlamps covered by a clear panel and a return to four circular taillights. Horsepower increased to 448, and Ferrari optimistically claimed a top speed of 196 mph. The F512M was in production until 1996, with just over 500 sold.

1988 F40

F40		
1987-1992		
Number made:	1311	
Engine:	2936cc twin-turbo V-8, DOHC, 478 hp @ 7000 rpm	
Transmission:	5-speed	
Wheelbase:	96.4 inches / 2450mm	
Weight:	2,425 lbs. (factory)	

1987-1992
F40

FULL CIRCLE: ENZO'S FINAL CAR REVISITS FERRARI'S BEAUTIFUL, BRUTAL ROOTS

"A little more than a year ago I expressed a wish to my engineers," an 89-year-old Enzo Ferrari said in the summer of 1987. Listening closely to his every word was the automotive media, all having journeyed to Maranello for the introduction of a new model. "Build a car to be the best in the world. And now that car is here."

With that last sentence spoken, a red cover was swept aside, revealing the jaw-dropping F40. The car was named to honor the company's 40th anniversary, and the journalists spontaneously broke into applause, mesmerized by a sensuous shape that screamed speed. A tall rear spoiler dominated the design, which showed a resemblance to the 288 GTO. But otherwise, the form was quite clean.

"To put it in perspective," observed *Road & Track*'s Dennis Simanaitis, "recall how jarring the Testarossa first looked. By contrast, the F40 looks immediately right."

That there was a 288 GTO "familiarity" was more than happenstance. To compete in Group B rally competition in 1986, Ferrari planned to make 20 GTO Evoluziones, a more-powerful ultralightweight version of the 288. Ferrari built five before the series was canceled, leaving the company the perfect starting point for the F40. Ferrari's engineers needed just over 12 months to radically rework the Evoluzione.

Like the 288 GTO, the F40 had a tubular steel chassis but differed in its extensive use of carbon-fiber composites on the floorpan, dashboard, front bulkhead, and other areas. The body was also made of composite materials employed in Ferrari's Formula 1 program, in this case a Nomex, Kevlar, and carbon-fiber weave.

The twin-turbo 2936cc V-8 was mounted longitudinally, and featured double overhead cams, twin intercoolers, and electronic engine-management systems. Ferrari quoted 478 horsepower, this in a car that tipped the scales at under 3,000 pounds in U.S. trim.

The interior was all business. The sliding windows were plexiglas, the doors and other panels were exposed carbon fiber. Seats were deep buckets, also made of carbon-fiber materials, and there was no carpeting. The only concession to luxury was a much needed air-conditioning system.

"We wanted (the F40) to be very fast, sporting in the extreme and spartan," Ferrari's Giovanni Perfetti told *Autocar* in 1987. "Customers have been saying our cars were becoming too plush and comfortable. The F40 is for the most enthusiastic of our owners who want nothing but sheer performance."

That's what the F40 delivered. *Road & Track* tested one in a "World's Fastest Cars" shootout; it hit 100 mph in 8 seconds flat, covered the quarter-mile in 11.8. That was quicker than both the Porsche 959 Deluxe and 959 Sport in the shootout. The test Ferrari topped out at 196 mph.

Customers lined up to purchase the F40 at a factory sticker of $470,000, and Ferrari responded. Three years earlier, at the

1990 F40

introduction of the 288 GTO, the firm announced how many GTOs it would produce. Prices skyrocketed in the secondary market. The lesson was not lost.

Initially, the company said it would make 400 F40s. But 3,000 customers were waving checkbooks, pen in hand. Production was increased. It was reported Ferrari planned to stop at 1,000. Production wound up being open ended—the company would build as many as the market would bear. Still, prices were driven up to three times sticker by "investors" in the speculator-driven hysteria of the late 1980s.

Values eventually came back to earth, and the speculator frenzy would be but a sidebar to the brilliance of the F40 itself. The car developed a devoted following among true enthusiasts. Its legend only grew when Enzo died in 1988, making the F40 the final Ferrari introduced under his watch.

1990 348ts

348 TB, 348 TS, 348 SERIES SPECIALE, 348 GTB, 348 GTS & 348 SPIDER
348 TB & TS 1989-1993
348 SERIES SPECIALE 1993
348 GTB & GTS 1993-1994
348 SPIDER 1993-1995

Number made:
348 tb:	2894
348 ts:	4228
Series Speciale:	100
GTB:	222
GTS:	218
Spider:	1146

Engine:
	3405cc, DOHC, 300 hp @ 7200 rpm
Series Speciale:	3405cc, DOHC, 312 hp @ 7200 rpm,
Spider:	3405cc, DOHC, 310 hp @ 7200 rpm
Transmission:	5-speed
Wheelbase:	96.5 inches / 2450mm

Weight:
348 tb:	3,292 lbs. (*Car and Driver*)
348 ts:	3,270 lbs. (*Road & Track*)
Series Speciale:	n/a
GTB:	n/a
GTS:	n/a
Spider:	3,252 lbs. (*Road & Track*)

1989-1995
348

AN IMPORTANT STEP FORWARD IN STRUCTURAL DESIGN IS ACCOMPANIED BY SOME UNSEEMLY STUMBLES

Ferrari's follow-up to the 328 series marked a radical departure in the way Maranello constructed its cars. Replacing a chassis of traditional steel tubes was a much stiffer monocoque structure with a tubular rear subframe.

Suspension remained independent front and rear with wishbones, springs, telescopic shocks, and antiroll bars, but with revised geometry. The ventilated disc brakes were much larger than those on the 328, and used antilock technology.

A midships-mounted V-8 returned, but it was larger and more powerful. Displacing 3405cc, it mounted longitudinally and mated to a transverse gearbox. The displacement accounted for the new car's 348 designation. The transverse gearbox gave it its suffixes—tb for the closed berlinetta body style, ts for the spyder (which actually had a lift-off targa roof panel).

A higher compression ratio and updated fuel injection helped generate 300 horsepower, 30-40 more than the 328, while a dry-sump oiling system gave the new Ferrari a lower center of gravity.

The 348 was the last design done under the supervision of chief stylist Leonardo Fioravanti. Taking cues from the Testarossa, its forms were softer than those of the 308/328 but still curvaceous, the side strakes being the most obvious Testarossa inspiration. Wheelbase was longer than the 328's and the track wider, giving the interior more space.

The 348, in tb and ts forms, made its debut at the 1989 Frankfurt Auto Show. "To many, it was Best in Show," said *Road & Track*. "Free of Testarossa excess—in width, overhang,

1993 348 Spider

styling—this 3.4-liter V-8 is compact, quicker on the track...ideal."

But the 348 proved not so ideal in the real world. Road-testers couldn't quite match Ferrari's claimed 5.6 seconds 0-60 mph and 171-mph top speed. Worse, they found the car a challenge to drive near or at the limit. Other shortcomings included a harsh ride, a wandering front end at high speed, and a stiff gearbox.

Then Acura released its NSX, and overnight the equation changed. The Honda-designed midengine V-6 two-seater equaled the 348's performance, had better-balanced road manners, greater comfort, and one-upped Ferrari with superior engineering and build quality. And it cost some $30,000 less.

"Has Honda bettered Ferrari?" *Road & Track* asked rhetorically in a January 1991 comparison. The magazine concluded the 348 was "the better exotic" and would later name it "one of the ten best cars in the world." But of the two, it believed the NSX was "the more successful car."

Well aware of the 348's shortcomings was Ferrari's new CEO, Luca Cordero di Montezemolo. "I had just bought a new 348," he said in an interview with *Automobile* a decade after he took the helm at Ferrari, "and with the exception of its good looks I was utterly disappointed. This was clearly the worst product Ferrari had developed for some time."

The company worked quickly to improve the 348. It upgraded the shift mechanism and climate system and installed new fuel injection and new shocks and springs. Magazines noted the improvements, but the 348 couldn't shake its reputation for hit and-miss build quality and dicey manners at the limit. Couple those perceptions with a global recession, and the result was a drop in Ferrari's overall sales from more than 4,000 in 1990 and '91 to 2,200 in '93.

The company's response for the U.S. market was the "Series Speciale." This was a 348 with slightly different cosmetics and seats, tuned exhaust, and 312 horsepower. Just 100 were made, each with a numbered plaque.

Ferrari also announced the 348 Challenge Series for 1994. Owners competed several times a year at racetracks around the world in specially prepared street-based 348s. A huge success, the concept was emulated by other manufacturers.

The berlinetta and targa models gained GTB and GTS designations in 1993 as part of the "relaunch" of the 348 line. But that year's real news was the 348 Spider. Introduced in Beverly Hills, California, it was Ferrari's first true two-seat convertible since the Daytona. Well-received by press and public alike, it survived the GTB and GTS by about a year, selling alongside the 348's successor, the 355, which bowed in spring 1994.

1995 456 GT

456 GT, 456 GT AUTOMATIC, 456 M GT & GTA		
456 GT 1992-1998		
456 GT AUTOMATIC 1996-1998		
456 M GT & GTA 1998-2003		

Number made:

456 GT:	1548
456 GT Automatic:	403
456 M GT & GTA:	1338
Engine:	5474cc V-12, DOHC, 442 hp @ 6250 rpm (436 hp for U.S. cars)

Transmission:

456 GT:	6-speed manual
456 GT Automatic:	4-speed automatic
456 M GT:	6-speed manual
456 M GTA:	4-speed automatic
Wheelbase:	102.3 in / 2600mm
Weight:	3,725 lbs. (factory)

1992-2003
456 GT

VITA NUOVA (NEW LIFE) FOR A CLASSIC CONSTRUCT: THE RETURN OF THE FRONT-ENGINE V-12 BERLINETTA

The unveiling of the 456 GT at the 1992 Paris Auto Show marked a shift in Ferrari's thinking. Balance and refinement replaced the excess and flamboyance that dominated the company's design direction and product personality during the second part of the 1980s. The 456 embodied the new direction.

Many of the greatest Ferraris were front-engine berlinettas, the last being the early 1970s Daytona. The 456 picked up the baton beautifully.

"It has been 20 years since we had a car like this at Ferrari," company CEO Luca di Montezemolo noted at the introduction. "I don't think it will bring speculators back to our order books—this is not a car for them."

He was right. Ferrari's traditional clientele queued up to buy the model for the right reasons. "(The 456 GT) is more refined, more comfortable and a sight more sophisticated than any car ever to be built at Maranello," said *Autocar* in its 1993 road

2000 456 M GT

test. "Whether you look at it, sit in it or drive it, it all adds up to one simple fact: The 456 is the greatest grand tourer the world has ever seen."

Indeed it was. This was Ferrari's first true four-seat model since the 412. Its aluminum coachwork was welded to its steel tube chassis using a new process. The 5474cc V-12 boasted 442 horsepower (436 for America) and a new six-speed manual transmission that was housed in unit with the transaxle. Top speed was listed at 185 mph.

A four-speed automatic joined the lineup in 1996 as the 456 GT Automatic. The automatic was also housed in unit with the transaxle and added about 170 pounds to the car. *Road & Track* said the GTA "gets the job done, but without the tautness and direct mechanical sensitivity of a manual Ferrari gearbox." The $255,000 test example did 0-60 mph in 5.1 seconds. In all, said *R&T,* the GTA was "a calm, civilized traveling companion with lots of power on tap, allowing fast travel with few demands on the driver." Ferrari sold nearly 2,000 456 GTs and Automatics in six years.

In 1998 came the 456 M GT and GTA. The "M" was for modificata, and marked revised coachwork with new bumpers, a crisper edge along the front fenders, and an updated interior. Clients also had the option of customizing the car with Ferrari's new Carrozzeria Scaglietti program.

The M closed out the 456 run in 2003. The line was in production 11 years, confirming the strength of Pininfarina's original shape, and how well Ferrari had designed and engineered the car.

1995 F355 Spider and 1997 F355 Berlinetta

1994-1999
F355

NO DEBATE: A V-8 MODEL FINALLY TAKES ITS PLACE AMONG THE ALL-TIME FERRARI GREATS

Ferrari in the early 1990s was a badly listing vessel. By 1993, production had dropped 50 percent over two years, the F40 was no longer the fastest car on the planet, and the 348 was an also-ran in magazine comparison tests. As England's *CAR* summed up in 1994, "When someone else makes the most coveted sports car in the world, you feel an injustice...."

Luckily, Maranello had the will, the talent, and the means to right its ship. First, in late 1992, came the stupendous 456 GT. The follow-up was better.

The F355 was a modern classic, so beautiful, so well-engineered, so well-received, that it marked the beginning of the end of the old-guard Ferraristi philosophy that the only "real" Ferraris were ones with 12-cylinder engines.

The F355 in closed Berlinetta and targa GTS form burst onto the scene in spring 1994. It shared most every dimension with its 348 predecessor. Yet it was virtually a new car, as its stunning coachwork indicated. More than 1800 hours of wind

F355 BERLINETTA, GTS, CHALLENGE, SPIDER, F1 & SERIE FIORANO

F355 Berlinetta 1994-1998
F355 GTS 1995-1998
F355 Challenge 1995-1998
F355 Spider 1995-1999
355 F1 Berlinetta, GTS & Spider 1998-1999
355 Serie Fiorano 1999

Number made:	
Berlinetta:	3829
GTS:	2048
Challenge:	104
Spider:	2664
F1 Berlinetta:	1042
F1 GTS:	529
F1 Spider:	1053
Serie Fiorano:	104
Engine:	3496cc V-8, DOHC, 380 hp @ 8250 rpm (375 hp for U.S. cars)
Transmission:	6-speed manual 6-speed paddle-shift manual (F1, Serie Fiorano)
Wheelbase:	96.5 inches / 2450mm
Weight:	2,976 lbs. (factory)

tunnel testing influenced the harmonious shape, which incorporated an F1-style flat bottom with an airflow channel that generated enough downforce to offset any lift.

Engine, transmission, and suspension received major upgrades. The longitudinally mounted 3496cc V-8 had five valves per cylinder and a stunning 375-380 horsepower at a spine tingling 8250 rpm. The gearbox was now a six-speed with a new type of synchromesh that made it much easier to shift. Electronically adjustable shocks varied stiffness within milliseconds to suit the road surface.

Around Ferrari's 1.86-mile Fiorano test track, the F355 was two seconds faster than the 12-cylinder 512 TR. That level of performance—and that sensational shape—landed the F355 on countless magazine covers. Testers were smitten.

In the hands of former Le Mans winner Paul Frere, an F355 Berlinetta took 4.9 seconds to 60 mph, 11.2 to 100, and 13.3 for the quarter-mile. Top speed was an estimated 183 mph. Frere asserted in his *Road & Track* report that the V-8 was "probably the best sports car engine ever made" and said the 355 was "the purest purebred yet from Ferrari's scuderia."

Autocar was just as direct: "At a stroke (this Ferrari) has created a new supercar class of its own, leaving 911s and NSXs for dead. The F355 is so good, in fact, that it makes the once peerless 512 TR look blunt."

Ferrari released a trio of new F355 models in 1995. The F355 Spider convertible broke cover on Rodeo Drive in Beverly Hills and was a huge sales success. Its electronically controlled power top retracted beneath a canvas cover.

Next was the F355 Challenge. Made to compete in Ferrari's popular Challenge Series, this berlinetta weighed approximately 200 pounds less than the street car. It had a more spartan interior; wire mesh "Challenge" rear grille; lower and stiffer suspension; and revised exhaust, brakes, and wheels.

The final '95 release was the one-off 355 Competizione shown in Geneva. It was approximately 500 pounds lighter than the F355 Berlinetta and featured a "paddle-shift" sequen-

1998 355 F1 GTS

1999 355 Serie Fiorano

tial manual transmission. This Formula 1-derived technology made its way into Ferrari's road cars in 1998 with the 355 F1. Its 6-speed gearbox used hydraulic actuators attached to the transmission's mechanical systems so that upshifts and downshifts were accomplished by tugging paddles situated just behind the steering wheel. The following year, the factory's Scaglietti customization program became available on all 355s.

The final F355 iteration was the "Serie Fiorano," introduced at 1999's Geneva Auto Show alongside the new 360 Modena. This unique 355 spider had special underpinnings, a Challenge rear grille, and Scuderia Ferrari shields on the front fenders. The interior used carbon-fiber inserts, a suede-covered steering wheel, and a dedication plaque stating its position in a promised 100 car run (the final number was 104).

The F355, in all its forms, was a benchmark of such renown that former Ferrari F1 champion Phil Hill named it as one of the 10 best Ferraris ever, placing it alongside such immortals as the 250 GTO and 250 SWB.

1995 F50

1995-1997
F50

INTOXICATING FORMULA: RACING TECHNOLOGY APPLIED TO THE ROAD

"Our market research says Ferrari customers believe F1 is the pinnacle of all automotive technology, the highest peak of their motoring aspirations," former Ferrari sales and marketing director Dr. Michele Scannavini said in the mid 1990s. "By offering them a chance to buy an F1 car dressed as a road car, we're going as close as we can to meeting those aspirations."

An "F1 car dressed as a road car" sums up the F50.

The idea for this F40 successor came from Piero Ferrari, then the company's vice chairman. He drove an F40 to the office daily, and with Ferrari concentrating its racing focus on Formula 1, that made F1 a perfect starting point for Maranello's highest performing new road car.

In 1990, when work on the F50 began, Ferrari's F1 cars used a carbon-fiber chassis, a naturally aspirated V-12 engine, pushrod suspension, and paddle-shift transmission. All would make it to the F50, save the shift paddles because of durability concerns.

The tub followed Formula 1 engineering principles. It was the central part of the car's structure and was made entirely of lightweight carbon composites and adhesive materials. Acting as a support for the rear suspension and for the carbon-fiber bodywork was the centrally mounted engine.

F50	
1995-1997	
Number made:	349
Engine:	4700cc V-12, DOHC, 513 hp @ 8500 rpm
Transmission:	6-speed manual
Wheelbase:	101.6 inches / 2580mm
Weight:	2,712 lbs. (factory)

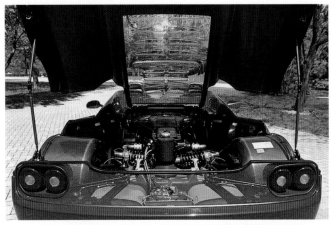

And what an engine it was. The 4700cc V-12 used the 1990 F1 car's block. It employed a similar design for the heads and crankshaft; this made the latter items easier to manufacture. Everything else was new so the engine could meet emissions laws and be drivable on the street. At 513 horsepower, the F50 was Ferrari's most-powerful road car ever.

The gearbox was a conventional six-speed manual mounted longitudinally. The suspension featured upper and lower wishbones, pushrods, and electronically controlled shocks managed by an ECU that took into account steering angles and lateral and longitudinal forces. This not only minimized body roll but made the ride more comfortable. The brakes were large ventilated Brembo discs and were not power assisted.

Originally, Ferrari wanted Pininfarina to make two different bodies for the car—a slinky aerodynamic coupe and a barchetta. Pininfarina's head of design was Lorenzo Ramaciotti, and the earliest F50 proposals drew from his stunning Ferrari Mythos show car of 1989. To pass U.S. crash tests, the body of the road car had to be lengthened, and once the general shape was decided, it underwent extensive aerodynamic testing.

"Our priority was to find a good balance between airflow on and inside the car by utilizing underbody aerodynamics," Ramaciotti said. Spoilers were added as necessary, and lessons learned developing the F50's flat underbody were tapped for the smaller F355.

A full-scale styling model was presented to Ferrari in 1991. At that point, Ferrari management told Pininfarina to merge the

coupe and barchetta into a single car. The design of the resulting open two-seater with a lift-off roof panel was barely
touched until shortly before the car's introduction at the 1994
Geneva Motor Show, when roll bars were added for additional
occupant protection.

Ferrari capped F50 production at just 349 units, one fewer
than it figured it would be able to sell. Most of the earliest cars
went to America, delivered before emissions regulations tightened in 1997. Ferrari had no trouble selling out the production
run, even at a factory sticker of nearly $520,000.

That was roughly half the asking price of the other preeminent supercar of the day, the McLaren F1. That the F50
couldn't quite match the McLaren's performance numbers was
of no importance to Ferrari. Its goal was to construct the
world's most involving drive, and that's exactly what F50 owners got.

Not that 0-100 mph in 8 seconds and the quarter-mile in
12.1 was slow. It was about the experience. As *Road & Track*
summed up in the test that recorded those figures, "More than
anything the F50 feels like a racing car."

Ferrari had hit its target, and the car was so special inside the
company that it had its own production line. When the last F50
rolled out in 1997, few were sadder to see it go than Ferrari
test driver Dario Benuzzi. "Developing the car has been a wonderful adventure," he told *Autocar*. "I do not want it to end."

1997 550 Maranello

1996-
550 & 575

WORTH THE WAIT: THE BEAUTY OF TWO SEATS BEHIND TWELVE CYLINDERS

For many years, a core of Cavallino enthusiasts reserved title of "the best all-around Ferrari" for the late-1960s 330/365 GTC. It's no wonder the next car to assume the mantle would follow a similar blueprint: mature but exciting styling, V-12 engine in the front, a two-seater built on a shortened 2+2 chassis.

This was the 550 Maranello, unveiled in July 1996 at Germany's Nurburgring racetrack. The name celebrated both its 5.5-liter V-12 and the Ferrari factory's hometown.

It essentially was the 456 GT four-seater rendered in tighter, lighter, sportier form. It also turned its back on the midengine layout that had defined Ferrari's performance flagships for more than a decade in the guise of the Testarossa through 512M. The attitude behind those supercars was no longer in fashion at Maranello.

"I was a little disturbed by a car that was too much of a showoff, too difficult to use," Ferrari CEO Luca Cordero di Montezemolo said at the 550's introduction.

Avoiding "showoff," circumventing "difficult to use" was the essence of the design and engineering brief. As usual, the recipe started with the engine, and the 550's 5474cc V-12 was a masterpiece. It had a variable-volume intake manifold, titanium connecting rods, forged aluminum pistons, four valves per cylin-

2002 550 Barchetta

550 MARANELLO, 550 BARCHETTA PININFARINA, 575M MARANELLO & 575 SUPERAMERICA

550 MARANELLO 1996-2001
550 BARCHETTA 2000-2002
575M MARANELLO 2002-
575 SUPERAMERICA 2005-

Number made:

550 Maranello:	3600
550 "World Record":	33
550 Barchetta:	448
575M:	n/a
575 Superamerica:	n/a

Engine:

550:	5474cc V-12, DOHC, 485 hp @ 7600 rpm
575M Maranello:	5748cc V-12, DOHC, 515 hp @ 7250 rpm
575 Superamerica:	5748cc V-12, DOHC, 533-540 @ 7250

Transmission:

550:	6-speed manual
575:	6-speed manual, 6-speed paddle shift manual

Wheelbase:	98.5 inches / 2500mm

Weight:

550 Maranello:	3,726 lbs. (factory)
550 "World Record":	n/a
550 Barchetta:	n/a
575M:	3,815 lbs. (factory)
575 Superamerica:	n/a

2002 575M Maranello

der, and four cams. Horsepower was an impressive 485 at 7600 rpm. With a great deal of its 420 pound-feet of torque available at 3500 rpm, it was also impressively user-friendly.

Its tubular chassis' wheelbase was four inches shorter than the 456's, but their underpinnings had much in common: independent suspension with double wishbones, coil springs, electronically adjustable shocks, and antiroll bars.

The largest engineering stride was the new ASR traction control. This featured three modes: Normal, Sport, and Off. It would cut back engine power if it sensed a rear wheel slipping, and if things got particularly unruly, the computer-controlled system would activate the ventilated disc brakes' antilock technology to intervene. The ABS also balanced braking effort between the front and rear brakes when deceleration reached more than 0.5g.

Sergio Pininfarina relished designing the 550, honing the shape with 4,800 hours in the wind tunnel. "It reminded me of how I felt in the 1950s, when I was first working with Ferrari," he said. "Ferrari returned to the front-engine configuration with this car because the progress of technology allowed us to reach the same level of performance of a midengine design with better comfort and luggage room."

A number of pundits (this writer among them) saw the 550's restrained styling as too conservative at the time of its launch. Such misgivings soon wore away as the purity of the shape gained recognition as a Pininfarina classic.

The design was also quite practical. Compared to the 512M, the 550 had three inches more leg room and 1.5 inches more head room, plus a larger trunk and a small storage area behind the seats. Yet it accelerated more quickly—4.3 seconds 0-60 mph. It was faster—a real top speed just shy of 200 mph. And it handled considerably better—the 550 was more than three seconds quicker than the 512M around Ferrari's Fiorano test track.

The idea of an open-air 550 was evident not longer after the

Maranello made its debut. Pininfarina had been building a number of custom-bodied Ferraris for Brunei's royal family, including cabriolets. Ferrari followed suit with the 2000 Paris Auto Show unveiling of the 550 Barchetta Pininfarina.

It was produced as a limited edition of 448 to commemorate 50 years collaboration between Ferrari and its great design partner. Distinguished from the coupe by a lower windshield, fairings and rollbars behind the seats, and a manually operated folding top, all were sold before production began in 2001.

In 2002, Ferrari introduced the 575M Maranello. The M stood for Modificata, which was borne out in a displacement bump to 5748cc, a horsepower kick to 515, and installation of an updated version of the paddle-shift F1 gear-change system first seen in the 355 F1. Cosmetically, more-aggressive headlights were integrated, and the interior was revised with a new dashboard and seats.

An open version of this car made its debut at the 2005 Los Angeles Auto Show. The 575 Superamerica conjured Ferrari's famed luxurious limited-production models of decades past. It opened its cockpit to the air via an intriguing rotating top of adjustable-tint electrochromic glass. The panel pivoted on points behind the passenger compartment and came to rest above the trunklid. It was a fitting exclamation point for a classic Ferrari.

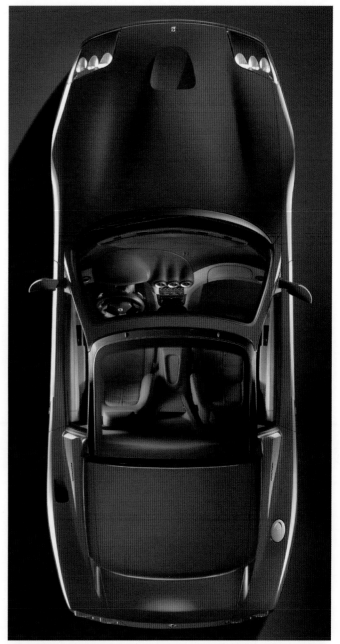

2005 575 Superamerica

1993 Pininfarina design study for the 360 Modena

1999-
360 & F430

THE MIDENGINE V-8 FERRARI SPEARS THE NEW CENTURY WITH A FRESH FACE AND UNCONCEALED POWER

If there were lingering doubts after the sensational F355 that an 8-cylinder car could be a real Ferrari, those doubts were obliterated by the 360 Modena.

Seen first at the 1999 Geneva Auto Show, the 360 Modena was named for its 3.6-liter engine and for the spiritual home of Ferrari. It had some large shoes to fill.

2000 360 Modena

The F355 been among the world's most beautiful and exciting pure sports cars. And it had become Ferrari's second-best-seller ever, with more than 11,000 produced.

Dimensionally, Modena was larger than the 355 in every way. A wheelbase stretched to 102.3 inches (2600mm) from 96.4 (2450) was the biggest difference, and resulted in a new cabin that was quite commodious for a midengine car. But even with its larger size, the Modena was some 80 pounds lighter than the 355.

The 360 had a lighter-weight aluminum monocoque/tubular chassis that increased bending stiffness and torsional rigidity more than 40 percent compared to the 355. Suspension was new double wishbones, coil springs, adaptive shocks, and anti-roll bars. The power-assisted rack-and-pinion steering needed

2001 360 Spider

360 MODENA, 360 SPIDER, 360 CHALLENGE STRADALE, F430 & F430 SPIDER

360 MODENA 1999-2004
360 SPIDER 2000-2004
360 CHALLENGE STRADALE 2003-2004
F430 2004-
F430 SPIDER 2005-

Number made:

360 Modena:	8761
360 Spider:	7483
360 Challenge Stradale:	1274
F430:	n/a

Engine:

360 Modena:	3586cc V-8, DOHC, 395-400 hp @ 8500 rpm
360 Spider:	3586cc V-8, DOHC, 395-400 hp @ 8500 rpm
360 Challenge Stradale:	3586cc V-8, DOHC, 425 hp @ 8500 rpm
F430:	4308cc V-8, DOHC, 483 hp @ 8500 rpm
Transmission:	6-speed manual, 6-speed paddle-shift manual
Wheelbase:	102.3 in / 2600mm

Weight:

360 Modena:	3,064 lbs. (factory)
360 Spider:	3,495 lbs. (factory)
360 Challenge Stradale:	2,822 lbs. (factory)
F430:	3,196 lbs. (factory)
F430 Spider:	3,351 lbs. (factory)

2003 360 Challenge Stradale

just 2.7 turns lock to lock, while the large power-assisted Brembo discs had ABS. Modena enlarged the 355's V-8 to 3586cc to produce 395-400 horsepower, some 20 more than the 355. Transmissions were an updated version of the F1 paddle-shift system or a conventional six-speed manual.

Finally, the 360 made the 355 look old in comparison. "The 355 was a car made by flat surfaces," Sergio Pininfarina explained. "With the Modena, it was one fluid shape, from beginning to end. So every place you look it is moving. It is dynamic."

The shape was subjected to considerable wind tunnel testing and generated four times the downforce of the 355's. Pop-up headlights were eliminated. Fresh air went to the engine via 250 LM-inspired air intakes on the rear fenders. And in a huge stylistic departure, the traditional circular air intake and grille up front was replaced by "nostrils" on either side of the fascia, a look that recalled Ferrari's early '60s shark-nose F1 design.

The 360 was also the first Ferrari with a clear glass engine cover. "Many times at the motorshows people were asking me on our stand, 'May I have a look at the engine?'" Pininfarina explained. "The 360's engine was a masterpiece, so we asked, 'Why must we keep the masterpiece in the car?'"

Still, some critics called the design a bit bloated. Others disliked the front end. But these quibbles faded once the Modena went into action.

It was a ballerina on the road—quicker, faster, more agile, and more comfortable than the 355. With a 0-60-mph time in the low-4-second range, a top speed of 180 mph and all that technology wrapped up in that flowing shape, it was clear that "real" Ferraris did indeed have V-8 engines.

Could any car be more alluring? It could if it were the 360 Spider. It repeated its closed sibling's mechanicals and even that clear engine cover. Its fabric top folded beneath a sculpted hard tonneau in little more than 20 seconds. The marketplace couldn't get enough: For years after its 2000 Geneva Show intro, the Modena Spider in America brought tens of thousands over list price in the secondary market.

In 2003, Ferrari introduced the most-focused 360. The Challenge Stradale used lessons learned with the "Challenge" Series and competition 360 GT. The 360 CS had a stripped out interior, greater downforce from revised aerodynamics, suspension updates, and carbon-ceramic brakes.

All this made for a lengthy waiting list for the Modena, one that still wasn't satisfied when, at the 2004 Paris Auto Show, Ferrari introduced its successor.

2004 F430

The F430 was based on the 360, yet Ferrari said 70 percent of its parts were new. Its body was new, too, but retained the family resemblance. The design was a collaboration between Pininfarina and Frank Stephenson, Ferrari's head of design. It was a tauter-looking machine, with Enzo styling cues.

Technologically, the F430 was a huge jump over the Modena. At 186 mph, the airflow-sensitive underbody produced 50 percent more downforce than the 360. On the steering wheel were two Ferrari road-car precedents: an ignition "start" button and the F1-derived manettino control. The latter dialed in five different driving modes affecting such variables as ride stiffness, traction-system response, and, with the F1 gearbox, shift points.

Visible again beneath a glass cover was the V-8 engine, but this was a 4308cc unit with 483 horsepower. It blasted the F430 to 60 in just 3.5 seconds, to 100 in 8.1, and through the quarter-mile in an astounding 11.7 seconds at 120 mph.

Ferrari followed up the F430 coupe with the 2005 Geneva Auto Show unveiling of the F430 Spider that delivered all this delicious performance in a luscious droptop form.

2005 F430 Spider

2003 Enzo

ENZO	
2002-2005	
Number made:	400
Engine:	5998cc V-12, DOHC, 660 hp @ 7800 rpm
Transmission:	6-speed paddle-shift manual
Wheelbase:	104.3 inches / 2650mm
Weight:	3,009 lbs. (factory)

2002-2005
Enzo

POWERFUL, POLARIZING, AND SOUL-STIRRING—MUCH LIKE ITS NAMESAKE

In 1998, Ferrari CEO Luca Cordero di Montezemolo began contemplating the company's next "extreme" model, a successor to the F50. He targeted three areas: the car must be "really impressive," he said, it must push the edge of the company's technology, and it must have a close relationship with Ferrari's racing programs as a celebration of their successes.

From those elements came what at the time was the world's most technologically advanced high-performance road car.

Its engine was the start of a new generation of Ferrari V-12s. At 5998cc and 660 horsepower, it followed Ferrari's Formula 1 thinking. It had four valves per cylinder and the variable-length induction system from 1995's F1 engine. It was also the first Ferrari powerplant to boast continuously variable exhaust-valve timing.

Along with the 6-speed paddle-shift gearbox, the V-12 was bolted onto a rear tubular subframe, which was then attached to the car's central carbon-fiber tub. The suspension was pushrod double wishbones front and rear, with coil springs and adaptive shock absorbers; this last item used four sensors on the body, two vertical wheel sensors, a speed sensor, and a brake switch to adjust the shocks' stiffness for superior ride comfort and body control.

But that was just the start of the electronic wizardry. In what it claimed was a world first, Ferrari integrated all the car's electronic control systems (engine, gearbox, suspension, traction control, aerodynamics, brakeforce distribution, and antilock braking) so they constantly communicated with each other to deliver optimal performance.

A bona fide world first was the Enzo's carbon-fiber brakes. The space-age material stopped the car more quickly than anyone imagined, while remaining impervious to fade in repeated use. Marveled one tester, "(The Enzo's) retardation is second only to hitting a brick wall...."

Pininfarina relished the challenge of creating a body for Ferrari's latest tour de force.

"The 250 SWB was our first quantum leap in design on Ferrari, the Dino the second," said Sergio Pininfarina. "I consider the Enzo our third."

In fact, the model marked a new styling direction.

From Day One, Montezemolo pushed the designers (and his engineers) to go a little too far, knowing they could always back off a bit if necessary. Pininfarina design chief Lorenzo Ramaciotti had an internal competition, stressing aerodynamics and a shape more aggressive than the F50 with a nose that had to resemble an F1 car's.

Initially, there were approximately two dozen proposals; these were then cut down to two. They were presented to Ferrari management in summer 1998, but Pininfarina and Ramaciotti decided to push the envelope even further with another model that had a nose much like the one that would grace the Enzo.

Ferrari management saw this, then asked for elements of all three design studies to be used. Then they threw in a new parameter—to eliminate the rear wing seen on all of the proposals.

The resulting extreme form was the production Enzo, a shape "determined by the car's high performance potential," Ramaciotti said, "rather than aesthetics." In essence, the wind tunnel ruled, and the shape was signed off on early in 2000.

By 2001, sharp-eyed residents around Modena were treated to a rare sight—menacing, angular prototypes leaving and entering the factory at odd hours. Then, in summer 2002, the Enzo broke cover when the factory released the first few authorized photos. This was followed by a lavish press kit that instantly became a treasured collector's item, then by the official Paris Show debut.

Once the Enzo was tested, journalists ran for the thesaurus to describe its performance. Magazines recorded 0-100 mph in the mid-6-second range. The quarter-mile came up in around 11 seconds. Top speed was 218 mph. Most impressive of all was how easy it was to drive this Ferrari in all situations.

"We have all known that somebody, someday, would build a better car than Britian's McLaren F1, which seemed so remarkable in 1994," Steve Cropley summed up in his *Autocar* road test. "Ferrari's Enzo is now that car. It is no faster in a straight line but its handling, roadholding, steering, brakes, and even its ride comfort are all comprehensively better. Ferrari has built the new supercar benchmark, and given it the greatest name of all."

2004 612 Scaglietti

612 SCAGLIETTI

2004-

Number made:	n/a
Engine:	5748 V-12, DOHC,
	533-540 hp @ 7250 rpm
Transmission:	6-speed manual
	6-speed paddle-shift manual
Wheelbase:	116.1 inches / 2950mm
Weight:	4,123 lbs. (*Car and Driver*)

2004-
612 Scaglietti

A CAR THAT COULD HARDLY BE NEWER STILL FINDS WAYS TO CELEBRATE THE PAST

Famed coachbuilder Sergio Scaglietti hadn't worked with Ferrari in 17 years when the phone call came. "I found out two hours before the presentation the car's name was Scaglietti," he beamed. "They called me and said to be sure to make it to the introduction of 'my car.' I was flabbergasted."

Ferrari indeed wished to honor the Modena stylist and coachbuilder associated with some of its most beautiful early sports cars. It chose for the purpose the new 612—six to suggest the liters displacement, 12 for its number of cylinders. Ferrari pitched this, its largest road car ever, as a genuine four-seater rather than a 2+2. Its long-hood, short-deck Pininfarina-styled body with its scalloped sides paid homage to the famous 375 MM "Berlinetta Aerodinamica" Pininfarina built in 1954 for Roberto Rossellini as a gift to Ingrid Bergman.

The car's unveiling at the 2004 North American International Auto Show in Detroit marked two Maranello milestones. It was the first time America was the site of the international launch of a Ferrari model. And it commemorated the 50th anniversary of the arrival of the first Ferrari road car into the United States.

Once the nostalgia and hoopla were satisfied, it became evident the 612 also represented a revolution in Ferrari construction through weight savings from its all-aluminum technology. The body was made in the Scaglietti body-construction facility, and it featured a space-frame chassis developed in conjunction with aluminum giant Alcoa. The chassis was of aluminum extrusions connected by aluminum casts that acted as joints. Sheet aluminum reinforced the structure, and special heat treatments made the alloy panels more resistant to deformation.

The 540-horsepower 5748cc V-12 had four valves per cylinder, light alloy construction, and a new exhaust system that reduced back pressure. It was positioned far behind the front axle for superb handling, a placement that dictated the car's somewhat controversial rearward cabin placement.

This was the first Ferrari with CST (Control for Stability and Traction) as a handling aid. The system, which worked with the antilock and antiskid functions, had Normal and Sport settings, or could be deactivated completely. Buyers could choose a traditional six-speed manual transmission or an updated version of the F1-derived paddle-shift system.

Despite being longer than a Mercedes E-class sedan and weighing 4,100 pounds, the 612 was a superb road car, perhaps the best Ferrari grand-tourer ever. *Car and Driver* in August 2004 compared it with the day's other premier four-place coupes and picked the 612 over the Bentley Continental GT, Mercedes-Benz CL600, and Aston Martin DB9. The Scaglietti stormed to 60 mph in 4.3 seconds, needed just 9.5 to hit 100, and clipped the quarter-mile in 12.5. Top speed was 192 mph.

"Drive our quartet hard," the magazine said, "...the Ferrari oozes character and dynamic ability to elevate the entire experience beyond its rivals...." That was the essence of the 612 Scaglietti's mission—to feel like a classic sports car even with two posti behind the driver.

The Sports-Racing Cars

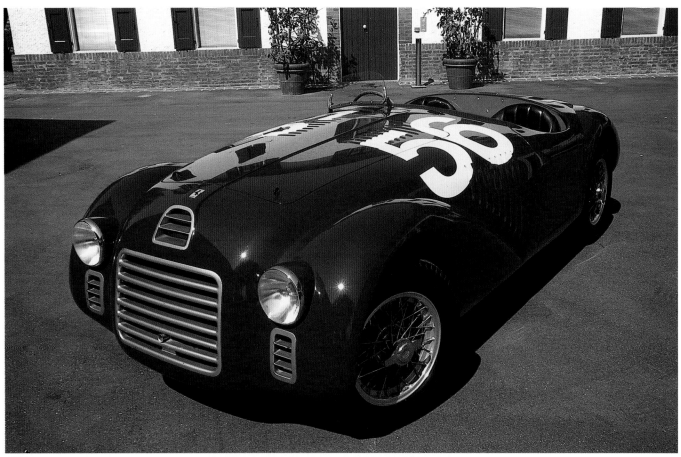

125 S

125 S, 159 S, 166 S & 166 S/C

125 S, 159 S, 166 S & 166 S/C	
125 S 1947	
159 S 1947	
166 S (SPORT) 1948	
166 S/C (SPORT CORSA) 1948	
Number made:	
125 S:	3 (approx.)
159 S:	1
166 S & S/C:	8 (approx.)
Engine:	
125 S:	1496cc V-12, SOHC, 72-118 hp @ 5600-6800 rpm
159 S:	1902cc V-12, SOHC, 125 hp @ 7000 rpm
166 S & S/C:	1996cc V-12, SOHC, 90-130 hp @ 6000-7000 rpm
Transmission:	5-speed
Wheelbase:	90.5 inches / 2300mm
Weight:	
125 S:	1,650 lbs. (factory)
159 S:	n/a
166 S:	1,760 lbs. (factory)
166 S/C:	n/a

MORE THAN MEETS THE EYE: THE LEGEND IS BORN ON THE TRACK WITH THE FIRST CAR TO WEAR THE FERRARI BADGE

The road to making his first cars was not an easy one for Enzo Ferrari. World War II had devastated Italy's infrastructure, material shortages were the rule, and political turmoil kept much of the country on edge.

Still, after securing the services of engineer Gioachino Colombo in the summer of 1945, Ferrari used his charisma and contacts to get the materials he needed and kept his cadre of men focused on the task of automaking. Haunting the team working on that first car were poorly machined components from suppliers, ignition problems, and myriad other maladies.

"I had to be ruthless in order to pull the 125 through its childhood illnesses, which were neither few, nor insignificant," wrote Giuseppe Busso in *Ferrari Tipo 166*. Busso was a talented technician who took over briefly for Colombo in early 1946.

Ferrari's first 125 ran under its own power on March 12, 1947. In early May, it raced in Piacenza, where it did not finish. Two weeks later in Rome, Franco Cortese's win started the legend that became Ferrari.

These first Ferraris were mostly homely looking machines

166 Sport Corsa

with crude bodywork formed into a torpedo-shaped fuselage with cycle fenders. Exceptions included the very first 125 and its two-seat roadster body, and the 1948 Mille Miglia winning Allemano coupe.

The 125 designation represented the swept volume in cubic centimeters of one cylinder of the all-aluminum V-12. Only the earliest Ferraris were 125s. Enzo's men quickly increased bore and stroke to create the 159. By early 1948, engine capacity grew to 2.0-liters so the V-12 could be used in Formula 2; the resulting 166 Sport won the Mille Miglia and numerous other races.

Even though victories were mounting, Ferrari's cars were just faces in the crowd. They looked much like everyone else's machines. It wouldn't be until the 166 MM "Barchetta" that Ferrari gained an identity.

166 MM Berlinetta

166 MM, 340 AMERICA & 212 EXPORT
166 MM 1948-1950 340 AMERICA 1950-1952 212 EXPORT 1951-1952

Number made:
166 MM:	32
340 America:	23
212 Export:	25

Engine:
166 MM:	1995cc V-12, SOHC, 140 hp @ 6600 rpm
340 America:	4101cc V-12, SOHC, 220 hp @ 6000 rpm
212 Export:	2562cc V-12, SOHC, 160 hp @ 6500 rpm
Transmission:	5-speed

Wheelbase:
166 MM:	86.6 inches / 2200mm
340 America:	95.2 inches / 2420mm
212 Export:	88.5 inches / 2250mm

Weight:
166 MM:	1,430 lbs. (Touring barchetta)
340 America:	1,980 lbs. (Vignale berlinetta)
212 Export:	1,870 lbs. (Touring berlinetta)

1948-1952

166 MM, 340 America & 212 Export

FERRARI FORGES AN IDENTITY WITH RACE-WINNING CARS AND A WINNING LOOK

While every early Ferrari blurred the line between street use and competition—most were, in fact, outright race cars—the 166 MM was the first Ferrari offered with equipment tailored to both needs.

Just as significantly, the seminal 166 MM "Barchetta" that made its debut at 1948's Turin Auto Show was also the model that gave Ferrari a "face."

"Ferrari was a very clever man," said Carlo Felice Bianchi Anderloni, who designed the Barchetta. "He knew if several [Ferraris] were at 1949's Mille Miglia, all looking identical, people would begin to recognize him as a true constructor."

The "Barchetta" name was applied by Italy's most-prominent automotive journalist, Giovanni Canestrini, who concluded the car looked like a "little boat," and used the Italian term for that—barchetta.

1949 166 MM Barchetta

212 Export

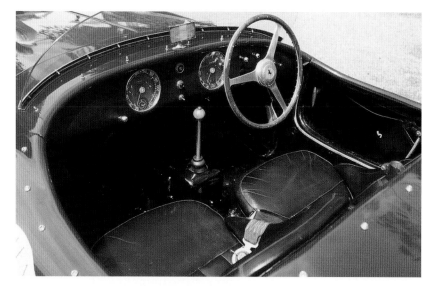

340 America

Road or racing, the Barchetta's body was built at Carrozzeria Touring, Anderloni's firm in Milan. It used Touring's patented Superleggera (super light) construction system in which the intricate frame of small thin tubes that supported the lightweight aluminum body was welded to the tubular chassis.

All Barchettas employed a front suspension of wishbones and transverse leaf springs. The rear had a rigid axle, semielliptic leaf springs, and an antiroll bar. Brakes were large drums with fins for cooling.

The 166's all-alloy V-12 displaced 1995cc, had a compression ratio of 10:1, and was crowned by three 32 DCF Weber carburetors. Ferrari claimed 140 horsepower at 6600 rpm, plenty for a machine with a factory-quoted weight of just 1,430 lbs.

It is no exaggeration to say the racing success of these early Barchettas helped secure Ferrari's future as a sports-car maker.

Nine Ferraris were entered in 1949's Mille Miglia. Four were Barchettas with Touring bodywork. One, chassis 0008 M, finished first overall, driven by Clemente Biondetti. A companion, chassis 0010 M, finished second overall.

Less than two months later, Barchetta 0008 M, driven by Ferrari's friend and future American importer, Luigi Chinetti, finished first overall in the 24 Hours of Le Mans, the world's most-important endurance-racing event. Chinetti capped that performance with a first overall in the 24-hours of Spa Francorchamps.

Touring also made a 166 berlinetta, a closed two-seater that used much of the same design language found on the Barchetta. "We had a lot of experience turning a coupe into

spider or a cabriolet into a coupe," Anderloni remembered. "So a Ferrari berlinetta was natural for us to try."

Dubbed the tipo "Le Mans" by Touring, the 166 berlinetta appeared at 1950's Geneva Motor Show. Within two months, the model would win the Mille Miglia. The barchetta that won 1949's event came in second.

In 1951, Touring's barchetta and berlinetta bodies were used on two new models, the 212 Export and 340 America. In general, these Ferraris had the same chassis as the 166, save a longer wheelbase and wider track. And they had larger, more powerful engines.

The Export's V-12 was a 2562cc derivative of the 166 MM's Colombo V-12. The 340 America used a 4.1-liter version of the Aurelio Lampredi designed 4.5-liter V-12 found in Ferrari's 375 F1 cars.

With the 212 and 340 America, other coachbuilders supplanted Carrozzeria Touring as Ferrari's preferred designer and body maker. Indeed, every Ferrari on display at the 1952 Geneva Motor Show was clad in bodywork by Ghia, an honorable old coachbuilder rescued after World War II by Mario Felice Boano.

Ferrari's fortunes were also being shaped by Vignale, a relative newcomer founded in 1946 by Alfredo Vignale and under the creative control of prolific stylist Giovanni Michelotti.

Vignale made a wonderful variety of spyders and berlinettas on both the 212 Export and 340 America chassis. The most significant was a one-off 340 America berlinetta (chassis 0082 A). It won the 1951 Mille Miglia.

Sicily hosted one of the first great road races

The Magic of Road Racing

Simply because no auto-racing tracks yet existed, the earliest motorized-vehicle competitions were held on public roads. With loud, colorful racing cars roaring through small towns and spectators watching from balconies or roadsides, road racing came to symbolize the romance—and the danger—of automotive competition.

Road racing existed in America at such venues as Watkins Glen in New York and Elkhart Lake in Wisconsin. But it was in Europe, where a few events ran the breadth of entire countries, that road racing was of most consequence. These contests attracted international competition and captured the national imagination. Among those they inspired was a 10-year-old boy from Modena whose father took him to an open-road race near Bologna in 1910. Enzo Ferrari credited the experience with sparking his lifelong passion for the automobile.

For the automakers, participation in these grueling trials of

stamina and strength was a great source of publicity, and winning one was vital to proving their cars were durable in an era when automobiles were anything but.

One of the first of the great road races was Sicily's Targa Florio. The brainchild of Vincenzo Florio, the son of a prominent and wealthy Sicilian, Florio traveled Europe and bought his first car around the turn of the century. He brought it back to Sicily, and a race against a cyclist and a horse infused him with the racing bug.

Florio was inspired to hold a race in Sicily, and the first Targa Florio was run in 1906. It comprised three laps around the island, each lap 92 miles. Fifteen years later, the Targa jumped in importance when Italy's leading performance-car maker, Alfa Romeo, participated with a factory team.

Various marques won in the early years, but Bugatti dominated in the late 1920s, Alfa and Maserati in the 1930s, and Ferrari and Porsche in the 1950s and '60s. When the Targa was last run in 1973, each of the 11 laps was approximately 45 miles long.

Bugatti scored its first Targa victory in 1926, the year another road race was born in Italy. The Mille Miglia ("Thousand Miles") was created in the apartment of prominent journalist

Giovanni Canestrini. "The Mille Miglia," he declared in the country's widely read newspaper, *Gazzetto dello Sport*, "will be the most important manifestation of Italian motor sport ever."

Initially there was tremendous public outcry against the idea until Arturo Turati, the Fascist government's No. 2 man, enlisted the support of police, civil, and military authorities. The Mille proved immensely popular, and soon Italians were lining the Brescia-Rome-Brescia route.

Alfa was master of the Mille during the 1930s, Ferrari in the postwar years, winning eight of ten until the event's cancellation after the 1957 contest when Alfonso de Portago crashed his Ferrari 315 S, killing himself, his codriver, and several spectators.

The U.S. never embraced the closing of public roads for auto competition to the extent that Europe did, though picturesque events, such as race through Pebble Beach in Northern California in the 1950s, did prove popular.

The most important road race in the Americas was Mexico's Carrera Panamericana. Launched in 1950, it celebrated the opening of a 2,000-mile highway that stretched from just south of the Texas border to the tiny village of El Ocotal in Guatemala.

That first contest was run over six days in nine legs, with 132 entries. Just 58 finished; an Oldsmobile was victorious. There were 91 starters for 1951, and Ferraris finished first and second of the 35 cars that survived the entire event. The Carrera Panamericana attracted some of the biggest drivers and teams in motorsport, including Ferrari and Mercedes-Benz, Lincoln and Cadillac.

The race was canceled before its running in 1955 due to financial and other considerations. Among those considerations was that year's horrendous crash in the 24 Hours of Le Mans in which Pierre Levegh's Mercedes 300 SLR went off course and into the crowd, killing 80 spectators.

The sheer joy...

... and the pageantry of early road racing

Enzo Ferrari at the wheel of an Alfa 6C thrills onlookers in the Circuit of Mugello, 1928

225 S

225 S & 250 S		
1952		
Number made:		
225 S:	21	
250 S:	1	
Engine:		
225 S:	2715cc V-12, SOHC, 210 hp @ 7200 rpm	
250 S:	2953cc V-12, SOHC, 230 hp @ 7500 rpm	
Transmission:	5-speed	
Wheelbase:		
225 S:	88.5 inches / 2250mm	
250 S:	94.5 inches / 2400mm	
Weight:	1,870 lbs. (factory)	

1952
225 S & 250 S

VIGNALE DRESSES A FERRARI FOR SUCCESS, AND GIOACCHINO COLOMBO CREATES A TIMELESS V-12

The brief, but significant, career of the 225 S and 250 S furthered the development of the Colombo V-12 and signified that Carrozzeria Vignale was the coachbuilder of choice for Ferrari's competition machines in the early 1950s. "S" stood for "Sport," and of the 22 made, 21 featured Vignale coachwork.

Both models had a tubular chassis and underpinnings quite similar to those of the 340 America. They also shared the 340 America's 88.5-inch (2250mm) wheelbase and its track of 50.3 inches (1278mm) front, 49.2 inches (1250mm) rear. The front suspension was independent with double wishbones and a transverse leaf spring. The rear had a rigid axle and semielliptic leaf springs.

In the 225 S, the Colombo "short-block" engine's bore increased 10mm over that in the 212 Export model to 70mm, for a total capacity of 2715cc. That and other modifications saw horsepower reach 210 at 7200 rpm.

Vignale's coachwork on the 225 was masterful. Of particular note was the restrained shape and stunning proportion of the 225 S spyders. Embellishment was minimal, and the front fenders were punctuated with three beautiful oval portholes that acted as air outlets.

One 250 S berlinetta (chassis 0156 ET) was built, and it would become one of the most important cars in Ferrari history.

Its engine was bored a further 3mm beyond the 225's, while the stroke remained at 58.8mm. No one could know it at the time, but the resulting 2953cc V-12 was the foundation for an integral part of the Ferrari legend. That displacement was used by Ferrari for another 12 years on some of its most famous road and racing cars.

Indeed, this powerplant's reputation for reliability in the heat of competition and its refinement on the street all but defined the unparalleled dual-purpose nature of Ferrari's cars. That 250 S was the first to demonstrate this achievement.

Finished by Vignale on March 1, 1952, it competed at the 1952 Mille Miglia just four days later. There, with Giovanni Bracco at the wheel, it handed Mercedes-Benz and its mighty 300 SL the only endurance-competition defeat the German company would suffer that year.

The 250 S berlinetta also won the 12 Hours of Pescara. It led most of the Carrera Panamericana before a transmission failure put it out on the seventh leg. And it led at Le Mans, where, driven by works pilots Alberto Ascari and Luigi "Gigi" Villoresi, it set a new lap record before differential troubles retired it in the third hour.

225 S

250 S

250 S

340 Mexico

1952
340 Mexico

FASCINATING AND FAMOUS: A ROLLING COMPENDIUM OF THE EARLY '50 SPORTS-RACING FERRARI

The 340 Mexico was the quintessential summary of Ferrari in the early 1950s: purpose-built for racing, very fast, with exotic styling that, in theory, would not look out of place on the street.

It rumbled out of the workshop in 1952, its name signifying the target venue, Mexico's grueling Carrera Panamericana race, which Ferrari won in 1951. The 2,000-mile competition was staged over five days and eight different legs. The results were well-publicized in America, an increasingly important market for Ferrari.

The Mexico's coachwork was some of the most extravagant designed by Giovanni Michelotti and constructed by Alfredo Vignale. It was yet another in their run of unique, often startling designs. How did they do it?

"The perfect analogy is they were like two people playing double's tennis," explained Franco Gavina, a friend to both men. "It was two people working together as a team, where they almost instinctively knew what the other was thinking and what they would do."

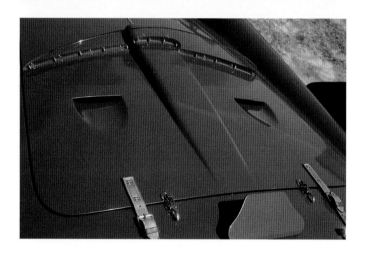

340 MEXICO		
1952		
Number made:	4	
Engine:	4101cc V-12, SOHC, 280 hp @ 6600 rpm	
Transmission:	5-speed	
Wheelbase:	102.3 inches / 2600mm	
Weight:	2,200 lbs. (approx.)	

Just four 340 Mexicos were produced: three coupes and one spyder. The engine was a revised version of the roadgoing 340 America's 4.1-liter V-12. A modified camshaft, different carburetors, and other changes added some 60 horsepower, for a total of 280. The transmission, a 4-speed in the 340 America, was a 5-speed here to handle the high speeds found in sections of the Carrera Panamericana.

The spyder was not entered in the race, leaving the three coupes to carry Ferrari's banner. One crashed on the first leg. A second lost its transmission during day three. The last, driven by Jean Lucas and three-time Le Mans winner Luigi Chinetti, soon to become Ferrari's U.S. importer, came in third overall, behind two Mercedes-Benz 300 SLs. Finishing fourth was a modified 340 America with Ghia coachwork.

Interestingly, it was the spyder that went on to have the longest competition career. Research by Ferrari historian Marcel Massini showed the car being raced in America into 1955. It frequently finished in the top five.

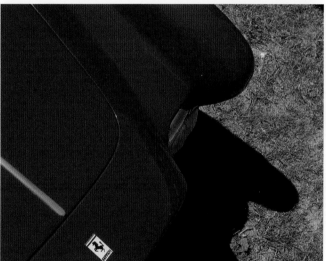

250 MM

250 MM, 166 SERIES II & 340 MM		
1953		
Number made:		
250 MM:	32	
166 Series II:	13	
340 MM:	10	
Engine:		
250 MM:	2953cc V-12, SOHC, 240 hp @ 7200 rpm	
166 Series II:	1995cc V-12, SOHC, 160 hp @ 7200 rpm	
340 MM:	4101cc V-12, SOHC, 300hp @ 6600 rpm	
Transmission:		
250 MM:	4-speed	
166 Series II:	5-speed	
340 MM:	5-speed	
Wheelbase:		
250 MM:	94.5 inches / 2400mm	
166 Series II:	88.5 inches / 2250mm	
340 MM:	98.4 inches / 2500mm	
Weight:		
250 MM:	2,200 lbs. (approx.)	
166 Series II:	n/a	
340 MM:	n/a	

250 MM, 166 Series II & 340 MM

RACE-CAR DESIGN INFLUENCES ROAD-CAR STYLING, AND A GOLDEN AGE OF SPEED AND BEAUTY BLOSSOMS

It was an extraordinary time in which a conduit was open between designs for road and for track, when sports cars intended for all-out competition were beautiful objects in and of themselves.

Such was the case with a trio of Ferraris from 1953. Built to run in long-distance races, the aptly named 250 MM and 340 MM were intended for such events as Italy's famed 1,000-mile enduro, the Mille Miglia.

The 250 MM was introduced at 1953's Geneva Motor Show. It was derived from the 250 S and used the same basic chassis and underpinnings: tubular frame with 94.5-inch (2400mm) wheelbase, independent suspension in front, rigid axle and leaf springs at the rear. Its 2953cc V-12 was modified to give another 10 horsepower, bumping output to 240.

The 340 MM's chassis and suspension basically mimicked the

166 Series II

250 MM's, but wheelbase was 98.4 inches (2500mm) and front track was 52.1 inches (1325mm) versus 51.1 (1300mm). Under its hood was a 4101cc V-12 nearly identical to the roadgoing 340 America's, but with new magneto-type ignition and other modifications to boost power by some 80 horses, to an even 300.

The 166 MM Series II was aimed at the popular under-2-liter racing class. Its tubular chassis continued the earlier 166 MM's 88.5-inch (2250mm) wheelbase, but the 1995cc V-12 had a higher compression ratio and different carburetors to boost output to 160 horsepower.

What all these cars had in common was their orientation toward competition and their use of Touring, Vignale, and Pinin Farina bodies.

For the most part, Touring's coachwork simply continued the landmark design of the 340 MM, properly enlarged to fit over the larger chassis and engines.

Vignale was at its creative zenith here, and Giovanni Michelotti's open-air design for a number of 250 MMs continued the lovely long-hood/short-rear-deck approach taken with the 225 S.

Road & Track, in May 1954, tested one such 250 MM (chassis 0260 MM) owned by future world champion Phil Hill. The magazine recorded 0-60 mph in 5.1 seconds, 0-100 in 13.7. "Never before have I accelerated so rapidly, traveled so fast, or decelerated so suddenly," marvelled *R&T*'s tech editor.

Hill won both the 1953 Pebble Beach and Stead Air Force Base races in that car. But such on-track prowess didn't stop

340 MM

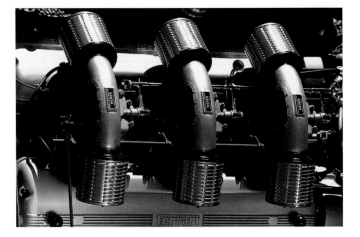

Road & Track from postulating that "...the addition of a complete windshield and fiberglass top might make this car a completely acceptable dual purpose vehicle." It would not be the last 250 to be so at home in both competition and touring.

A number of other 250 MM and 340 MMs enjoyed yet another, even more splendid, Vignale design. This voluptuous body had rounded curves that followed the lead of Touring's Barchetta, but with a uniquely Michelotti flair that employed both exposed and covered headlights. Count Giannino Marzotto drove one such 340 MM (chassis 0280 AM) in 1953 to his second Mille Miglia victory.

The 166 Series II, 250 MM, and 340 MM are also noteworthy for their use of Pinin Farina coachwork. To now, the famed carrozzeria had done just a handful of conservative designs for the 212 Inter road car. That changed in the fourth quarter of 1952, when the company used a 340 MM (chassis 0236 MM) as the basis for its first competition berlinetta. The design would influence the shape of Ferrari's racing coupes for years to come.

Company founder Battista Pinin Farina and his men had begun experimenting in the 1930s with the fastback theme in search of better aerodynamics. His radical Lancia Aprilia Berlinetta Aerodinamica of 1935 stunned everyone.

"I was aiming for essentiality," "Pinin" wrote in his autobiography, *Born with the Automobile*. "[W]hat you take off counts for more than what you put on...I had drawn the Aprilia's shape to be like an airplane wing."

World War II delayed his creative experimentation for several years, but it all came together in his first postwar masterpiece, the Cisitalia 202. That landmark berlinetta proved so influential in defining post-World War II automotive styling that one was prominently displayed in New York's Museum of Modern Art in its famous 1951 exhibit, "Eight Automobiles."

The Cisitalia's form and proportions inspired Pinin's first competition 340 MM, which in turn evolved into a small series of 250 MM berlinettas with a lower roofline and shorter tail.

The successful shape also continued on several more Pinin Farina-bodied 340 MMs. These had a wheelbase of 98.4 inches (2600mm), split windscreen, and larger air intake over the rear wheel for cooling the brakes. One of three entered in 1953's Le Mans, and driven by Giannino Marzotto and his brother Paolo, finished fifth and was the only Ferrari to complete the 24 hours.

340 MM

375 MM

375 MM

375 MM & 375 PLUS	
1953-1955	
Number made:	
375 MM:	24
375 Plus:	8
Engine:	
375 MM:	4522cc V-12, SOHC, 340 hp @ 7000 rpm
375 Plus:	4954cc V-12, SOHC, 330 hp @ 6000 rpm
Transmission:	4-speed
Wheelbase:	102.3 inches / 2600mm
Weight:	2,000 lbs. (approx.)

1953-1955
375 MM & 375 Plus

PININ FARINA TO THE FORE AS INTERNATIONAL SPORTS-CAR TITLES FALL TO FERRARI

Conceived and built as a pure endurance race car, the 375 MM also further propagated Ferrari's growing reputation as a maker of true dual-purpose machines. At the same time, it cemented Pinin Farina as Ferrari's coachbuilder of choice.

The 375 MM appeared first at Le Mans in 1953. It essentially was a 340 MM chassis fitted with a 340-horsepower 4.5-liter V-12 derived from the engine used for Ferrari's aborted Indianapolis 500 project.

Pinin Farina designs clothed virtually every one, and a 375 MM berlinetta (chassis 0318 AM) set a lap record in the '53 24 Hours, but retired after its clutch failed. A later 375 MM (0358 AM), with slightly revised bodywork and grille, finished fourth overall at Mexico's Carrera Panamericana road race. That gave Ferrari the first international sports-racing title, the Constructors Sports World Championship.

In addition to 375 MM berlinettas, Pinin Farina made a series of 375 MM spyders. The first, for American driver James Kimberly, had a "pontoon" front-fender design that would become a feature on later Ferrari endurance-racers. The balance of 375 MM spyder production used a traditional fender treatment.

375 MM

375 Plus

The 375 MMs played an integral role in securing Ferrari another Sports World Championship in 1954. One was victorious in the season's first race at Buenos Aires. Another was a top-10 finisher at the Carrera Panamericana.

Winning both Le Mans and the Carrera Panamericana in 1954 was the 375 Plus. This open-cockpit Ferrari also had Pinin Farina coachwork. It looked nearly identical to the 375 MM spyders save revised rear coachwork with a larger center bulge to accommodate a new fuel tank nestled above the De Dion rear end. Underhood was a V-12 of 4954cc.

So desirable were the 375 MM and 375 Plus that a number of berlinetta and spyder versions were made for the street. The chassis was also used for several stupendous one-off design exercises, all helping to nourish Ferrari's standing as a constructor of the world's foremost high-performance cars.

500 Mondial

500 MONDIAL	
1953-1955	
Number made:	30 (20 Series I, 10 Series II)
Engine:	1985cc inline-4, SOHC, 160 hp @ 7000 rpm
Transmission:	5-speed
Wheelbase:	88.5 inches / 2250mm
Weight:	1,715 lb. (*Autocar*)

1953-1955
500 Mondial

A SWEET AND POTENT FOUR-BANGER PLEASES THE PROFESSIONALS AND THE PRIVATEERS

Ferrari's fortunes in the early 1950s were rising along with those of Europe. The continent was just regaining its economic health after the devastation of World War II. For Ferrari, that meant a surge in demand for its competition cars by both professional drivers and gentlemen racers.

The 500 Mondial was born during the formative stages of this yeasty period. Ferrari was already well-known for its V-12s, but Enzo and chief engineer Aurelio Lampredi were cognizant of the success other manufacturers were having with four-cylinder engines.

A four-cylinder could furnish better low-end torque than a 12, allowing for more acceleration out of corners. Its lighter weight could help a car handle better, too. For its new four-cylinder sports-racing car, Ferrari tapped the development it had done on the four-cylinder engine for its 500 F2. That open-wheel mono-posto dominated Grand Prix racing in 1952 and 1953.

The resulting 500 Mondial was an extremely well-balanced machine. This was illustrated in its first race, the 12 Hours of Casablanca, in December 1953. Factory drivers Alberto Ascari and Luigi (Gigi) Villoresi finished first in class and second overall behind one of Ferrari's considerably more powerful 375 MMs.

There were two series of 500 Mondials, and both were popular with factory drivers and privateers alike. All had a jewel of an all-alloy 2.0-liter based on Ferrari's F2 engines. First-series cars had mostly Pinin Farina coachwork and resembled the coachbuilder's voluptuous 375 MM berlinettas and spyders.

A handful of the first-series cars, and all of the second series used Scaglietti coachwork. The Modena designer and body maker had done a number of "rebodies" on Ferrari chassis for clients in the early 1950s. "Enzo Ferrari liked what he saw on those cars," Sergio Scaglietti recalled, "so he began sending me rolling chassis."

Ferrari also appreciated Scaglietti's relationship with his son, Dino. Accounts over the years credited Dino with the basic Scaglietti design for the 500 Mondial. But Scaglietti, a modest man who preferred to give credit to others, told this author that this was untrue. He said Dino, who had muscular dystrophy and thus spent the majority of his days at Scaglietti's rather than trying to keep up with his energetic father, was responsible only for the headrests used on the Mondial and other competition Ferraris.

The Mondial played an integral role in Ferrari winning its second Sports World Championship in 1954. That type of success caused Enzo to funnel even more work toward Sergio Scaglietti, the talented, and humble, coachbuilder.

250 Monza

250 MONZA, 750 MONZA & 860 MONZA
250 MONZA 1954-1955
750 MONZA 1955
860 MONZA 1956

Number made:

250 Monza:	4
750 Monza:	37
860 Monza:	3

Engine:

250 Monza:	2953cc V-12, SOHC, 240 hp (approx.) @ 7000 rpm
750 Monza:	2999cc inline-4, DOHC, 260 hp @ 6000 rpm
860 Monza:	3431cc inline-4, DOHC, 310 hp @ 6200 rpm

Transmission:

250 Monza:	4-speed
750 Monza:	5-speed
860 Monza:	5-speed

Wheelbase:

250 Monza:	88.5 inches / 2250mm
750 Monza:	88.5 inches / 2250mm
860 Monza:	92.5 inches / 2350mm

Weight:

250 Monza:	n/a
750 Monza:	1,680 lbs. (*Auto Age*)
860 Monza:	n/a

1954-1956
250, 750 & 860 Monza

MONZAS SPAN THE GLOBE, SPREADING THE FERRARI LEGEND AND BRINGING HOME THE GOLD

Ferrari's Monzas were named after the famous racetrack on the outskirts of Milan and illustrated the incredible engineering diversity and talent the firm possessed in the mid 1950s.

The first Monza, the 250, had a 2953cc V-12. The 750 and 860 that followed were powered by inline-fours and were even more potent and well-balanced than the 250. Each drew its numerical designation from the cubic-centimeter capacity of one of its cylinders.

The 250 Monza had approximately 240 horsepower and used a four-speed gearbox to the other Monzas' five-speed. Its tubular chassis was similar to that of the 500 Mondial. Coachwork was by Pinin Farina and Scaglietti; the former's looked very similar to its 375 MM and 500 Mondial spyders. Scaglietti's work continued his evolution of the long, low aerodynamic body style seen on the Mondial.

In 1955, journalist Hans Tanner went to Mexico to test one of the two Scaglietti 250 Monzas. After fighting Mexico City traffic, Tanner recorded 145 mph on an empty freeway. "Great car," a policeman commented as Tanner paid a toll on the return trip. "And by the way, I forgot to mention the speed limit on the Autostrada is 60 mph!"

Generating 260 horsepower from 2999cc, the 750 Monza was the most popular of the trio with privateers. Almost 40 were made, all but one having a Scaglietti spyder body. The 750 was a frequent class winner, and placed second overall at 1954's Tourist Trophy Race in England and in 1955's 12 Hours of Sebring in Florida.

The 860 Monza competed in 1956 with great success. Using a tube frame much like that of the 250 and 750 Monza, its 3431cc four was good for more than 300 horsepower. In 1956, Ferrari team drivers Juan Manuel Fangio and Eugenio Castellotti won Sebring in an 860 Monza, with Luigi Musso and Harry Schell finishing second in another 860. The car also placed second and third in the Mille Miglia, and in the top three at two other championship races. Thanks to such consistency, Ferrari handily won 1956's Sports World Championship with double the points of second-place Maserati, its crosstown rival.

750 Monza

860 Monza

121 LM

118 LM
& 121 LM

A FORAY INTO THE SIX-CYLINDER FORMULA ADDS UP TO SOMETHING LESS THAN VICTORY

Ferrari's foray into four-cylinder engines yielded success with several models that by the end of 1954 had contributed to two Constructors Sports World Championships, as well as wins in Formulas 1 and 2.

That good fortune didn't accompany his six-cylinder sports-racing cars. They were very fast, but did not prove reliable enough for the crucible of the day's endurance races, grueling battles contested on a cruel mix of racetracks and come-what-may public roads.

The 118 LM had a 3747cc inline-six based on the Lampredi four-cylinder design. It featured two plugs per cylinder, magneto type ignition, and three Weber carburetors. Unlike the four-cylinder's double overhead cams, however, the six made do with a single overhead cam. Final output was 280 horsepower, and four 118 LMs were made.

These same four cars, fitted with an enlarged version of the engine, became the 121 LM. Bore increased 12mm to 102mm while stroke remained at 90mm. Power bumped to 330 horses.

The LM's underpinnings were similar to Ferrari's four-cylinder endurance-racers. The tubular chassis was lengthened to accommodate the longer engine, and the front suspension was independent with wishbones and coil springs. The rear had a De Dion tube.

118 LM & 121 LM	
1954-1955	
Number made:	4 (all converted to 121 specs)
Engine:	
118 LM:	3747cc inline-6, SOHC, 280 hp @ 6400 rpm
121 LM:	4412cc inline-6, SOHC, 330 hp @ 6000 rpm
Transmission:	5-speed
Wheelbase:	94.5 inches / 2400mm
Weight:	n/a

Sergio Scaglietti's coachwork developed themes seen on the 500 Mondial and Monzas. The front end—longer, lower, and with covered headlights—was now sleeker, though the rear continued the ubiquitous headrest fairing.

Scaglietti's shop was getting more work from Ferrari, and had increased in size as a result. But his coachbuilding techniques were those he learned before the war.

"We formed the lines of the cars by placing a thin metal tubing over the chassis to get an idea of what the body would look like," Scaglietti recalled. "Ferrari left the design up to me and we never did a drawing. Instead we relied on this wire 'maquette,' which normally took about three days to make. Once completed, we constructed the body panels."

Ferrari had hoped the 118 LM and 121 LM would help him contest a wider range of sports-car races, including those that didn't hinge on V-12-style high speed. Plus, the Mercedes-Benz SLRs were applying unrelenting pressure that his four-cylinders couldn't always handle.

As it turned out, the six-cylinder sports-racers weren't up to the task. Their best finish was a respectable third overall at 1955's Mille Miglia, though in the handful of other championship events in which they competed, the cars failed to finish.

121 LM

410 S

1955
410 S

A PRETTY AND POTENT FERRARI STORMS THE STATES; SHELBY'S IMPRESSED

Long before Carroll Shelby became a famed sports-car constructor he was a successful racing driver. The car he called "the best Ferrari I ever drove" was the 410 S.

This model was a tour de force from both Ferrari and body builder Sergio Scaglietti. As with most of Enzo's competition cars, the 410 S used the best of lessons already learned. The chassis and underpinnings started with the Le Mans-winning 375 Plus, but the frame was strengthened and the wheelbase reduced for better handling. The front suspension replaced leaf springs with coils.

The mighty V-12 was derived from the 410 Superamerica's and was Ferrari's largest yet, at 4962cc. It had a twin-ignition system with four distributors for the two-plugs-per-cylinder heads. Output hit the 400-horsepower mark, and was transmitted to the rear wheels via a five-speed gearbox.

By 1955, Sergio Scaglietti's design themes had matured so that the 410 S was truly rolling art. Its proportions were superb, having the right curves to give it an almost feminine shape. Yet, it was extremely aggressive, thanks in part to the large air intake necessary to cover the engine's three 46 DCF/3 Webers.

410 S		
1955		
Number made:	4 (includes 2 Speciales)	
Engine:	4962cc V-12, SOHC, 400 hp @ 7000 rpm	
Transmission:	5-speed	
Wheelbase:	92.5 inches / 2350mm	
Weight:	2,640 lbs. (factory)	

The model first appeared in January 1956 at the 1,000 km of Buenos Aires. Two competed, and one set a new lap record, but both retired with broken transaxles.

That type of performance potential caught the eye of John Edgar, one of Ferrari's most active American clients. He wound up with one of the two Buenos Aires cars and went on to win 1956's SCCA Championship with Carroll Shelby driving.

"It was the best Ferrari I ever drove," Shelby told Edgar's son, William, in *FORZA* magazine. "We never even changed the plugs that came in it, not for about the first seven or eight races! The car had a different timing system. It didn't even sound like other Ferraris."

While the 410 S may not have made much of an impact in Europe, it helped cement Ferrari's reputation as the machine to beat in U.S. endurance sports-car racing.

500 TR

500 TR, 625 LM & 500 TRC		
500 TR 1956		
625 LM 1956		
500 TRC 1957		
Number made:		
500 TR/625 LM:	17	
500 TRC:	19	
Engine:		
500 TR:	1984cc inline-4, DOHC,	
	180 hp @ 7000 rpm	
625 LM:	2498cc inline-4, DOHC,	
	225 hp @ 6200 rpm	
500 TRC:	1984cc inline-4, DOHC,	
	180 hp @ 7000 rpm	
Transmission:	4-speed	
Wheelbase:	88.5 inches / 2250mm	
Weight:		
500 TR:	1,500 lbs. (factory)	
625 LM:	n/a	
500 TRC:	1,500 lbs. (factory)	

1956-1957
500 TR, 625 LM & 500 TRC

A FERRARI BY ANY NAME IS SPECIAL, BUT A HINT OF AMORE NEVER HURTS

The Ferrari legend has many ingredients: The cars' shape and the engines' sound, the race-winning ways and the rich and beautiful buyers. Not to be underestimated are the provocative model names.

"TR" stands for "testa rossa," red head in Italian. Red was the color of the valve covers on a new Ferrari four-cylinder engine introduced for 1956. The car in which it made its debut was christened the 500 TR. It brought to the world what would become a classic Ferrari model name.

Like a number of Ferrari's other four-cylinder engines, this 1984cc unit was based on Aurelio Lampredi's 500 F2 powerplant. The great engineer left Ferrari in 1955 to join Fiat, so development was carried out by Andrea Fraschetti and Vittorio

Bellentani, two stalwart engineers who had worked with Enzo Ferrari for years.

The 180-horsepower Testa Rossa engine used the same 90mm bore and 78mm stroke as Lampredi's 500 Mondials, but the bottom end was strengthened and new connecting rods were used. The Weber carburetors were also changed, and distributors replaced magnetos.

Bodywork continued Scaglietti's basic racing-spyder form, though Touring built some 500 TRs distinguished by pontoon fender-style front-wheel openings. Most had more orthodox shapes by Scaglietti.

From Monza to California, Carroll Shelby, Peter Collins, Mike Hawthorn, and Phil Hill all drove 500 TRs to race wins in 1956. The car also was the basis for Ferrari's entry in that year's 24 Hours of Le Mans, but with a larger displacement to fit new rules.

Reeling from the 1955 Le Mans tragedy in which Pierre Levegh's Mercedes 300 SLR went off course and into the crowd, killing 80 spectators, race organizers in effect limited low-production cars like Ferrari's sports-racers to 2.5-liters displacement.

So Modena created a new 2.5-liter four-cylinder for a model it called the 625 LM. This engine did not have the red heads, so the 625 was no TR. Bore remained 90mm while stroke was lengthened to 94mm. Compression increased slightly and horsepower jumped to 225.

Touring did the bodies for three of the 625 LMs, and one of these placed third overall at Le Mans with works drivers Olivier Gendebien and Maurice Trintignant. It was the only Ferrari to finish in the top ten in a race that went to Jaguar's D-Type, which was able to run a 3.4-liter engine by virtue of its higher production numbers.

500 TRC

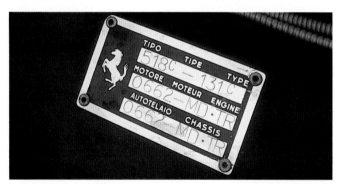

For 1957, the FIA revised dictates governing sports-racer bodywork. These so-called Appendix C regulations resulted in Ferrari offering the 500 TRC for clients. Engine and chassis were essentially those of the 500 TR, but Scaglietti updated the body to include a full-width windscreen. Along with slightly rounded contours, it was among the prettiest competition Ferraris.

It was also a most-capable performer. The 500 TRC was especially effective in the U.S., scoring a class victory at Sebring and dominating the Sports Car Club of America's Class E Modified division.

290 MM

1956
290 MM

**"THE MORE AERODYNAMIC A CAR WAS, THE MORE
BEAUTIFUL IT BECAME." — SERGIO SCAGLIETTI**

The 290 MM marked several turning points in Ferrari history.

Engineer Aurelio Lampredi, the architect of many Ferrari four-cylinder engines and the "long block" V-12, left the company in late 1955 and was replaced by Vittorio Jano. This legendary figure in the automotive world was an extremely gifted engineer Ferrari knew from his prewar days at Alfa Romeo. He came to Ferrari in mid 1956, when Lancia pulled out of racing.

Another change was the return of the V-12 as Ferrari's powerplant of choice for endurance competition. Engineers Andrea Fraschetti and Vittorio Bellentani worked closely with Jano on the design and development of the 290 MM's engine. The team utilized the best features found in both the Gioachino Colombo V-12 "short blocks" and in Lampredi's designs.

The resulting 3490cc V-12 had four distributors, two plugs per cylinder as found in Lampredi's V-12s, and modified connecting rods similar to those in Colombo's engines. Output was 320 horsepower at 7300 rpm.

Scaglietti made another masterful creation to clothe the 290 MM's tubular frame. His flowing lines, covered headlights, and headrest fairing were styling cues that gave Ferrari as much a

290 MM	
1956	
Number made:	4
Engine:	3490cc V-12, SOHC, 320 hp @ 7300 rpm
Transmission:	4-speed
Wheelbase:	94.5 inches / 2400mm
Weight:	1,936 lbs. (*Autosport*)

"face" during the mid to late 1950s as did Touring's 166 Barchetta in 1949.

"Aerodynamics were an important consideration in designing the cars," Scaglietti said. "The more aerodynamic a car was, the more beautiful it became. We understood that less air underneath made a car go faster."

And go fast is exactly what the 290 MM did. *Autosport* estimated its top speed at 180 mph, which made the 290 MM a formidable machine. The model retired in its first race at the Tour of Sicily, but was a force for the balance of the '56 season.

Two 290 MMs were among Ferrari's five entries in the Mille Miglia. The Maranello cars swept the top five spots in a race run in a torrential downpour. Works driver Eugenio Castellotti took his 290 MM to first place overall; its companion finished fourth. A 290 MM placed third at Germany's Nurburgring.

Finally, Frenchman Maurice Trintignant and American Phil Hill won the Swedish Grand Prix for sports cars in a 290 MM and were followed to the checkered flag by a second 290 MM. This was the season's final race and clinched for Ferrari another Constructors Sports World Championship, its third in four years.

250 GT Tour de France

250 GT TOUR DE FRANCE
1956-1959

Number made:	77
Engine:	2953cc V-12, SOHC, 240 hp @ 7000 rpm
Transmission:	4-speed
Wheelbase:	102.3 inches / 2600mm
Weight:	2,300 lbs. (factory)

1956-1959
250 GT
Tour de France

NAMED FOR A SINGLE RACE, IT DEFINED THE ESSENCE OF THE THOROUGHBRED GRAN TURISMO

Ferrari never officially used it as a model name, but when a 250 GT berlinetta won the Tour de France in 1956, another Maranello legend was born.

"Tour de France" came to identify a series of competition-oriented Ferrari berlinettas built over the next three years, all based on the 250 GT, all with 3.0-liter V-12s and all based on Ferrari's "long-wheelbase" 102.3-inch (2600 mm) chassis. These TdFs cemented the 250 GT as the heart of the Ferrari mystique.

The event Tour de France was a multiday competition over several diverse circuits, and Ferrari followers quickly seized on the '56 win by Alfonso de Portago to nickname his winning mount.

The timing was perfect. The FIA had just created a Gran Turismo category as another response to the 1955 Le Mans tragedy. It sought to emphasize a more civilized performance perimeter exemplified by the "GT," a sporting car at home on the road as well as the track. The category capped displacement at 3.0-liters. That bode well for Ferrari: It had been competing with Colombo-designed 3.0-liter V-12s since the 250 S in 1952.

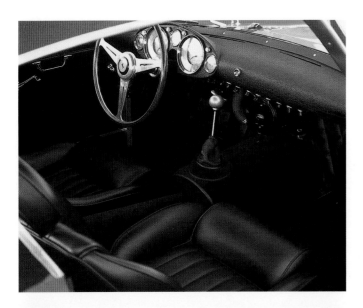

250 GT Tour de France by Zagato

The development of what would become the TdF began in 1954 with a series of striking, custom-coachwork competizione coupes from Pinin Farina. These used a new, stronger tubular chassis with suspension updated from previous 250s by replacing elliptic leaf springs with wishbones, coil springs, and shocks.

The "prototypes" for the TdF series appeared in 1954-55 on 250 GT competiziones that had aluminum bodywork, plexiglass side windows, and other race-oriented features. These cars sometimes are referred to as 250 Europa GT berlinettas. The handsome form derived from Pinin Farina's 375 MM berlinettas, but with a slightly wider track.

For 1956, body construction switched to Scaglietti because Pinin Farina's plant was bursting with work for Ferrari, Alfa, and others; Pinin Farina would move to a new factory in 1958. "The shop divided into two sectors," Sergio Scaglietti recalled of the period. "One group did repair work for Pinin Farina, while another, the larger group, made body panels."

Though initial TdF designs were Pinin Farina's, Scaglietti spoke often with his Turin counterparts and made modifications as he saw necessary.

The 1956 Tour-winning TdF closely resembles earlier 250s. TdFs made during '56 and '57 had a more tapered nose, a new tail, and a louvered sail panel. They are often called "Fourteen Louver" cars for the number of slats.

Late in 1957, Pinin Farina designed a new TdF body that Scaglietti built. It had yet another nose highlighted by covered headlights and a new sail-panel treatment with vents instead of louvers. These make up the majority of TdFs and are referred to as "three" and "single" outlet or slot cars, depending on the number of vents. The very last TdF's had open headlights in accordance with 1959 Italian regulations.

Fangio and Frere; Collins and Moss; Spa and Monza; Goodwood—and the Tour de France nine times. The list of drivers and events won by 250 GTs in the TdF family reads like a racing dream book. These timeless competition berlinettas were immensely popular with serious amateurs, too, and some drove them on the street. They were, afterall, GTs.

250 GT Tour de France

315 S

315 S & 335 S		
1957		
Number made:		
315 S:	2	
335 S:	4	
Engine:		
315 S:	3783cc V-12, DOHC, 360 hp @ 7000 rpm	
335 S:	4023cc V-12, DOHC, 390 hp @ 7800 rpm	
Transmission:	4-speed	
Wheelbase:	92.5 inches / 2350mm	
Weight:	n/a	

1957
315 S & 335 S

"[T]HE GREATEST FRONT ENGINE RACE CAR FROM FERRARI." DISAGREE? DIRECT COMMENTS TO PHIL HILL

The 315 S and 335 S were a natural evolution of the 290 MM in Ferrari's quest for even greater speed at the pinnacle of sports-racing competition. The cars' engines were as spectacular as Scaglietti's stupendous coachwork and were Ferrari's first V-12s to use double overhead cams.

The 315 S appeared in 1957 at Sebring, its heart a 3783cc engine with 360 horsepower, or 95 horsepower per liter. Mated to a four-speed gearbox, this engine was actually lighter than the 290 MM's smaller, less-powerful V-12.

Suspension followed Ferrari practice: independent up front with double wishbones and coil springs; in the rear, a De Dion tube and transverse leaf springs. Brakes were large drums.

The 315 S had an integral role in Ferrari's 1957 Constructors Sports World Championship, winning what would be the last Mille Miglia. Works driver Piero Taruffi promised his wife he'd retire if he won, and he did.

Just as important to the world championship was the 335 S. It looked nearly identical to the 315, but had a V-12 given more bore and stroke to reach 4023cc and 390 horsepower. It finished second at that ill-fated Mille Miglia, the scene of another '50s racing tragedy. It was Alfonso de Portago's accident in another 335 S, which took the life of the dashing Ferrari driver and those of a number of spectators, including five children, that caused the event to be discontinued.

The 335 S placed second in two other races, then won the season's last event at Venezuela to take the makes title away from crosstown rival Maserati.

No less than future F1 World Champion Phil Hill considered the 335 S "the greatest front engine race car from Ferrari." Writing in the 50th Anniversary issue of *Road & Track*, Hill said the 335 S "was a driver's dream, one of those points when a car's development in both power and handling peaked at the same time. Not only did the V-12 have more top end power than we had known, but the chassis dealt better on a variety of road surfaces and was more predictable, something Ferrari race cars hadn't been in the previous few years...."

335 S

250 Testa Rossa

250 Testa Rossa, TRI & 330 LM

FASCINATING TO LOOK AT, FANTASTIC IN COMPETITION, THESE FULL-BLOODED RED HEADS WERE HISTORY MAKERS

The Testa Rossa was one of history's greatest racing cars. Its various iterations helped Ferrari win four Constructors Sports World Championships. And its four wins at Le Mans included the last victory for a front-engine car at the Sarthe circuit.

Development of the TR began in 1957, likely as a reaction to a rules change under consideration by the FIA. Ferrari, Aston Martin, Jaguar, and particularly Maserati were making ever-faster, more-powerful sports-racers, and the horrendous Pierre Levegh crash two years earlier at Le Mans was still a fresh wound.

When the FIA announced a 3.0-liter limit for the top echelon of sports-racers competing for the 1958 championship, Ferrari was ready. His successes with 3.0-liter spyders and berlinettas stretched back to the 250 S, and recently included the TdF.

So in the first half of 1957, a 3.0-liter V-12 was installed in a chassis similar to that of the 500 TRC and 290 MM. As with the four-cylinder engines in the 500 TR and TRC, Ferrari painted the valve covers red. Instead of just TR initials, however, he

bestowed upon his new sports-racer the full "Testa Rossa" name.

The prototype of this TR made its racing debut in the 1,000 kilometers at Germany's demanding Nurburgring, where it finished 10th overall. A second prototype ran as high as second at Le Mans before retiring. The two prototypes finished 1957 placing third and fourth at Venezuela.

Those results convinced Ferrari of the model's potential, and rightly so. In 1958, factory-team 250 Testa Rossas captured for Maranello its third consecutive Constructors Sports World Championship, winning four of that year's six endurance races. Outright victories included Le Mans (Olivier Gendebien and Phil Hill driving), the Sebring 12 Hours (Peter Collins and Hill), and the Targa Florio (Luigi Musso and Gendebien).

Designed and built by Scaglietti, the body of this 250 TR 58 was a masterpiece in its originality, and was especially notable for its distinctive pontoonlike front fenders. The 250 TR 58 was among the coachbuilder's very favorite cars.

"Formula 1 was the inspiration for its shape," Sergio Scaglietti explained. "There were pods on the sides of the F1 cars, and while I wouldn't call them aerodynamic, they went well. We used a similar idea by designing the body to bring air in towards the brakes to cool them. In many ways the Testa Rossa was a Formula 1 car with fenders."

For '59, Scaglietti was occupied with Ferrari's burgeoning order bank for 250 berlinettas and Spyder Californias. So the TR was redesigned by Pinin Farina but built by Medardo Fantuzzi. Another of Modena's talented craftsmen, Fantuzzi had a coach-building business inside the Maserati works, his main client.

When Maserati withdrew from F1 and endurance racing in 1958, Fantuzzi moved off-site and soon picked up Ferrari.

The TR 59 had an all-enclosed body and was undoubtedly more aerodynamic than its pontoon-fender predecessor. It was also about 100 pounds lighter. Mechanical improvements included a new five-speed gearbox in place of a four-speed, a limited slip differential, and disc brakes.

The season was an epic battle between the TR and Aston Martin's DBR1. The TR 59 won at Sebring and finished in the top five at the Nurburgring and Goodwood in England. But that wasn't enough to offset the DBR1's Le Mans win and two other

250 TESTA ROSSA, TRI & 330 TRI/LM		
250 Testa Rossa 1957-1958		
TR 58 1958		
TR 59 1959		
TR 60 1960		
TRI 60 1960		
TRI 61 1961		
330 TRI/LM 1962		

Number made:

250 Testa Rossa:	21	
TR 58:	2	
TR 59:	5	
TR 60:	3	
TRI 60:	2	
TRI 61:	2	
330 TRI/LM:	1	

Engine:

250 Testa Rossa, TR 58, TR 59, TR 60, TRI 60, TRI 61:	2953cc V-12 SOHC, 300 hp @ 7200 rpm
330 TRI/LM:	3967cc V-12, SOHC, 360 hp @ 7800 rpm

Transmission:

250 Testa Rossa & TR 58:	4-speed
TR 59, TR 60, TRI 60, TRI 61, 330 TRI/LM:	5-speed

Wheelbase:

250 Testa Rossa, TR 58 & TR 59:	92.5 inches / 2350mm
TR 60:	89.7 inches / 2280mm
TRI 60:	88.5 inches / 2250mm
TRI 61:	91.5 inches / 2324mm
330 TRI/LM:	95.2 inches / 2420mm

Weight:

250 Testa Rossa:	1,760 lbs. (factory)

TR 59

TR 60

victories. Ferrari lost the constructors championship by two points.

For 1960, Ferrari improved the TR by shortening the wheelbase, while Fantuzzi gave it lower coachwork and a full windshield to meet new regulations. Gendebien and Paul Frere won Le Mans in this TR 60, leading Ferrari to its sixth Constructors Sports World Championship in eight years.

The 1960 Le Mans race also saw the unveiling of the TRI 60. This had a shorter-still wheelbase and the model's first independent rear suspension. It showed tremendous potential by running in the top five, often second or third, for 16 hours before retiring with gearbox problems.

The Testa Rossa was fully redesigned for 1961 with a new aerodynamic shape by Ferrari chief engineer Carlo Chiti. He had come to Ferrari in 1958 from Alfa Romeo. Chiti brought with him a new degree of engineering sophistication, as evidenced by the scale model that was subjected to wind tunnel testing before Fantuzzi finalized the slippery new shape that became the TRI 61.

Two TRI 61s were built. Hill and Gendebien won Le Mans and Sebring in one, the other finished second in both those marquee events. Coupled with successes by the 250 SWB, Ferrari captured another sports-car world championship.

In 1962, the FIA decided the world championship for makes would be contested by GT cars of no more than 3.0-liters. But it also created a new category that allowed "prototypes" of up to 4.0-liters to run at Sebring, Nurburgring, and Le Mans.

Led by its new 250 GTO, Ferrari's 3.0-liter racers would dominate this Constructors International Grand Touring Championship. But Ferrari couldn't resist modifying a TRI 61 by installing a 4.0-liter V-12, fitting a double wishbone suspension front and rear and slightly modifying the body.

This one-off 330 TRI/LM won Le Mans, with Hill and Gendebien leading 19 of the race's 24 hours on their way to Ferrari's sixth win there. That victory was a fitting finale to the Testa Rossa saga, for it closed the curtain on front-engine winners of world's most prestigious endurance event.

TRI 61

330 TRI/LM

250 GT Spyder California LWB

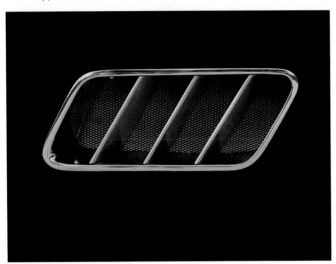

1958-1963
250 GT
Spyder California

UNMATCHED PROVENANCE, UNWAVERING CLASS: THE OPEN-AIR SPORTS-RACING GT AT ITS PINNACLE

Ferrari's earliest open-air sports-racing cars were hardly distinguishable in specification or appearance from the "touring" versions of the same models. Maranello swayed from that "dual-purpose" path with the 375 MM and 500 Mondial of 1953, which had no direct roadgoing counterparts.

The dual-purpose spyder returned in 1958, however, and in spectacular fashion with the Spyder California. It would become an integral part of the 250 legend for its suave looks and competition prowess.

Popular belief holds that the "Cal Spyder" was inspired by Ferrari's American importer Luigi Chinetti. In reality, the motivation came from Ferrari's Southern California dealer, Johnny von Neumann, according to Girolamo Gardini, Ferrari's influential sales manager at the time.

Von Neumann and the rest of the Ferrari universe got something decidedly more sporty than the 250 Cabriolet Series I, which was launched for 1957. The 250 Cabriolet Series I was tame by comparison, basically an open-air version of the pretty Pinin Farina 250 GT coupe.

By contrast, the Cal Spyder was a competitor at heart, with underpinnings borrowed from the 250 Tour de France. In Ferrari tradition, the frame was welded steel tubes and retained the TdF's 102.3-inch (2600mm) wheelbase. Unequal-length wishbones, coil springs, and an antiroll bar were in front. Rigid axle, semi-elliptic leaf springs, and radius rods were in back. Brakes were initially large steel drums.

250 GT SPYDER CALIFORNIA	
1958-1963	
Number made:	
LWB:	50
SWB:	54
Engine:	
LWB:	2953cc V-12, SOHC, 260 hp @ 7000 rpm
SWB:	2953cc V-12, SOHC, 280 hp @ 7000 rpm
Transmission:	4-speed
Wheelbase:	
LWB:	102.3 inches / 2600mm
SWB:	94.5 inches / 2400mm
Weight:	
LWB:	2,200 lbs.
SWB:	2,300 lbs.

Underhood was a 3.0-liter V-12 with single overhead cams and an initial compression ratio of 9.0:1. Soon improved to 9.5:1, and with different Weber carburetors, the engine produced 240-260 horsepower.

Carrozzeria Scaglietti manufactured the car's aluminum coachwork, but the humble man wouldn't take credit for the design. Asked who designed the 250 Spyder California, Sergio Scaglietti told this author "Pininfarina." When the author posed the question to Sergio Pininfarina, he answered "Scaglietti."

Production started in early summer 1958. Versions intended primarily for road use had steel bodies. Those aimed principally for competition had skins of lightweight aluminum and a larger gas tank identified by a fuel filler visible on the trunklid.

A 250 GT Spyder California finished first in class and ninth overall at Sebring in 1959's first race. Three months later, at Le

250 GT Spyder California SWB, chassis 2383

Mans, one placed a remarkable fifth overall. At Sebring in 1960, three Cal Spyders finished among the top ten; one was fifth overall.

Despite such successes, it was evident that less chassis flex would mean better handling. The easy solution was to use the shorter-wheelbase chassis just introduced on the 250 GT SWB Berlinetta.

With that, the SWB Spyder California was born. It demanded a sharp eye to distinguish from its long-wheelbase brethren. Versions of each were produced with both open and covered headlamps, and competition-oriented models of both tended to alloy bodies and trunklid fuel fillers.

The SWB could be identified from the LWB by a hood scoop slightly inset at its leading edge. Its front-fender openings had two vertical vanes versus three, and it had conventional door handles, rather than flush-type. Inside, the SWB Cal Spyder was more luxurious, with better carpeting and a dash covered in leather rather than a black crinkle finish.

The shorter wheelbase did deliver a tauter chassis for a more nimble car, but just one SWB Spyder California competed in international endurance competition. It had an aluminum body, covered headlights, and the outside filler cap. The engine had more radical cams, a higher compression ratio, and large Weber carbs. It ran as high as 11th at Le Mans in 1960, but did not finish the race.

Other competition SWB Cal Spyders, such as chassis 2383 GT, were used by their owners both as road cars and as hill-climb specials. This particular example also had a hopped-up engine and alloy body.

Spyder California production continued into 1963, with just over 100 made. It was the last true dual-purpose open-air Ferrari, and it attained near-mythic status as a sports car of rare beauty and genuine performance.

Drivers sprint to their cars in the famous Le Mans start, circa 1951

Le Mans:
The Ultimate Endurance Test

The 24 Hours of Le Mans is arguably the most important contest in motorsport. It's made reputations, influenced racing and car design, and helped shape automotive history.

It began in 1923, over rural roads in central France. Structured tracklike sections were inserted over the years, but the 8.1-mile (13km) circuit retains the flavor of a classic Grand Touring dash through the European countryside. And though it started as a competition for four-seat touring cars, then in the 1930s, for the two-seaters still mandated today, the goal is the same: finish as many miles as possible in 24 hours.

Over the years, victory in the race has been essential to a manufacturer's reputation. This was especially true for, among others, England's Bentley, which dominated Le Mans in the late 1920s, Alfa Romeo (early '30s), Jaguar (early '50s), Ford (mid '60s), Porsche (1970s), and Audi (2000s).

Ferrari's international reputation for unparalleled speed and style was born in 1949, when its 166 MM followed up a victory in the Mille Miglia with one at Le Mans.

The importance of victory at Le Mans cannot be overemphasized, especially in the immediate postwar years. Unlike the purpose-built prototypes that came to the fore in the late 1950s, many of the top-echelon machines up until then were quite

similar to their production counterparts or used many of the same components and technology.

And that was central to the Ferrari legend, which was stoked white-hot by its dominance of Le Mans in the late 1950s and first half of the 1960s. Piero Ferrari lists endurance racing, not Formula 1, as one of the key elements to Ferrari's success in the company's formative years. Not only were its sports cars faster than any competitor's, Le Mans demonstrated that they were also quite reliable in a day when automobiles, especially European exotics, still had much to prove.

"In the 1950s and '60s," explained one of Europe's leading automotive designers, Giorgetto Giugiaro, "long-distance driving was still an adventure. Cars weren't as reliable as they are today, so on such trips you didn't know if you would indeed arrive at your final destination or not."

But to finish Le Mans was more than an illustration of reliability. After World War II nationalistic pride ran very high, and a Le Mans win was widely viewed as a victory for that car's country. The stakes got no higher.

Former Jaguar employee Geoff Turner was a teenager in the 1950s, and recalled "that decade was really the Le Mans years. I used to listen late at night with my father to the radio and the racing reports....when Jaguar went there and won, it felt great! For a British car company to go into international motorsport was incredible, for we hadn't been doing well at it for a long time. Jaguar was fielding sports cars that would go out and beat the world: in those days, companies like Alfa Romeo, Maserati, and particularly Ferrari who also made sports cars. For us it was incredible."

The particular demands of Le Mans helped shape car design itself. The long Mulsanne straight, where racing speeds reached more than 200 mph, influenced automotive aerodynamics. And bringing cars down from such velocities led to innovations such as Jaguar's use of disc brakes in the 1950s. Racing rules world-wide were reexamined after the 1955 Le Mans crash in which Pierre Levegh's Mercedes 300 SLR went off course and into the crowd, killing 80 spectators.

And how would automotive history have been different had Henry Ford II, eager to enhance his company's sporting credentials, not tried to take a shortcut to that goal by attempting to buy Ferrari in 1963?

No sooner was his offer spurned than Ford said "let's go beat them," the target being victory at Le Mans. That set up the marvelous Ford-Ferrari wars of the mid 1960s, when Ford showed the might of the American auto industry by winning the event four times, pushing Ferrari and other European manufacturers to redouble their efforts to win the world's most important race.

A Ferrari 330 P3 in the 1966 race

Why the world watched: Ford GT40, Ferrari 250 LM, Porsche 917, 1969

250 GT SWB

1959-1962
250 GT SWB Berlinetta

THE ULTIMATE ROAD-AND-RACE FERRARI TAKES TO THE TRACK, WITH MAGNIFICENT RESULTS

Examine sports-racing results from the early 1960s, and it's obvious why the 250 GT SWB Berlinetta was such an integral part of the Ferrari legend.

The record is riddled with class victories, rife with top-10 finishes. It's rich with such names as Stirling Moss, Mike Parkes, and Graham Hill, and with myth-making runs at storied places like Le Mans, Sebring, and Brands Hatch.

The SWB Berlinetta was a natural continuation of the 250 GT Tour de France. Its competition incarnation was seen first at Le Mans in June 1959 in the form of two cars called the 250 GT Interim. Their shape was by Pininfarina (who in 1961 began using his name as one word) and employed the TdF's 102.3-inch (2600mm) chassis and virtually identical mechanicals. The Interims placed fourth and sixth overall, then, in September, won the Tour de France itself with Olivier Gendebien and Lucien Bianchi. This assured the design's continuation. Scaglietti subsequently received the wooden body buck and constructed five more examples.

The definitive 250 GT SWB Berlinetta broke cover at the

250 GT SWB	
1959-1962	
Number made:	
	90 (steel bodies)
	75 (aluminum coachwork)
Engine:	2953cc V-12, SOHC,
	260-280 hp @ 7000 rpm
Transmission:	4-speed
Wheelbase:	94.5 inches / 2400mm
Weight:	2,100 lbs.

250 GT SWB

250 GT SWB "Breadvan"

1959 Paris Auto Show. Wheelbase was now 94.5 inches (2400mm) for better handling and less weight, though to the eye the body differed from the Interim only in the absence of rear quarter windows. Over the life of the model, about 75 of the total 165 produced were earmarked for serious competition and were typified by a comparatively sparse interior, aluminum instead of steel body, more-aggressive engine tuning, and a stiffer suspension.

Street or track, underpinnings were similar to those of the TdF: independent with double wishbones and coil springs in front, the proven rigid axle and leaf springs in back. Besides the shorter wheelbase, the big difference was installation of disc brakes.

The 3.0-liter V-12 was reaching the pinnacle of its development. The SWB's had a new block and heads. Competition SWBs received additional modifications, such as cylinder heads similar to those in the Testa Rossa, and higher compression ratios. Depending upon state of tune, horsepower was between 240 and more than 280. All used a four-speed transmission.

On the track, the race-tune 250 SWB Berlinetta picked up where the TdF and Interim left off. In its competition debut at Sebring in 1960, it took three of the first ten places, including fourth overall. At Le Mans, the SWB of Fernand Tavano and Pierre Dumay came in fourth overall and first in GT; other SWBs finished sixth and seventh on distance. Later that season, an SWB won outright at Goodwood in England and at Monza in Italy, helping Ferrari secure another sports-racing endurance championship.

The results were much the same in 1961. Significant showings included the Le Mans performance by Pierre Noblet and Jean Guichet in Noblet's SWB. They won the GT category and finished third overall, covering 25 miles more in 24 hours than the previous year's outright winner, a full-race Ferrari TR 60. Another SWB took sixth overall.

Among other '61 SWB successes were overall victories at Goodwood and Monza. At the 1,000-kilometer race at Montlhery outside Paris, SWBs swept the first five places and accounted for 11 of the top 13 finishers. Ferrari's little GT came in fourth at Germany's challenging Nurburgring, second at Pescara in Italy.

Throughout, there were no major changes to the poised-to-pounce appearance that made the SWB Berlinetta among the most arresting cars at any track. Small alterations included the addition of air outlets on front and rear fenders for 1960. For '61, side windows gained wing vents and lost the subtle kink at their upper rear corners.

Several SWBs did however get wholesale rebodies in an effort to make them even faster. Most famous was the "Breadvan," a one-off funded by Giovanni Volpi, a European Count and Ferrari racing privateer. Volpi had staffed his team with engineers hired from Ferrari, and in retaliation, Enzo refused to sell him Maranello's sports-racing successor to the SWB, the 250 GTO.

So Volpi took an SWB that had finished second in the 1961 Tour de France and had engineer Giotto Bizzarrini create a form with a truncated vertical Kamm tail; some thought it resembled a bakery delivery truck. "Bizzarrini made the Breadvan in two weeks," marveled the Count.

Volpi's Scuderia Serenissima raced the Breadvan during 1962. Early in the 24 Hours at Le Mans, it lead all GTOs before retiring with driveshaft failure. At Montlhery, it finished third, behind two GTOs, but ahead of seven others. It was first in class at Brands Hatch.

Then, in a demonstration of why the SWB was one of history's great dual-purpose machines, the Count retired it from competition and used it as his road car starting in 1963.

196 SP

196 SP, 246 SP, 248 SP, 268 SP & 286 SP		
1961-1962		
Number made:		
196 SP:	3	
246 SP:	2	
248 SP:	2	
268 SP:	3	
286 SP:	1	
Engine:		
196 SP:	1983cc V-6, SOHC, 210 hp @ 7500 rpm	
246 SP:	2417cc V-6, DOHC, 270 hp @ 8000 rpm	
248 SP:	2458cc V-8, SOHC, 250 hp @ 7400 rpm	
268 SP:	2644cc V-8, SOHC, 260 hp @ 7500 rpm	
286 SP:	2862cc V-6, SOHC, 260 hp @ 6800 rpm	
Transmission:	5-speed	
Wheelbase:	91.3 inches / 2320mm	
Weight:	n/a	

1961-1962

196 SP, 246 SP, 248 SP, 268 SP & 286 SP

ENZO PUTS THE CART BEFORE THE HORSE: FERRARI'S FIRST MIDENGINE SPORTS-RACING CARS

The Sports Prototype was the sports-racing car taken to its extreme. These pure-competition machines dropped all pretense of the dual-purpose road-and-race ideal.

Liberated from the commercial motives and regulatory necessities that forced them to link track cars and street machines, manufacturers switched to a design that was required in order to win at the highest levels of competition: the midengine layout.

The movement at Ferrari had its seeds in Formula 1, in the first half of 1958, when a midengine Cooper beat its larger-engine Ferrari rivals at Buenos Aires and Monaco.

The benefits of placing the engine behind the driver to provide greater cornering power were obvious to Ferrari chief engineer Carlo Chiti. But Enzo Ferrari was a traditionalist at heart, and he resisted. It took three years of lobbying from Chiti and others, including designer Vittorio Jano, to get The Old Man to consent to a midengine design.

Finally, in 1961, the company unveiled its first midengine sports-racer, the 246 SP, for Sports Prototype. Its open body was developed in the wind tunnel and clothed an all-independent suspension with inboard brakes. In a nest of tubes behind the two-seat cockpit was a 2.4-liter V-6 with double overhead cams and a five-speed gearbox in unit with the differential.

Despite its sleek-looking skin, the track tests proved the shape unstable. Driver Richie Ginther concluded it could be improved by the addition of a small rear spoiler. This was the first use of the appendage in a competition car, and the results were dramatic. Within weeks, the 246 SP would win Sicily's grueling Targa Florio in the hands of Olivier Gendebien and Wolfgang von Trips. It later placed third at Germany's Nurburgring, another course known for its numerous tight turns.

Development of the SP continued full pace in 1962 with several variations. Coachwork was revised in accordance with new FIA regulations to create a series of nearly identical-looking SPs with a parade of engines that gave them different designations: a 1.9-liter V-6 (196 SP), a 2.4-liter V-8 (248 SP), a 2.6-liter V-8 (268 SP), and a 2.8-liter V-6 (286 SP).

The 196 SP took second in the Targa Florio with Lorenzo Bandini and Giancarlo Baghetti, and won the inaugural European Championship for Mountain Driving. The updated-coachwork 246 fared even better, winning the Targa Florio (Gendebien/Ricardo Rodriguez/Willy Mariesse) and at the Nurburgring (Phil Hill/Gendebien). The stage was thus set for Ferrari's midengine V-12 Sports Prototypes, which would appear in 1963.

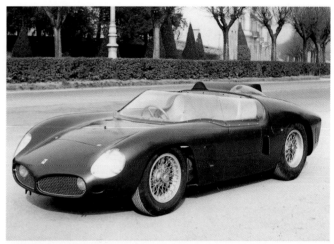

246 SP

268 SP

286 SP

250 GT

1962-1964
250 GTO

THE PASSION AND PRIDE OF MARANELLO EMBODIED IN A SINGLE CAR: GRAN TURISMO OMOLOGATO

In its development and refinement of the long-running 250 series, Ferrari saved the best for last with the immortal 250 GTO.

All told, just 39 examples of this voluptuous coupe were produced. All were built to race, but were theoretically usable on the street by virtue of sports-racing rules that required road versions of competition cars. That regulation, in fact, gave rise to the car's name: gran turismo omologato—a GT homologated, or sanctioned, for racing.

And race it did, propelling Ferrari to the Constructors International Grand Touring Championship in 1962, 1963, and 1964.

Surprisingly, the GTO could be said to owe its existence to Britain's Jaguar. In March 1961, Ferrari sales manager Girolamo Gardini watched Jaguar unveil the E-type at the Geneva Motor Show and returned to Modena, sounding the alarm. "Gardini was going around the factory, telling everyone 'They are going to beat us with their new GT,'" engineer Giotto Bizzarrini recalled.

Once Gardini convinced Ferrari of the urgency, Enzo instigated a full-court press. Bizzarrini was put in charge of the project and operating in complete secrecy, handpicked several workers and technicians outside normal Ferrari circles.

250 GTO		
1962-1964		
Number made:	39	
4-liter:	3	
Series II:	3	
Engine:	2953cc V-12, SOHC, 300 hp @ 7500 rpm	
4-liter:	3967cc V-12, SOHC, 340 hp @ 7000 rpm	
Transmission:	5-speed	
Wheelbase:	94.5 inches / 2400mm	
Weight:	2,315 lbs.	

Bizzarrini's starting point was the 250 GT SWB, which he helped develop. A passion for aerodynamics and proper weight distribution caused him to relocate the entire engine behind the front axle. This improved weight balance for better handling while allowing him to create a lower, more-aerodynamic hood line. A new steeply raked windshield and a hand-formed fast-back completed the silhouette.

Intense trial and error distinguished the prototype's development. Enzo was on the shop floor daily, pushing the men to speed up. Bizzarrini's group worked around the clock, seven days a week. He recalled the many midnight phone calls, the voice on the line telling him, "Ingengere, the car is ready for testing." Bizzarrini would drag himself out of bed and, with no regard for hour or weather, complete another series of tests.

In September 1961, the prototype was taken to the Monza racetrack near Milan for its first real tests. An SWB was brought along for comparison. The GTO was consistently several seconds faster a lap than the 250 SWB, Bizzarrini remembered.

Two months later, Bizzarrini became embroiled in "The Walkout." He found himself on the outside of Ferrari, along with fellow engineer Carlo Chiti, sales manager Gardini, and a handful of others. Ferrari promoted Mauro Forghieri, a young engineer, to complete the GTO's development, with stalwart Sergio Scaglietti assigned to refine the body. In the process, the tail was fitted with a small rear spoiler, as found on the new midengine 246 SP.

250 GTO

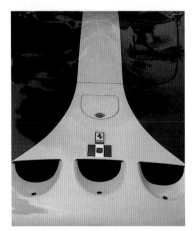

250 GTO Series II

The 250 GTO proved a design pinnacle for front-engine race cars. Its 2953cc V-12 featured Testa Rossa heads and larger valves and was topped with an impressive row of six double-barrel Weber carburetors. A five-speed transmission replaced the SWB's four speed.

The SWB chassis was modified with smaller tubes for lighter weight and additional bracing for extra stiffness. Double wishbones, coil springs, Koni shocks, and an antiroll bar comprised the front suspension. A Watts linkage, Koni shocks, and semi-elliptic leaf springs made up the rear. Disc brakes were used all around. The interior was unusually well-turned-out for a car intended for the track, being roomy and dressed up with chrome-trimmed gauges.

Indeed, the car's qualification for GT-class competition revealed much about Enzo Ferrari's gamesmanship. The FIA allowed body modifications to already-homologated production cars. Ferrari successfully positioned the GTO as simply a modi-fied-body 250 GT SWB. Thus, he slipped this limited-production purpose-built competition coupe into a class meant for volume-built sports cars. It was a wolf among lambs.

The first one was sent to Florida for the 1962 running of the 12 Hours of Sebring. Phil Hill and Olivier Gendebien won the GT class, and finished second overall. GTOs thereafter were a fixture in the winner's circle and among the top ten. Outright victories came in England at Goodwood and in France at Auvergne and Monthlery, where GTOs took four of the top five spots. At Le Mans, Jean Guichet and Pierre Noblet won the GT class and finished an astounding second overall, their 113.077-mph (182.673km/h) average bettered only by the winning Ferrari 330 LM's 115.245 mpg (185.469km/h). Other GTOs came in third and sixth on distance. Additional second-place finishes that year were turned in at Nurburgring and at Bridgehampton in America.

The results were much the same in 1963. Counted among overall victories were Daytona in Florida (Pedro Rodriguez), Spa in Belgium (Willy Mairesse), two major Goodwood events (Mike Parkes and Graham Hill), and the Tour de France (Guichet/Jean Behra). Again at Le Mans, a GTO won the GT class and placed second overall.

Ever-escalating speeds called for still-lower, wider bodywork that in 1964 resulted in the "Series II" GTO, its new green-house inspired by the 250 LM. The original body shape contin-ued in the form of three "Series I" GTOs with 4.0-liter engines.

These cars staved off Carroll Shelby's Ford-powered Cobras and Daytona coupes to win another world GT championship. Victories at Daytona, Spa, and in the Tour de France helped put Ferrari over the top. For '65, weary rulesmakers doubled the allowable engine displacement in its class, neutralizing the 250 GTO as a consistent podium threat. This was Ferrari's last successful front-engine race car, and an uncompromised classic.

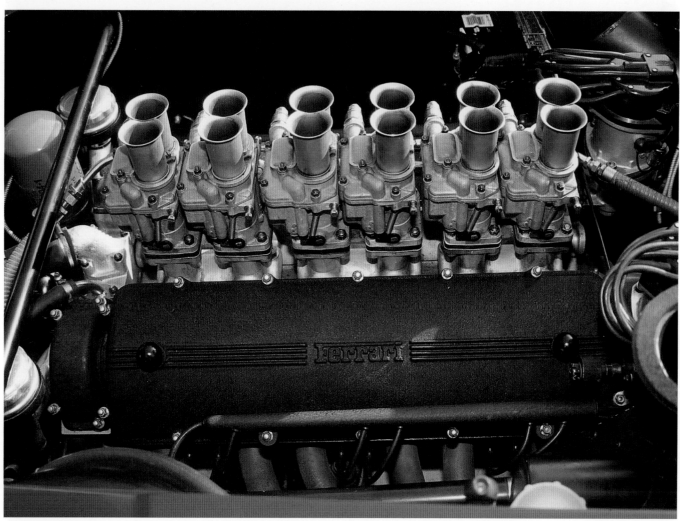

250 GTO 4.0-liter V-12

330 LMB

1963
330 LMB

A MIX-AND-MATCH STAB AT STAVING OFF THE MIDENGINE ONSLAUGHT

The midengine revolution was in full swing, but that didn't stop Ferrari from one last stab at success with the proven front-engine formula.

The 330 LMB (Le Mans Berlinetta) sports-racer was another mix-and-match job in which Ferrari employed existing components and design features to create a new model in the continual quest for speed. The car also allowed Ferrari to compete in a new prototype class that allowed an engine displacement of 4.0-liters rather than 3.0.

The 330 LMB used a modified powertrain out of Ferrari's luxurious 400 Superamerica. The 4.0-liter V-12 replaced three Webers with six to help bump horsepower to 390 from 340. Like its roadgoing cousin, the LMB used a four-speed gearbox.

The chassis and underpinnings also found their origins in the Superamerica. Both cars' tubular frames rode on a wheelbase of 98.4 inches (2500mm), though the 330 had wider front and rear tracks. The suspension was nearly identical, with double wishbones and coil springs in front, rigid axle and semielliptic leaf springs in back.

Pininfarina designed the coachwork, a successful amalgam of existing Ferrari models. Forward of the windshield, the LMB was a near dead ringer for a 250 GTO. From the A-pillar back, it was a double of Pininfarina's 250 Lusso, though with rear fenders sliced by lower vents and topped with intakes that funneled air to the brakes and provided greater tire clearance.

330 LMB		
1963		
Number made:	4	
Engine:	3967cc V-12, SOHC, 390 hp @ 7500 rpm	
Transmission:	4-speed	
Wheelbase:	98.4 inches / 2500mm	
Weight:	n/a	

The mix of street- and competition-car styling proved surprisingly slippery. The model's first appearance was at Le Mans, where its near-190-mph showing on the long Mulsanne straight was actually faster than that of Ferrari's first midengine V-12 prototype, the 250 P.

Four 330 LMBs were entered in that '63 24 Hours; just one survived, finishing fifth overall. That turned out to be the car's only true success. It was now clear: There was no stopping the midengine revolution.

250 P, 275 P, 330 P, 275 P2, 330 P2, 365 P & 365 P2		
250 P 1963		
275 P 1964		
330 P 1964		
275 P2 1965		
330 P2 1965		
365 P 1965		
365 P2 1965		
Number made:		
250 P:	4	
275 P:	3	
330 P:	3	
275 P2:	5	
330 P2:	5	
365 P:	1	
365 P2:	1	
Engine:		
250 P:	2953cc V-12, SOHC, 300 hp @ 7500 rpm	
275 P:	3285cc V-12, SOHC, 320 hp @ 7700 rpm	
330 P:	3967cc V-12, SOHC, 370 hp @ 7500 rpm	
275 P2:	3285cc V-12, DOHC, 350 hp @ 8500 rpm	
330 P2:	3967cc V-12, DOHC, 410 hp @ 8200 rpm	
365 P:	4390cc V-12, SOHC, 380 hp @ 7200 rpm	
365 P2:	4390cc V-12, SOHC, 380 hp @ 7200 rpm	
Transmission:	5-speed	
Wheelbase:	94.5 inches / 2400mm	
Weight:		
250 P:	1,520 lbs.	
others:	n/a	

250 P

1963-1965

250 P, 275 P, 330 P, 275 P2, 330 P2, 365 P & 365 P2

THE FIRST MIDENGINE DESIGN—AND THE LAST FACTORY FERRARI—TO WIN THE 24 HOURS OF LE MANS

Le Mans marked a milestone in 1963, and Ferrari was responsible. Its 250 P became the first midengine car to win the world's greatest road race.

The winning mount traced its origins to the 246 SP, the V-6 model that launched Maranello's midengine prototype line in 1961. For the 250 P, the 246's tubular frame was lengthened slightly to fit a Testa Rossa-derived 300-horsepower 3.0-liter V-12. The engine, five-speed gearbox, and final drive were located behind the two-place cockpit in what was technically a mid/rear-engine layout.

That chief engineer Mauro Forghieri would pursue such a design was a given. The trend in all forms of top-flight motorsport was to rear-engine placement for better handling and

aerodynamics. Moreover, Le Mans had teamed up with Sebring, the Targa Florio, and the Nurburgring to create world constructors championships for prototypes.

Then there was the atmosphere in Ferrari itself. The company had already done well with non front-engine cars in Formula 1 and endurance racing, and Forghieri had Ferrari's confidence. This was important to the young engineer, for prior to the 1961 "Walkout," he had primarily been responsible for engines and gearboxes. That was a far cry from running everything. Now, Forghieri's creative talent was let loose while Enzo himself handled all the corporate politics. The results spoke for themselves.

The 250 P ran 1-2 in its first outing at Sebring, then took first overall at the Nurburgring. At Le Mans, the 250 P of Ludovico Scarfiotti and Lorenzo Bandini was first overall, marking Ferrari's seventh win in the 24 Hours. Another 250 P was third.

For 1964, Ferrari updated this successful formula with the 275 P and 330 P, which, unlike the 250 P, were made available to privateers. The basic design was similar to the 250 P's, with increased engine capacity the biggest change. For the 275 P, the V-12 was bored to 3285cc for 320 horsepower. For the 330 P, stroke increased for a capacity of 3967cc and 370 hp.

Visually, the new cars were identified by fuel caps on the front fender forward of a more steeply raked windshield. They had a larger rollbar and smaller air intakes located higher on the rear fenders.

Race results for 1964 were much like in '63. At Sebring, 275 Ps went 1-2; a 330 P was third. Another 275 P won the Nurburgring. At Le Mans, the 275 P driven by Jean Guichet and Nino Vaccarella gave Ferrari its eighth outright win in the 24 Hours, a victory that would be the last for a Ferrari factory car at the historic track. Finishing second and third were 330 Ps, which later in the year tasted victory at England's Tourist Trophy and in the season finale at the 1,000 km of Paris.

Pressured as never before in international endurance racing by the full weight of Ford and its GT40 and by the fierce Chevrolet-powered Chaparrals, Ferrari for 1965 dug deep for new technology and more horsepower. The result was the 275 P2, 330 P2, 365 P, and 365 P2.

The 275 P2 and 330 P2 had basically the same appearance, but were quite different from their prototype predecessors. Designed with the aid of a wind tunnel and built by Carrozeria Fantuzzi, they were lower and wider, with a fresh nose, more upright windscreen, larger rollbar structure, and a new tail with a pronounced ducktail spoiler. The wheels were cast magnesium rather than wires, and were staggered in width—eight inches front, nine rear—instead of six inches at each corner.

Chassis and suspension utilized Formula 1 technology. Body panels were riveted to the tubular frame for additional rigidity, and the rear suspension got new geometry and employed two supporting struts.

275 P

330 P

The P2s used double overhead cams and twin plugs per cylinder. Horsepower was 350 for the 275 P2's 3285cc V-12, and 410 for the 330 P2's 3967cc V-12.

The 365 P was introduced just before Le Mans and displayed yet another new skin. Its 4390cc V-12 retained single overhead cams, one plug per cylinder, and made 380 horsepower.

All these cars saw the winner's circle. A 275 P2 won at Monza and the Targa Florio. The 330 P2 was victorious at the Nurburgring. The 365 P2 took the checkered flag at Reims. All told, Ferrari won makes world titles for prototypes in 1963, '64, and '65. And though it won Le Mans in 1965, it wasn't with a P2. Maranello had some momentum, but the challenges of sports-racing were not about to get any easier.

250 LM

250 LM	
1964-1965	
Number made:	32
Engine:	3286cc V-12, SOHC, 320 hp @ 7500 rpm
Wheelbase:	94.5 inches / 2400mm
Weight:	1,874 lbs.

1964-1965
250 LM

PERSEVERING AND VERY TOUGH ON COMPETITORS, LIKE THE RACE FOR WHICH IT WAS NAMED

That the 275 P2, 330 P2, and 365 P did not chalk up a win at Le Mans in 1965 can be traced to two reasons—reliability and another Ferrari model, the 250 LM.

The 250 LM made its debut at the Paris Auto Show in 1963 and was in essence a 250 P with a roof. Pininfarina did the design, using a small wooden model in the wind tunnel to hone the shape.

As he had done with the 250 GTO, Ferrari attempted to have the 250 LM homologated for the 3.0-liter GT class. In his mind, it was another Ferrari "250." In fact, its roof design was similar to that of the Series II 250 GTO. But this time, the FIA was not fooled, and it refused to homologate the LM as a GT car. Thus, it raced as a prototype.

Ironically, even the name "250 LM" was a misnomer. Only the development example of the LM had a proper 3.0-liter V-12 that went with the 250 nomenclature. Every other LM had a 3.3-liter V-12, effectively making them "275" LMs. Ready for the 1964 race season, 250 LMs were entered in 35 races and won 10.

Then, in 1965, when it was arguably old technology out-gunned by true, more-cutting-edge prototypes, the 250 LM finished 1-2 at Le Mans. Both cars were run by private teams. First overall was the entry by Luigi Chinetti's North American Racing Team, driven by Masten Gregory and Jochen Rindt. Second was a French entry driven by Pierre Dumay and Taf Gosselin.

Throughout its career, the LM was the warrior that wouldn't die. It often proved more reliable than Ferrari's faster but more delicate P cars. It beat Ps in 1965 at Le Mans, and also out-performed them by winning in 1964 at Reims. The LM recorded five top-10 finishes in 1966, and it was still winning as late as 1967.

And while it never did justify Enzo's insistence that it was a Grand Touring car, a version did make it to the street...after a fashion. In 1965, Pininfarina created a one-off 250 LM Berlinetta Speciale (chassis 6025 GT) as a road car. Unveiled at the New York Auto Show, this lovely machine featured fastback rear glass and cowling and boasted a comfortable interior with proper upholstery and carpets. It was painted in NART's racing livery of white with blue stripes.

250 LM Berlinetta Speciale, chassis 6025 GT

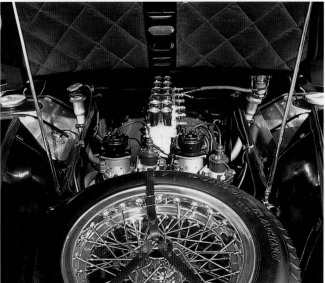

275 GTB Competizione

1964-1966
275 GTB Competizione & 275 GTB/C

CONDITIONED FOR COMPETITION: THE ASTUTELY MODIFIED ROAD FERRARI WAS STILL A GT-CLASS FORCE

The roadgoing 275 GTB spawned two competition versions: the 275 GTB Competizione and the 275 GTB/C.

Like the purely street 275 GTB, the Competizione's body was designed by Pininfarina and built at Scaglietti's plant in Modena. But it had extra-thin aluminum body panels and windows of weight-saving plastic instead of glass. Curb weight was under 2,200 pounds, some 500 pounds less than a steel-body road 275 GTB.

Subtle styling differences included fared-in fog lights below the headlights, and a hood bulge that mimicked that of the Series II 250 GTO. The Competizione shared the stock 3.3-liter V-12, but was fitted with hotter cams and six carburetors instead of three.

Ferrari made 14 Competiziones, and among these were a trio of a quite audacious edition built in 1965. These had radical coachwork—in effect, a blend of 250 GTO and 275 GTB styling—with louvers behind the rear-wheel openings. Fenders were expanded to cover larger wheels, and the tail sported a more prominent spoiler.

275 GTB COMPETIZIONE & 275 GTB/C	
275 GTB COMPETIZIONE 1964-1966 **275 GTB/C 1966**	
Number made: 275 GTB	
Competizione:	14
275 GTB/C:	14
Engine:	3285cc V-12, SOHC, 280-300 hp @ 7000 rpm
Transmission:	5-speed
Wheelbase:	94.5 inches / 2400mm
Weight:	2,178 lbs.

Underneath was a special lightweight chassis and a six-carb, dry-sump 3.3 V-12 similar to that found in the 250 LM and producing over 300 horsepower. It was a formidable setup. One of these cars, driven by Willy Mariesse and Jean Blaton, took GT honors at the 24 Hours of Le Mans in 1965, and finished third overall.

Ferrari's encore for 1966 was the 275 GTB/C. These returned to the basic road-car body appearance, but followed the Competizione's lead with ultrathin-gauge aluminum body panels and plexiglass windows (only the windshield was glass). Inside, they had proper carpeting and trim, but no insulation.

Their 3.3-liter V-12 had a dry-sump oiling system like the three radical Competizones, but with three carburetors instead of six. This dropped output to approximately 280 horsepower.

That didn't keep the GTB/C from having more overall success than the Competizones. Highlights included a fourth in class and 24th overall at 1966's Targa Florio.

At Le Mans, the GTB/C of Roy Pike and Piers Courage was eighth overall and first in GT. Another GTB/C was second in GT, 10th overall. Though Ferrari fielded 14 cars in the '66 event, these GTB/Cs were the only Ferraris to finish the race.

Dino 166 P

DINO 166 P, DINO 206 P, 206 S & 206 SP
DINO 166 P & DINO 206 P 1965 206 S & 206 SP 1966-1967

Number made:
DINO 166 P
& DINO 206 P: 4
206 S & 206 P: 15
Engine:
166 P: 1592cc V-6, DOHC,
                180 hp @ 9000 rpm
206 P: 1986cc V-6, DOHC,
                205 hp @ 8800 rpm
206 S & SP: 1986cc V-6, DOHC,
                218 hp @ 9000 rpm
Transmission: 5-speed
Wheelbase: 89.7 inches / 2280mm
Weight: 1,300 - 1,600 lbs.

1965-1967

DINO 166 P, DINO 206 P, 206 S & 206 SP

THE LITTLE DINOS THAT DID: FERRARI DEMONSTRATES ITS MIDENGINE VERSATILITY

While Ferrari's midengine mantle was being carried into battle by mighty V-12 prototypes with engines up to 4.4-liters, the company was at the same time pursing a smaller, lighter interpretation of the midengine motif.

In 1965, for the race at Monza, it released the curvaceous Dino 166, an enclosed sports-racer with a 1592cc V-6. It was fast in practice, but the engine expired after just one lap. The Dino 166 reappeared at the Nurburgring to finish fourth overall before a dismal Le Mans, where it lasted just two laps.

Two months later, the Dino reappeared at Germany's Freiburg-Schaunisland course, now powered by a 1986cc V-6. This Dino was called the 206 P, and it won the race, beating a number of Porsche 904s, Abarths, and Lotuses. Three weeks later, at the Hillclimb Ollon-Villars Hillclimb in Switzerland, it won again, besting a 275 P2 and a 250 LM in the process.

The 166/206 served as the basis for Pininfarina's one-off 166

Dino Speciale show car, unveiled at the 1965 Paris Auto Show. Using the race car's mechanicals, the Speciale was so well-received that Pininfarina continued to develop it, eventually turning it into the 206/246 Dino, which, for all intents, qualified as Ferrari's first midengine road car.

Replacing the 206 P in 1966 was the more-refined 206 S. It had a beautiful body done at Carrozzeria Sports Cars in Modena and looked much like the larger, more powerful 330 P3. The 206 S's chassis was a semimonocoque: Following techniques used in the 275 and 330 P2, its aluminum coachwork was riveted to the tubular chassis for additional stiffness.

The 1986cc V-6 in the 206 S kept much of the architecture of the 206 P's engine, though with revised combustion chambers and, on some examples, Lucas fuel injection in place of three Weber carburetors.

The 206 S—registered alternately with S and SP suffixes—was quite capable on tighter courses and hillclimbs. First-place finishes in 1966 included Italy's Enna City Cup and Switzerland's Sierre Montana-Crans Hillclimb. They finished second and third at the Nurburgring behind a Chaparral. One also was runner-up in the Targa Florio.

Ferrari's V-6 Dino sports-racers were produced in both open and closed bodies, and demonstrated the company's versatility within the midengine formula. Weighing 1,300-1,600 pounds, and with more than 100 horsepower per liter, they ably represented Ferrari in the 2.0-liter prototypes classes while proving capable of beating far-more-powerful competition.

206 S

206 S

330 P3

330 P3, 365 P2/3, 330 P3/4 (412 P) & 330 P4
330 P3 1966 365 P2/3 1966 330 P3/4 1967 330 P4 1967

Number made:
330 P3:	3
365 P2/3:	2
330 P3/4:	3
330 P4:	3

Engine:
330 P3:	3967cc V-12, DOHC, 420 hp @ 8000 rpm
365 P2/3:	4390cc V-12 SOHC, 380 hp @ 7200 rpm
330 P3/4:	3967cc V-12, DOHC, 450 hp @ 8200 rpm
330 P4:	3967cc V-12, DOHC, 450 hp @ 8200 rpm

Transmission:	5-speed
Wheelbase:	94.5 inches / 2400mm

Weight:
330 P3:	1,588 lbs.
365 P2/3:	n/a
330 P3/4:	1,762 lbs.
330 P4:	1,762 lbs.

1966-1967
330 P3, 365 P2/3, 330 P3/4 & 330 P4

FERRARI GOES NOSE-TO-NOSE WITH FORD FOR THE BIGGEST PRIZES IN ENDURANCE RACING

Development of Ferrari's 12-cylinder prototype racers accelerated in 1966 and '67, and with good reason.

With Carroll Shelby running its sports-racing program, Ford in 1965 wrested from Ferrari the Constructors International Grand Touring Championship. Now the American company was knocking on the door of Ferrari's domination in the sports prototypes class, with the Chevrolet-powered Chaparrals serious threats, as well.

Ferrari mounted its 1966 offensive with the 330 P3. A stunning machine to behold, it looked menacing in a way Modena's earlier prototypes did not. Supporting the look were sophisticated mechanicals that benefited from a more-intensive cross-pollination with Ferrari's Formula 1 technology. An updated suspension with different geometry teamed with a monocoque chassis that used some stressed body panels in the center section.

330 P3/4

The V-12 got new heads to take the Lucas indirection injection system that replaced the predecessor 330 P2's Weber carburetors. A new Borg & Beck three-disc clutch was used with a ZF five-speed gearbox; most of Ferrari's earlier "P-car" gearboxes had been made in-house. Finally, there was a drop in weight: The P3 was more than 200 pounds lighter than the P2.

Only Ferrari "works" drivers drove the 330 P3. Privateers were offered an updated version of the 365 P2, the 365 P2/3. Save some suspension and brake updates, mechanically the model was a near-twin of the 365 P2. The coachwork was a different story, combining as it did the lines of the 365 P2 with the driver's compartment of the 330 P3.

The '66 prototype championship was a dogfight. In the top class, Ford GT40s won the first two races, then a 330 P3 scored a victory at Monza. In the 2.0-liter category, a Dino 206 S took second at Monza to a Porsche 906. Then a 330 P3 won at Spa. A Chaparral was victorious at the Nurburgring. Then Ford scored its biggest victory, GT40s running 1-2-3 at Le Mans. Ford went on to win the Constructors International Sports Prototype Championship, with 38 points to Ferrari's 36.

For 1967, Enzo Ferrari and chief engineer Mauro Forghieri responded with the 330 P4. It would come to be considered by many the greatest Ferrari endurance race car. The P4 looked nearly identical to the 330 P3, but had some significant mechanical changes. The engine block was strengthened, the heads got three valves per cylinder instead of two, and the fuel-injection pipes were repositioned.

330 P4

The chassis was modified and used a shorter wheelbase and wider track. The brakes were repositioned for improved cooling, and the gearbox was redesigned.

Privateers in '67 were offered the 330 P3/4, also known as the 412 P. These were 330 P3s brought up to 330 P4 specifications, though they had Weber carburetors rather than fuel injection and continued with an updated version of the P3's gearbox. Visually, the 330 P4 and 412 P were identical.

Endurance ace Chris Amon joined Ferrari as a works driver for the 1967 season. Quoted in *Scarlet Passion*, by Anthony Pritchard, he said, "The P4 was a very pleasant car to drive, as it was a great deal more nimble than the Fords I was used to. Although it lacked the ultimate top end pace of the 7-litre Ford, it gave you the feeling that you could drive it to the maximum for the whole race, which really wasn't the case for the Fords, especially the brakes...."

The 330 P4 underwent a number of days testing at Daytona, and the preparation paid off. In the season's first race at the Florida track, Amon teamed with Lorenzo Bandini to win the 24 Hours. Another P4 was second, and a 412 P was third. A Ford GT40 won at Sebring, then P4s finished 1-2 at Monza, Amon and Bandini again the victors. Le Mans went to a GT40, but P4s ran 2-3. It was another donnybrook of a season, but this time Ferrari emerged on top to recapture the prototypes world title.

However, rulesmakers delivered an unpleasant surprise when they threw cold water on a tremendous three-way rivalry among Ferrari, Ford, and Porsche. They effectively neutralized the biggest weapons of Ford and Ferrari by limiting the top prototypes class to cars with no more than 3.0-liters displacement. For the Sports Car Championship, engine size was limited to 5.0-liters and manufacturers had to build a minimum of 50 cars to qualify.

"I remember when I heard that, for I was screaming," said Franco Lini, who was then Ferrari's team manager. "I found myself saying 'Next year you will not see any Ferrari cars.' When the organizers asked why, I said 'Because Ferrari is a small factory and we don't have the money to build 50 cars for homologation....'"

Indeed, there were no "works" Ferraris entered at any FIA-sanctioned endurance events in 1968, only older cars run by privateers. But that didn't mean Ferrari had abandoned endurance racing altogether.

350 Can Am

1968-1971
350 CAN AM, 612 P & 712 P

LOST IN TRANSLATION: FERRARI'S SPORTS-RACING ACUMEN DOESN'T CONVERT TO CAN AM SUCCESS

The Canadian/American Challenge Cup was inaugurated in 1966, kicking off some of the most unbridled competition in the annals of motorsport.

Taking place on road courses in Canada and the United States, Can Am was open to invention and allowed most any innovation. Engines were huge, made even more powerful by liberal use of supercharging and turbocharging. Aerodynamic invention was rampant. Can Am machines, for a number of years, were faster than Formula 1 cars.

Ferrari's entry into the series was the idea of Luigi Chinetti, its American importer. Ferrari's most-powerful prototypes had been benched by regulations changes after Le Mans in 1967, so Chinetti had his North American Racing Team's 412 P sent to Ferrari for modifications that would enable it to compete in Can Am.

The body's center section was lengthened, the nose streamlined, the roof removed, and the rear shortened. Mechanicals were largely unaltered, however, and Ferrari knew that with only 450 horsepower, it would likely be down on power compared with top Can Am rivals, and it attempted to make up for it with light weight.

Christened the 350 Can Am, the car was seventh in its maiden outing, at Bridgehampton in New York, then couldn't finish its second race, at Mosport outside Toronto. Ferrari subsequently converted two 330 P4s to 350 Can Am specifications and sent them over to be campaigned by Ferrari West Coast

distributor Bill Harrah. The two finished fifth and eighth in their first appearance at Laguna Seca. One then came in eighth at Riverside.

For 1968, Ferrari returned to the Can Am with the 612 P. This had the series' characteristic air-foil wing mounted midships on struts. And it used what was then Ferrari's largest-ever engine, a 6.2-liter 620-horsepower V-12 mated to a four-speed gearbox. Alas, the 612 competed in only the season's last race, at Las Vegas, where it didn't last a lap. It survived a multicar pileup, only to have its big V-12 stall in the resulting sandstorm.

The 612 was returned to Ferrari where the body was modified and engine output increased to 640 horsepower. It returned to America for the '69 season and finished third in its first race, at Watkins Glen. Later that year, Ferrari shipped over a 6.9-liter V-12, giving the model the designation 712 P. It competed in just one race, and was black-flagged for a rules infraction.

Ferrari never seemed to have its heart in Can Am, and the results were the evidence.

612 P

350 CAN AM, 612 P & 712 P

| 350 CAN AM 1968 |
| 612 P 1968-1969 |
| 712 P 1971 |

Number made:

350 Can Am:	3
612 P:	1
712 P:	1

Engine:

350 Can Am:	3967cc V-12 DOHC, 450 hp @ 8200 rpm
612 P:	6222cc V-12, DOHC, 620-640 hp @ 7000 rpm
712 P:	6780cc V-12, DOHC, n/a

Wheelbase: 98.4 inches / 2500mm

Weight:

350 Can Am:	1,750 lbs.
612 P:	1,543 lbs.
712 P:	n/a

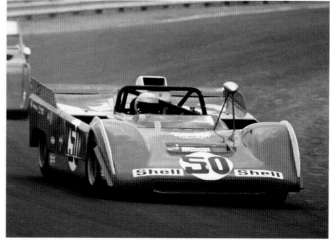

712 P

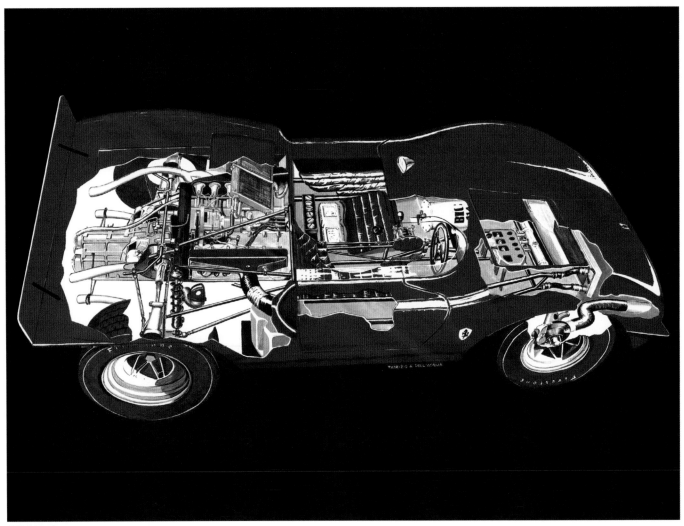

212 E Montagna

1969
212 E MONTAGNA

UP, UP, AND AWAY: AN AMALGAM OF ELEMENTS JELLS TO CREATE AN UNCOMMONLY SUCCESSFUL FERRARI

These were no mere sprints up a hillside, but soaring ascents of real mountains. It was the European Mountain Championship and it attracted some of the biggest names in motor racing. Thousands of spectators lined the twisting, miles-long climbs, cheering on all manner of machinery, from purpose-built sports-racers to the occasional F1 single-seater.

Ferrari, Porsche, and Abarth were the principal rivals in the late 1960s. Piloting a 196 SP in 1962 and a Dino 206 S in 1965, Ferrari team driver Ludovico Scarfiotti won two mountain championships during the decade. But it was another performance, a dominating exhibition in the decade's final season, that has entered into Ferrari lore.

In many ways the 212 E was a throwback to the old days, when Ferrari personnel borrowed ideas from disparate cars to

212 E MONTAGNA	
1969	
Number made:	1
Engine:	1991cc flat-12, DOHC, 320 hp @ 11,800 rpm
Transmission:	5-speed
Wheelbase:	94.5 inches / 2400mm
Weight:	1,002 lbs.

make a new one. The 212 E's chassis and suspension were largely taken from the 206 S. The car's open bodywork resembled the 350 Can Am's. Like the 206 S, the 212 E used a 2.0-liter engine, but instead of a V-6, it was a remarkable flat-12.

This was Ferrari's first use of a "boxer" twelve since 1964, and the powerplant was a testament to the brilliance of company chief engineer Mauro Forghieri.

"[He] was the finest engineer that I worked with," remembered driver Chris Amon in *Scarlet Passion*. "He was capable of engineering the whole car, including the engine and gearbox, something that few others have ever done."

Once Forghieri laid down the basics, he put engineer Stefano Jacaponi in charge of the project. Jacaponi started with the 1.5-liter flat-12 from Ferrari's '65 F1 campaign. He kept the stroke basically untouched, but enlarged the bore for a total displacement of 1991cc. The engine boasted double overhead cams, four valves per cylinder, and Lucas fuel injection for an output of 320 horsepower at 11,800 rpm.

And, as in the glory days of the 1950s and early '60s, the melding of ideas that created the 212 E was immensely successful. With works driver Peter Schetty at the wheel, the car won all seven races it entered during 1969, setting a course record at each outing, and taking the series championship.

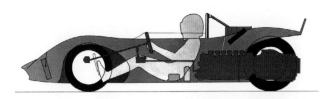

512 S

1969-1971
512 S & 512 M

A BRAVE BUT LESS-THAN-BRILLIANT BIG-BORE RETURN TO ENDURANCE RACING'S MAJOR LEAGUES

512 S & 512 M	
512 S 1969-1970	
512 M 1970-1971	
Number made:	25
Engine:	
512 S:	4994cc V-12, DOHC, 550-575 hp @ 8500 rpm
512 M:	4994cc V-12, DOHC, 600 hp @ 8500 rpm
Transmission:	5-speed
Wheelbase:	94.0 inches / 2390mm
Weight:	1,850 lbs.

Enzo Ferrari and his company were in the midst of a maelstrom in 1969. He successfully negotiated the sale of his firm to Fiat, competed in Formula 1, Formula 2, the mountain championship, and Can Am, all while building road cars and battling the unions.

That makes Ferrari's return to the endurance-racing campaign in 1970 with the 512 S all the more remarkable. Porsche was already competing with its 917 when Mauro Forghieri and his men designed and developed the 512. "As usual," Forghieri remembered, "Ferrari gave me no technical directive. Instead, there was the imposition to use existing tools for the engine, gearbox, and suspension."

Forghieri explained that "the 512 had the same chassis as the 612 P Cam Am car, but with a different body," and the car's 5.0-liter V-12 was developed much the same way. Bore and stroke were reduced, and once the engine was completed, a five-speed gearbox developed in-house was bolted to its rear. The body was developed by Giacomo Caliri in both coupe and spyder form.

It was a valiant effort by Ferrari, but 1970 proved to be a long season. A 512 finished third to two 917s at Daytona, then scored a victory in the 12 Hours of Sebring driven by the works team of Ignazio Giunti, Nino Vaccarella, and Mario Andretti. That was the car's only win, though other highlights included a second at Francorchamps and a 2-3-4 finish at Monza.

Early in the season, Forghieri said, he and his crew realized the 512 S "was not competitive on high-speed circuits" so they began developing a new model. The result was the 512 M (Modificato). "It was essentially a 512 S with a new body done by Caliri," Forghieri said.

As was typical Ferrari, engine development continued and the 512 M went into action with 600 horsepower, some 25 more than the S. The car retired in its first outing, then Giunti and Jacky Ickx easily beat the 917s at the season's final race at Kyalami in South Africa.

That victory proved the swan song for the 512. New regulations for 1972 made 5.0-liter cars ineligible for the championship, so Ferrari instructed Forghieri to concentrate on further developing the company's 3.0-liter V-12.

512 M

312 P

312 P

1969-1973
312 P & 312 PB

GOING OUT ON A HIGH NOTE: FERRARI WEAVES 3.0-LITER MAGIC FOR A ROUSING SPORTS-PROTOTYPE FINALE

Displacement limits that outlawed 5.0-liter sports-racing proto-types caused Ferrari to skip 1968's endurance-racing season. But Maranello was back for the 1969 campaign with the 312 P.

Its chassis and underpinnings were derived from those of the V-12 612 Can Am. For power, it used a 3.0-liter V-12 similar to the twincam unit found in 1969's 312 F1 car, though the proto-type had different heads and single overhead cams. Both the F1 and prototype cars had a quoted output of approximately 430 horsepower, though the 312 P peaked at lower rpm in the interest of longevity.

Initially, the bodywork was a stark-but-curvy spyder shell that resembled the 612 P. This edition made its racing debut at Sebring, where Chris Amon put it on the pole, only to finish second because of a minor accident. This 312 P also finished second at Spa and fourth at Brands Hatch.

For Le Mans 1969, Ferrari entered a pair 312s, each fitted with a roof to create strikingly low-slung coupes. Neither fin-ished; one crashed, the other had gearbox problems. The 312 Ps then went to America, where Ferrari's U.S. rep Luigi Chinetti refitted them with new open bodies; one finished fourth overall at Daytona in 1970.

Ferrari's plan for 1971 was to use the season for testing, then make an all-out assault on the endurance crown in '72. His sports-prototype "test bed" was the 312 PB.

312 P & 312 PB	
312 P 1969	
312 PB 1971-1973	
Number made:	
312 P:	3
312 PB:	12
Engine:	
312 P:	2989cc V-12, DOHC, 420 hp @ 9800 rpm
312 PB:	2991cc flat-12, DOHC, 450 hp @ 10,800 rpm
Transmission:	5-speed
Wheelbase:	
312 P:	93.3 inches / 2370mm
312 PB:	87.4 inches / 2220mm
Weight:	
312 P:	1,497 lbs.
312 PB:	n/a

This was another stark spyder, in many ways an F1 car with a body. In fact, its flat-12 engine, gearbox, and suspension came directly from Ferrari's 312 B single-seater. Its body was efficient, but not as dramatic in appearance as the 312 P coupes. It didn't matter.

In the first year of Ferrari's test-then-assault plan, 312 PBs counted among their moderate successes the Clay Regazzoni/Brian Redman win at Kyalami. But in 1972, PBs dominated what was now called the Sports World Championship for Makes. Every race they entered, they won.

It started with a first by Ronnie Peterson and Tim Schenken at Buenos Aires. Jacky Ickx and Mario Andretti then went on a tear, winning the Daytona 6 Hours, the Sebring 12 Hours, and the 1,000 km at Brands Hatch. Regazzoni and Ickx were first at Monza. Redman and Arturo Merzario won at Spa-Francorchamps. Merzario and Sandro Munari finished first in the Targa Florio. It was Peterson and Schenken again at the Nurburgring, and Ickx and Andretti at Watkins Glen. Other PB victories included Imola and Kyalami.

The 312 PBs returned pretty much unchanged for 1973. Ickx and Redman were victorious at Monza and at Nurburgring, and while the car consistently dotted the top-10 finishers, Ferrari narrowly missed the championship. And that spelled the end of its full-works participation in sports-prototype racing.

The 312s, especially in PB form, sent Maranello out of an endurance-racing era with its head held high. Now the factory turned its concentration to Formula 1.

312 PB

365 GTB/4 Competition

365 GTB/4 COMPETITION

1971-1973

Number made:	15
Engine:	4390cc V-12, DOHC,
	352-450 hp @ n/a rpm
Transmission:	5-speed
Wheelbase:	94.5 inches / 2400mm
Weight:	2,712 lbs.

1971-1973
365 GTB/4 COMPETITION

ONE OF MARANELLO'S ALL-TIME ROADGOING GREATS SHOWS THAT IT'S NO ONE-TRICK CAVALLINO

Though Ferrari's efforts in sport-car racing in the early 1970s were focused on the pure-competition prototypes, that didn't stop the clamoring from its clients to continue the tradition of customers racing Maranello's road-based GTs.

They were rewarded with special versions of the company's leading street performer of the day, the 364 GTB/4 Daytona. The Daytona had been introduced at the 1968 Paris Auto Show, and shortly thereafter an aluminum-body version was prepared for U.S. distributor Luigi Chinetti to race at Le Mans in 1969. It crashed in practice, returned to the factory, and was sold.

More than a year passed before production began on what were officially the Competition Daytonas. Ferrari built them in three batches, for a total of 15 cars. Five were made in late 1970 and '71, another quintet was constructed in 1972, and the final five were built in 1973.

Each had a lighter-than-stock body—as much as 400 pounds lighter—with extensive use of aluminum and fiberglass. They also used plexiglass side windows.

All retained the Daytona's 4.4-liter twincam V-12. The first batch was rated at the stock 352 horsepower. The second group was tweaked with different heads and a higher compression ratio, sending horsepower over 400, while handling was improved with wider wheels. The third series was the most heavily modified. Horsepower rose to around 450, antiroll bars and brakes were changed, and a roll cage was installed.

Still, the 1970s were a far different era than the 1950s and early '60s, when Ferrari catered to the racing needs of prominent importers, distributors, and clients. Now, factory support was minimal at best. Owners thus took matters into their own hands, and had racing shops such as Holman and Moody modify their cars. Chinetti even had stylist Giovanni Michelotti construct an entirely different body for his North American Racing Team's 1975 Le Mans entry.

Competition Daytonas began racing in the 1971 season. Notable placings that year included 12th overall at Sebring, fourth and ninth at the Tour de France, and third at the Paris 1000 km.

The cars fared even better in 1972. Highlights included a first-in-GT at Le Mans for the team of French Ferrari importer Charles Pozzi. Other privateer GTB/4s finished fifth through ninth in the 24 Hour classic. At the Tour de France, it was an outright win for Jean-Claude Andruet, with another Competition Daytona finishing second.

Usually a bit overweight, but durable and powerful, racing GTB/4s continued to compete through the 1970s. At Le Mans, they were sixth overall in 1973 and fifth and sixth overall in 1974. At Daytona, it was a seventh overall in 1975 and a sixth overall in 1976.

Then, in 1979, five years after production had stopped, a series-three model driven by Americans John Morton and Tony Adamowicz capped the Competition Daytona story at the 24 Hours of Daytona with a first in the GTO class and a remarkable second overall behind the winning Porsche 935.

512 BB LM

512 BB LM	
1979-1980	
Number made:	24
Engine:	4942cc flat-12, DOHC, 480 @ 7200 rpm
Transmission:	5-speed
Wheelbase:	98.5 / 2500mm
Weight:	2,380 lbs.

1979-1980
512 BB LM

EVER-OPTIMISTIC PRIVATEERS LEARN HOW DIFFICULT IT HAD BECOME TO MAKE A RACE WINNER OF A ROAD CAR

No sooner had Daytona production ended than Ferrari's energetic U.S. distributor Luigi Chinetti began eyeing the company's first midengine 12-cylinder road car, the 365 GT4/BB, as a potential endurance-racer.

With minimal to no factory input, one was modified for use by his North American Racing Team. Rear body work was widened, larger wheels and tires were fitted, and weight-adding luxury amenities were removed. These race-prepped 365s were good performers, but not good enough. The car's highest finish in several seasons of competition by NART and others was a sixth overall at Sebring in 1975.

Its flat-12 enlarged from 4.4-liters to 5.0, the 365 GT4/BB became the 512 BB in 1976, and it was only a matter of time before it was seen at Le Mans and elsewhere. This go-round, the factory was slightly more involved in preparing cars that would be campaigned by privateers. Some were heavily modified, with wings and spoilers; others looked relatively stock. Four lined up at Le Mans in '78. They were joined by a 365 GT4/BB fitted with the 5.0-liter engine; it was the only Boxer to complete the 24 Hours, finishing 16th overall.

365 GT4/BB

For 1979, a more thoroughly prepared set of competition 512 BBs was made available. Known as the 512 BB LM, these factory-developed machines had new bodies shaped in the Pininfarina wind tunnel. The nose was extended, a new roofline ran to the back of the extended tail, and a wing for additional downforce was placed at the rear. They were almost 18 inches longer than the roadgoing 512 Boxer, and weighed some 1,235 pounds less. Flared fenders covered 10-inch wheels up front, 13s in back. The fuel-injected 5.0-liter flat-12 pumped out 480 horsepower, 120 above the stock motor.

They raced first at Daytona, in the form of two entries for the team of Ferrari's French importer, Charles Pozzi, and one for NART. The results were a harbinger of things to come. Two cars were withdrawn. The last ran for six hours before being sidelined in an accident. Four BB LMs lined up for Le Mans that year, with similar results. One finished 12th overall, the other three retired.

In 1980, six BB LMs ran at Le Mans. One finished 23rd overall, with the Pozzi entry coming in 10th for the best finish for a BB LM in any 24-hour race.

All this was more evidence of how difficult it had become for a production-based car to compete at the highest levels of endurance racing, especially without full factory participation.

288 GTO Evoluzione

288 GTO EVOLUZIONE, F40 LM, F40 GT & F40 GTE		
288 GTO EVOLUZIONE 1985-1986 F40 LM 1989-1994 F40 GT 1993-1994 F40 GTE 1994-1996		

Number made:
288 GTO
Evoluzione: 5
F40 LM: 20
F40 GT: 7
F40 GTE: 7

Engine:
288 GTO
Evoluzione: Longitudinally mounted 2855cc twin-turbo V-8, DOHC, 650 hp @ 7800 rpm
F40 LM: 2936cc twin-turbo V-8, DOHC, 720 hp @ 7500 rpm
F40 GT: 2936cc twin-turbo V-8, DOHC, 560 hp @ n/a rpm
F40 GTE: 2936cc (est.), 3500cc (est), or 3600cc twin-turbo V-8, DOHC, 660-780 hp @ n/a rpm

Transmission: 5-speed
F40 GTE: 5-speed sequential
Wheelbase: 96.4 inches / 2450mm
Weight:
288 GTO
Evoluzione: 2,050 lbs
F40 LM: 2,310 lbs.
F40 GT: 2,200 lbs. (approx.)
F40 GTE: n/a

1985-1996
288 GTO EVOLUZIONE, F40 LM, F40 GT, & F40 GTE

ITS KILLER-B GROUNDED, FERRARI RECOVERS TO CREATE A SERIES OF ENTERTAINING PRODUCTION-BASED RACERS

Ferrari's 288 GTO broke cover at 1984's Geneva Motor Show to great fanfare, for it marked a return to endurance competition for Ferrari. This, however, was sports-prototype racing of a different stripe. It was the first time Ferrari tackled the world of rallying.

Specifically, it would compete in a rallye category known as Group B. Incredibly popular in the early and mid 1980s, Group B attracted some of the world's wildest cars to a series of events staged on circuits that combined paved and unpaved sections.

The GTO that Ferrari intended to use was cut from a different cloth than its already quite-exotic street counterpart. The use of carbon-fiber composites was even more extensive, and the V-8 was greatly modified, with larger turbochargers and a higher compression ratio for more than 600 horsepower.

The body was considerably different from that of the production 288 GTO, as well. It had a different nose, cabin, and sides, and a rear with a high wing for downforce. Weighing just over 2,000 pounds, its top speed was reported at 225 mph.

It was called the GTO Evoluzione, but it never competed in Group B. As development continued, fatal accidents on the circuit caused the series to be canceled.

The Evoluzione thus became the starting point for 1987's F40 road car. In 1989, its racing offspring, the F40 LM, appeared. Done at the instigation of France's influential importer, Pozzi Ferrari, the model was developed by renowned Ferrari GT and sports-prototype tuner Michelotto. It featured a reinforced chassis, revised suspension, larger brakes and wheels, different rear wing, and a much more powerful engine. It raced with moderate results in America's IMSA series.

Three years later, Michelotto developed the F40 GT in response to the renewed interest in sports and GT racing. Aimed at the Italian Supercar Championship, the F40 GT used many lessons learned on the LMs. New suspension pieces and settings helped handling. A different exhaust and turbos with slightly higher boost lifted horsepower to around 560.

The F40 GT fared well in competition in Italy, winning eight of 10 races in 1993, and 14 of 20 in 1994.

The final variation on the theme that started with the 288 GTO Evoluzione was the F40 GTE. Made by Michelotto, it was aimed in part at a series formed essentially as a venue for priva- teers to race competition versions of the day's fastest road- based GTs. Called the BPR GT Championship, it eventually attracted such supercars as the McLaren F1.

The GTE had a stronger chassis and bigger brakes than the F40 GT. And in addition to the 3.0-liter twin-turbo V-8 used by its predecessor, at various times, it was fitted with 3.5- and 3.6-liter versions and a sequential manual gearbox. Running at tracks such as Suzuka, Spa-Francorchamps, Le Mans, and Monza, the seriously fast GTE placed in the top three 13 times and won four races from 1994 to 1996.

F40 LM

F40 GTE

F40 GTE (left)

333 SP

1994-1998
333 SP

CURTAIN CALL: A TRIUMPHANT RETURN TO SPORTS-RACING WITH A SHOWCASE FOR MODERN FERRARI

The 333 SP was born from a vision shared by two stalwart figures in Ferrari history—Piero Ferrari and racing driver Giampiero Moretti, who had founded the MOMO accessory company.

In early 1993, Moretti was in Ferrari's office, telling him he wanted to end his racing career in a Ferrari. From that conversation was born the 333 SP, the factory's first pure sports-racing car since the 312 PB was launched 20 years earlier.

The America International Motor Sport Association series was changing its rules for the 1994 season, making it the perfect venue for a new Ferrari. This exposure was important to Maranello because, at that time, there were no Formula 1 races on American soil.

Piero Ferrari remembered telling Moretti, "The problem will be convincing others in management that this is a good idea. In short, the effort has to be successful as well as make economic sense." Ferrari put together a brief, crunched some numbers, and pitched the idea to company CEO Luca Cordero di Montezemolo. He bit, and greenlighted the project.

Ferrari then turned to Gianpaolo Dallara, a gifted engineer who started his career at Ferrari in 1959, but had subsequently worked with Maserati, Lamborghini, and others. Dallara assigned his engineers to work with Ferrari personnel. One group developed the chassis, engine, and gearbox, another the body. All understood the cars would be sold to privateers, meaning the design had to take into account discrepancies in

333 SP, 333 SP EVOLUZIONE & 333 SP MICHELOTTO		
333 SP 1994-1995		
333 SP EVOLUZIONE 1995-1996		
333 SP MICHELOTTO 1997-1998		
Number made:		
333 SP:	9	
333 SP Evoluzione:	5	
333 SP Michelotto:	25	
Engine:	3997cc V-12, DOHC, 650 hp @ 11,500 rpm	
Transmission:	5-speed	
Wheelbase:	108.2 inches / 2750mm	
Weight:	1,956 lbs.	

the abilities of the mechanics and pit crews.

The 333's V-12 derived from the 4700cc 513-horsepower engine in the roadgoing F50. The stroke was reduced to bring capacity within IMSA's 4.0-liter limit, and the heads had five valves per cylinder instead of four. Digital fuel injection topped it off. Final horsepower rating was 650 at 11,500 rpm.

The chassis was effectively a Formula 1 tub made wider to meet IMSA's two-seat requirement. It was constructed of carbon-fiber composites and an aluminum honeycomb core. Suspension also followed Formula 1 techniques with pushrods front and rear. Brakes were large Brembo discs.

The bodywork employed carbon-fiber composites as well, and was developed with the help of Dallara's wind tunnel. As the 333 project was under way, Ferrari hired British engineer Tony Southgate as a consultant. This initially concerned Dallara. "Though we chose the way we felt was best," he recalled, "what would have happened if this guy came in and said, 'No,

we don't go that way?'" But the instant the two men met, Dallara knew Ferrari had made a good decision, as Southgate contributed to the design's aerodynamic efficiency.

Piero Ferrari recalled that a number of engineers inside his company had a twinkle in their eyes as the 333 SP was developed. It had been two decades since their last purpose-built sports-racing car, and all remembered how victories at Le Mans and other 24-hour races spoke volumes about the reliability of Ferraris.

To the delight of all involved, the 333 SP did not disappoint. Its first race was in April 1994, at Road Atlanta, and the SPs finished 1-2-5. American Jay Cochran drove the winning car, with Moretti the second-place finisher. In the following race, at Lime Rock, Moretti won, and he scored two more victories that year. But because the car had not competed in the season's first two races, Ferrari narrowly missed winning the IMSA world sports-car championship.

Things started poorly in 1995, when only one of the four 333 SPs at Daytona finished. But that race was the exception. The Ferraris won at Sebring, Shearwater, Lime Rock, Texas World Speedway, and Phoenix International Raceway. Ferrari easily won the 1995 IMSA championship.

Dallara continued to develop and build the model into 1997, at which time construction was taken over by Ferrari tuner Michelotto. This was the version that helped Moretti achieve a dream finish to his career. In 1998's opening contest, the 24 Hour race at Daytona, he shared outright victory with 333 SP codrivers Mauro Baldi and Didier Theys. Then, just weeks later, in the 12 Hours of Sebring, the trio's 333 SP finished first again.

333 SP

575 GTC

550 GTS & 575 GTC

550 GTS & 575 GTC	
2000-	
Number made:	
550 GTS:	10 (approx.)
575 GTC:	n/a
Engine:	
550 GTS:	5993cc V-12, DOHC, 585 hp @ 6250 rpm
575 GTC:	5997cc V-12, DOHC, 600 hp @ 6000 rpm
Transmission:	6-speed sequential
Wheelbase:	98.5 inches / 2500mm
Weight:	
550 GTS:	2,350 lbs.
575 GTC:	n/a

2000-
550 GTS & 575 GTC

EUROPE AND AMERICA GET A TASTE OF FERRARI V-12, AND THE FACTORY DEVELOPS A NEW GT-RACING APPETITE

The 550 Maranello's 1996 introduction marked a return to the front-engine two-seat V-12 Ferrari. Its spiritual predecessor, the Daytona of some two decades earlier, had a successful track carrier. Could history repeat itself?

The first competition 550 appeared in 2000, in response to customer demand and a recent change in endurance-racing rules. No longer could thinly disguised full-race prototypes compete as "GT" cars. GT racers had to be just that, and the rules encouraged individuals, as well as automakers, to create competition versions.

That gave rise to the 550 GTS, constructed outside Ferrari by experienced companies such as Prodrive. The target was to compete at Le Mans for the FIA GT Championship and in North America in the American Le Mans Series.

Roadgoing 550s were stripped of several hundred pounds through the use of composite body panels. The new body featured a fresh front and larger fenders to cover bigger wheels and tires. Engine displacement and compression ratio were increased, bumping output to more than 580 horsepower. A new six-speed gearbox was installed.

In the 2000 FIA GT Championship, the 550 GTS suffered a string of race-ending failures. It fared considerably better in '01, garnering a number of top-10 finishes. In 2002, it dominated the GT Championship, chalking up four wins, plus two more in the American Le Mans Series.

This piqued the factory's interest, and in 2003, Ferrari introduced its own version, the 575 GTC. It was designed in-house and built by a factory-approved subcontractor, N-Technology.

The 575 GTC also had a composite body with bulging fenders, a new front end, and a large wing mounted on the rear deck. The 5997cc V-12 pumped out 600 horsepower, and the gearbox was a six-speed sequential. Brakes were large Brembo discs.

The 575 GTC scored a victory straight out of the box in its first race, the October 2003 event in Portugal. But in a tribute to the skills of the nonfactory efforts, the older 550 GTS proved more consistent: It won the FIA GT Championship in 2004.

360 GT

360 GT & 360 GTC	
2002-2004	
Number made:	
360 GT:	20
360 GTC:	n/a
Engine:	
360 GT:	3586cc V-8, DOHC, 430 hp @ 8500 rpm
360 GTC:	3586cc V-8, DOHC, 445 hp @ 8750 rpm
Transmission:	6-speed sequential
Wheelbase:	102.3 inches / 2600mm
Weight:	2,425 lbs.

2002-2004
360 GT
& 360 GTC

YOU CAN TAKE THE FACTORY TEAM OUT OF SPORTS-CAR RACING, BUT YOU CAN'T KEEP RACERS OUT OF FERRARIS

In the early 1990s, Ferrari's sales were lagging, particularly for its "entry-level" 348 line. To boost interest in the midengine two-seater, Ferrari launched its popular "Challenge" Series. Production 348s were given a slight massage, then pitted against one another in a series of races, often on major tracks in support of top-flight pro events.

The racing was highly competitive and the series proved so popular with Ferrari's clientele that the tradition continued with the 348's successors, the F355 and 360 Mondial.

In 2000, the year after the 360 was introduced, several 360 Challenge cars found their way into the FIA GT Championship. The 360 Challenge was in essence a road car, but with fewer amenities to lighten weight, with grippier tires, and different wheels and brakes. The 3.6-liter V-8 was not significantly altered, but racing shock absorbers replaced the road car's electronic suspension control, and ride height was lowered with racing springs and aluminum bushings. Several 360 Challenges, prepared and raced by outside firms, finished GT Championship races in the top-10 in class.

This led to creation of the 360 GT. Done in conjunction with Ferrari tuner Michelotto, the 360 GT was some 200 pounds lighter than the 360 Challenge. It got further suspension upgrades, massive Brembo brakes, and a large rear wing. The 3.6-liter V-8 was boosted slightly to 430 horsepower, and used the available six-speed sequential gearbox. It scored multiple class wins in the FIA's N-GT class in 2002 and 2003. Another highlight was a second overall placing at the 24 Hours of Daytona in 2003.

In 2004, Ferrari introduced the 360 GTC, also done in collaboration with Michelotto. Like the 360 GT, the GTC weighed 2,425 pounds—the minimum allowed by class rules—but was an even more-aggressive machine. The GTC used the basic, mildly race-prepped bodywork of the 360 Challenge Stradale, but added a new, large rear-mounted wing, giving the GTC a different appearance from the 360 GT.

Steel disc brakes were fitted, the front with six-piston calipers, the rears with four-piston calipers. The 3.6-liter V-8 made 445 horsepower at 8,750 rpm, thanks in large part to new Magneti Marelli electronics. The car garnered a class victory at the Czech Republic's Brno raceway in 2004.

In racing, Ferrari's focus had for some years clearly been on Formula 1. But thanks to a cooperative effort between factory-affiliated engineers and tuners, and a legion of always-enthusiastic competition-oriented Ferrari owners, Cavallino sports cars were once again an exciting presence on the world's premier race courses.

360 GTC

The
Formula 1
Cars

125 F1

1948-1950
125 F1

**ENZO'S FIRST GRAND PRIX CARS SHOW PROMISE, BUT THE
PROUD OLD GUARD WOULD PROVE TOUGH TO BEAT**

After World War II, Formula 1 took longer to gel than sports-
car competition. It was called Grand Prix racing prior to the war,
when it was a technological tour de force and teams benefited
from government backing as part of the political propaganda
machine. After the war, financing for proper engineering, materials, fuel, and even the venues was in short supply.

When Ferrari entered the fray in 1948, he used his 125 S
sports-racer as the starting point for the first Ferrari Grand Prix
racer, the 125 F1. Like the sports-racer, it used Ferrari's compact, high-revving 1497cc V-12. But chief engineer Gioachino
Colombo exploited F1 rules and followed the era's typical practice of supercharging. This boosted horsepower from 118 in the
125 S to 230. Both used a five-speed gearbox.

Known originally as the 125 Grand Prix, this was the first single-seater to wear the Ferrari badge. Its torpedo-shaped body
was a pleasing design, with a large eggcrate grille, long nose,
exposed wheels, and proper proportions. The frame was of
steel tubes with struts and crossmembers. The front suspension
followed the lead of the 125 S, with double wishbones, a transverse leaf spring, and shock absorbers. In the rear were longitudinal struts, a torsion bar, and shock absorbers.

125 F1	
1948-1950	
Number made:	10
Engine:	
1948:	1497cc V-12, SOHC, 230-260 hp @ 7000 rpm
1949-1950:	1497cc V-12, DOHC, Roots-type Supercharger, 280 hp @ 7500 rpm
Transmission:	
1948-1949:	5-speed
1950:	4-speed
Wheelbase:	
1948:	85.0 inches / 2160mm
1949:	93.6 inches / 2380mm
1950:	91.3 inches / 2320mm
Weight:	1,540 lbs.

The 125 F1 first appeared in September at the race in Turin. Three started, and the one driven by Raymond Sommer finished third overall. A month later, Giuseppe "Nino" Farina drove a 125 F1 to Ferrari's first Grand Prix victory, at Garda, in Italy.

The winner at Turin, and the cars to beat during this period in F1, were the Type 158s from Alfa Romeo. Four of the sophisticated monopostos had survived the war, and with a bit of refurbishment, they were dominating the competition. Ironically, it was Enzo himself who had helped build the foundation for this dominance in his prewar stint at the helm of Alfa's racing effort.

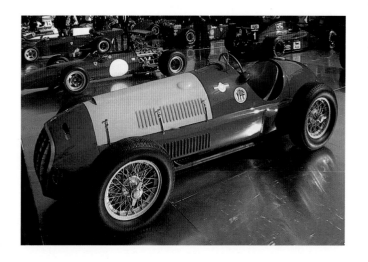

For the 1949 Italian Grand Prix at Monza, Ferrari introduced a new 125. This car had a longer chassis with similar underpinnings, but the big news was the engine. It now had double overhead cams and a two-stage Rootes supercharger, boosting horsepower to 280.

Formula 1 as a description for Grand Prix racing came into use in 1947, with the establishment of the sport's governing body, the Federation Internationale de l'Automobile (FIA), headquartered in Paris. In 1950, the FIA established F1's World Championship of Drivers, based on points per race. The FIA would not designate an F1 constructors championship until 1958, so in these early years, the manufacturers looked to the drivers for reflected glory.

Late in 1950, Ferrari shortened the 125's chassis and modified the rear suspension by using a de Dion tube and leaf springs. The new four-speed gearbox became integral with the final drive. That made the car extremely competitive, but it still wasn't enough to unseat Alfa Romeo. Alfa won all six Grand Prix races it entered and its driver Nino Farina, who had left Ferrari after the 1949 season, was F1's first world champion.

375 F1

1950-1951
375 F1

FERRARI PUNCTURES ALFA'S F1 DOMINANCE, AND TAKES A SIDE TRIP TO THE INDY 500

The final 125 served as the basis for the 375 F1, the model that broke Alfa Romeo's stranglehold on Formula 1.

Rules allowed use of a 1.5-liter engine with supercharger or a maximum of 4.5-liters with natural aspiration. Supercharging generated incredible power, and had been Alfa's strength. But supercharging also consumed lots of fuel, and Ferrari now felt it was his principal rival's Achille's heel.

And so was born the 375 F1. It continued use of the 125's tubular chassis in its longer wheelbase form of 91.3 inches (2320mm). The suspension and four-speed gearbox were carried over. But instead of a supercharged 1.5, the V-12 was a naturally aspirated 4.5-liter of 330-380 horsepower. This was the culmination of an Aurelio Lampredi-designed series of unsupercharged Ferrari F1 V-12s that began as a 3322cc unit in the 275 F1, followed by a 4101cc engine for the 340 F1.

The 4.5 made its debut at the all-important Italian Grand Prix at Monza in September 1950. It just missed setting the pole, and ran a close second for the majority of the race before retiring with six laps to go.

But the die had been cast, and the man who punctured Alfa's F1 dominance was a young Argentinean in his first year as a Ferrari works driver. Froilan Gonzalez, 29, was the son of a Chevrolet dealer and an immensely talented driver who originally came to Europe as a companion for countryman Juan Manuel Fangio. Fangio was now driving for Alfa, and the turning point was July 14, 1951, at the British Grand Prix.

"Two to three days before the British Grand Prix Juan drove me around the Silverstone circuit in the Alfa," Gonzales recalled in *Ferrari 1947-1997.* "'Pepe,' he said after we had studied the course, 'I think you are going to win this one.'"

Fangio was right. The Alfas were extremely thirsty, averaging just 1.8 mpg, giving Ferrari the advantage of one fewer fuel stop, critical in what for the period was a short race.

"I still have a photograph of us looking across at each other as we drove side by side down the main straight," Gonzales remembered. "But his advantage went away at his first pit stop when his crew put in too much fuel, making his car too heavy."

The stocky Argentinean beat Fangio to the checkered flag. That ended an amazing run in which Alfa Romeos had finished

375 F1		
1950-1951		
Number made:	7	
Engine:	4494cc V-12, SOHC,	
	330-380 hp @ 7000-7500 rpm	
Transmission:	4-speed	
Wheelbase:	91.3 inches / 2320mm	
Weight:	1,870 lbs.	

first in every postwar Grand Prix event in which they were entered, more than two dozen races in all. The triumph over his former employer was a satisfying, if poignant, start to Enzo Ferrari's F1 legacy.

An interesting footnote to F1's first decade was that all its races, typically eight or so per season, were run in Europe—with one notable exception. From 1950 to 1960, America's Indianapolis 500 was among the events counted toward the F1 world championship. Thus, fabled Indy 500 winners such as Bill Vukovich and Rodger Ward are listed among drivers with F1 points.

For the traditional F1 field, travel to America for one race was impractical, and Indy was never treated seriously as a points opportunity. But Ferrari's U.S. importer and chief promoter, Lugi Chinetti, saw the publicity possibilities.

Ferrari thus prepared a variation of the 375 F1 to run in the Memorial Day classic. Called the 375 Indy, its naturally aspirated 4.5-liter was tuned for 400 horsepower, the chassis was strengthened, and aerodynamics were improved. As a shakedown run, three were sent to the 1953 Turin Grand Prix, where Luigi "Gigi" Villoresi's finished first.

A fourth was prepared for Ferrari works driver Alberto Ascari, and he qualified it for the '52 Indy 500 at just over 134 mph, good enough to start in 19th position. The red 375 proved ill-suited to a long afternoon of punishment at the Brickyard, however. It lasted 40 laps, spinning in the fourth turn when a wheel hub collapsed. It was the only Ferrari to compete in an Indy 500.

375 Indy

Grand Prix racing, 1930: Achille Varzi muscles an Alfa P2

Formula 1: At the Pinnacle of Motorsport

Formula 1 racing was some five decades old before it became known by that name. Motor racing's history stretches back to the late nineteenth century, and most early contests were lengthy point-to-point affairs, from Paris to Madrid, for example. Then, in 1906, the French coined the term "Grand Prix" to describe a motor competition in which participants started and finished in the same place, though still rarely on purpose-built tracks.

At about the same time, various national motor clubs established the Association Internationale des Automobile Clubs Reconnus (AIACR) to oversee international motor sport. The AIACR issued a calendar and rules for international motoring competition in 1908, and in 1924 constituted a Commission Sportive Internationale (CSI) to organize Grand Prix and other forms of international racing.

Up to World War II, it was quite normal to see a car compete in both a Grand Prix, on road or track, and in a long-distance road race. All that was needed were minor modifications—sometimes little more than simply removing the fenders—and the machine was ready to go.

Wheel-to-wheel at Watkins Glen, 1966

By the early 1930s, however, a competitive Grand Prix car was a purpose-built single-seater with a dedicated racing engine.

The first postwar Grand Prix was held in Nice in 1946, but shortages of gas and materials, coupled with the lack of capital, made these races few and far between. They did spread to other countries as the decade rolled on, but Grand Prix needed a shot in the arm to bring it to international prominence.

Then, in 1947, the term Formula 1 came into use when the AIACR reorganized itself as the Federation Internationale de l'Automobile (FIA). The World Championship of Drivers was begun in 1950.

For the first few seasons, races were run exclusively in European countries, except for the inclusion of the Indianapolis 500. Argentina joined the circuit in 1953, and the FIA established a world constructors championship in 1958.

That year's race in Argentina marked a turning point in Formula 1 competition. Stirling Moss won in an underpowered Cooper-Climax, the key to victory being the engine's placement: It was behind the driver. The rear-engine configuration has been *de rigueur* in all forms of open-wheel racing since the mid 1960s.

Formula 1 today is a multibillion-dollar enterprise, with circuits in Europe, North and South America, Australia, Asia, the Far East, and the Middle East and boasts a rabid, worldwide TV audience. It is considered the most technically demanding form of auto racing.

The crown jewel of the season is the Monaco Grand Prix run through the streets of ritzy Monte Carlo on the shores of the Mediterranean Sea. The course is one of the most challenging on the F1 circuit, and with a history traced to 1929, has Grand Prix's most evocative legacy.

World Champion driver, World Champion team, 2004

Formula 1 is the world's most-watched, most-lucrative, and most-controversial racing series

500 F2

1952-1953
500 F2

ALFA ROMEO IS VANQUISHED, AND FERRARI ENTERS THE REALM OF WORLD CHAMPIONS

After the 375 F1 victory at Silverstone in 1951, Ferrari easily defeated Alfa Romeo's 159s in the next two races, setting up a showdown at the season's final race in Spain. Alfas finished first and third, Ferraris second and fourth. That gave the championship to Alfa driver Juan Manuel Fangio.

But it was evident that the 159 and its supercharged engine were no longer capable of holding off Ferrari and its larger, naturally aspirated V-12. Alfa's owner, the Italian government, was unwilling to contribute funds to the company to develop an all-new car, so at the end of the season, Alfa Romeo reluctantly withdrew from racing.

With Alfa gone, the FIA recognized that Formula 1 faced a serious shortcoming. There were no other strong competitors to challenge Ferrari, let alone fill the grid. In April 1952, a decision was made to use the less-expensive Formula 2 series for the World Championship. F2 had been popular since its inception in 1948, due in part to its limiting maximum engine capacity to 2.0-liters.

500 F2	
1952-1953	
Number made:	11
Engine:	1985cc inline-four, SOHC, 185 hp @ 7500 rpm
Transmission:	4-speed
Wheelbase:	85.0 inches / 2160mm
Weight:	1,230 lbs.

Ferrari was ready. He began competing in F2 with the V-12-powered 166 F2. This was, in essence, a modified 166 Spyder Corsa sports-racing car. For 1949, the 166 F2 used a 125 F1 chassis, winning every race in which it entered. In 1950 it won 13 of 17 races.

In charge of 1952's F2 project was Ferrari chief engineer Aurelio Lampredi. "I would go into the factory on Sunday mornings to look over my affairs," he recounted in *Ferrari I Quattro Cilindri*. "Ferrari turned up and told me they'd launched the new project, an F2 with 2000cc capacity.

"'What would you do?' he asked.

"'I'd make a 4-cylinder,' I replied.

"'Do make me a sketch then, now.'"

A few intense hours later, Lampredi was finished. The 185-horsepower 1985cc inline-four was placed in a chassis that followed lessons learned in F1. The combination was virtually unbeatable.

The 500 F2 won seven of eight races in 1952, and made team driver Alberto Ascari Ferrari's first world champion. The car won seven of nine races in 1953, and Ascari was again world champion. On the way to his two titles, the former motorcycle racer from Milan finished first in nine consecutive races in which the 500 F2 competed. It was a Grand Prix record that would last the century, and beyond.

D50

1955-1956
D50

FROM THE ASHES OF LANCIA'S PROGRAM—AND THE DRIVER'S SEAT OF MERCEDES'—COMES A CHAMPIONSHIP

In 1954, the Grand Prix world championship ended its two-year hiatus under Formula 2 rules and was reconstituted under revised Formula 1 regulations. Now, engine capacity was limited to 2.5-liters naturally aspirated or 750cc supercharged.

Like most competitors, Ferrari went the naturally aspirated route. He continued use of Lampredi-designed four-cylinder engines in an update of his 553 F2 machines called the 553 F1. (The 533 F1's generous midsection reminded some of a shark's torso, and the car was nicknamed "Squalo.")

But there were two thorns in Ferrari's side that season. First, the 250 F from crosstown rival Maserati was a masterfully balanced machine, and it won the year's first two races. Then Mercedes-Benz entered F1 in the season's fourth race, and thereafter dominated the proceedings, winning the championship behind the driving of Juan Manuel Fangio.

At 1954's last race, in Spain, Lancia entered the fray. The Turin automaker's innovative Vittorio Jano-designed D50 showed considerable promise, setting fastest lap before retiring with mechanical problems. No one could know that Lancia would influence Ferrari's fortunes in a most unexpected way.

For 1955, Ferrari revised his cars' chassis, suspension, and

D50		
1955-1956		
Number made:	5	
Engine:	2486cc V-8, DOHC,	
1955:	250 hp @ 8100 rpm	
1956:	265 hp @ 8000 rpm	
Transmission:	5-speed	
Wheelbase:	89.7 inches / 2280mm	
Weight:		
1955:	1,360 lbs	
1956	1,420 lbs.	

bodywork and coaxed more horsepower out of the engine. The new racer was called the 555 F1 "Super Squalo," but it was to no avail. Mercedes dominated the season, the "Super Squalo's" lone victory coming at Monaco.

Soon after the start of the season, racing lost one of its immortals. Two-time world champion Alberto Ascari died at Monza in the wreck of a Ferrari he had borrowed for practice. Ascari was at the time Lancia's lead F1 driver. Lancia was already experiencing financial troubles, and Ascari's death was another layer of misery. In July, after protracted negotiations, Lancia handed over to Ferrari six D50s and the services of engineer Vittorio Jano. Fiat agreed to offer financial support so Ferrari could compete against the German onslaught.

The D50 was loaded with innovations. It boasted F1's first V-8 engine. Its gearbox and clutch were in unit with the final drive. And it wore its fuel tanks as bodyside pods. The tanks' placement helped in weight distribution and acted as aerodynamics aids.

Still, it wasn't enough to unseat Mercedes, and Fangio again won the 1955 world championship. But in the wake of the 1955 carnage at Le Mans, Mercedes decided to withdraw from Grand Prix and sports-car racing.

Fangio came over to Ferrari for the '56 F1 campaign. The D50 evolved, with Ferrari's men creating a modified body that incorporated the main fuel supply in the tail while retaining the side pods as auxiliary tanks. The suspension was altered, and additional bracing was employed in the engine compartment.

Fangio and the D50 claimed the world championship for Ferrari, its first since Ascari's in 1953. It was a thrillingly tight title charge, the great Argentinean finishing with 30 championship points to 27 for Stirling Moss in the Maserati. Ferrari's Peter Collins was third, with 25.

555 F1 "Super Squalo"

246 F1

1957-1960
Dino 246 F1
& Dino 256 F1

THE DINO V-6 GOES GRAND PRIX RACING, AND RUNS INTO THE FUTURE OF FORMULA 1

For 1957, Ferrari continued modifying the Lancia D50, now calling it the 801. But the car had changed so much it was unrecognizable from its original guise.

The coachwork was completely different, the front and rear suspension changed, the V-8's bore and stroke modified. Alas, its best individual race results were three second-place finishes, and Ferrari came in a distant runner-up to Maserati in the Grand Prix season.

But there were benefits to what appeared to be a bleak campaign. Ferrari was having great success in Formula 2 with its superb Dino 156 (1.5-liters, 6-cylinders). Named for Ferrari's first son, the 156 served as the basis for 1958's Dino 246 F1.

In Formula 1 guise, the six-cylinder engine was enlarged to 2417cc, good for 280 horsepower. The model was first tried at the final F1 race of 1957, then returned for 1958 with a number of modifications. These included telescopic shocks in front, and disc brakes in place of large drums in the rear.

Identified by the clear cover over its sextet of carburetor stacks, the 246 F1 propelled team driver Mike Hawthorn to the F1 world championship, the third for a Ferrari driver. The title was won through consistency. Over the 10 races, Hawthorn had only one victory, at Reims in France, but his five seconds and one third were enough to snare the championship by one point over fellow Brit Stirling Moss, who had four victories driving the Cooper-Climax and Vanwall cars. (This was the first year in which the FIA established an F1 Constructors Championship to go along with the driver's crown. Vanwall beat out Ferrari for the '58 title.)

DINO 246 F1 & DINO 256 F1	
DINO 246 F1 1957-1960	
DINO 256 F1 1959-1960	
Number made:	
246:	9
256:	1
Engine:	
246:	2417cc V-6, SOHC, 280 hp @ 8500 rpm
256:	2474cc V-6, SOHC, 290 hp @ 8800 rpm
Transmission:	
246:	4-speed, 5-speed (1960)
256:	5-speed
Wheelbase:	
246:	85.0 inches / 2160mm 90.5 inches / 2220mm (1960)
256:	90.5 inches / 2220mm
Weight:	1,230 lbs.

The Dino returned in 1959 as the Dino 256 F1. It was a prettier car, with more aerodynamic bodywork, and was fitted with Dunlop disc brakes at each corner, a new suspension, and a 2474cc V-6.

Ferrari ran both the 246 F1 and 256 F1 during 1959, but was still at a disadvantage in a season that marked a watershed change in motorsport.

Brit Tony Brooks was a Ferrari team driver that year, and piloted the 256 F1 to victories in the French and German Grands Prix. But he finished second in the points hunt to Australian Jack Brabham, 31 to 27. Brabham's championship was the first in F1 to be won in a rear-engine car.

As Brooks explained in *Ferrari 1947-1997:* "Our Dino-engined V6 cars were strong and reliable, but on slow and medium-speed circuits they were no match for the lightweight rear-engine British cars. Even at the fast Reims circuit Jack Brabham was quick enough to split Phil Hill and me on the front row of the grid. It was only thanks to our superior power that I was able to pull away from Brabham at the start and lead all the way to the finish."

In 1960, it wasn't even close. The lone Dino victory was Phil Hill's at Monza, as Brabham and the rear-engine Cooper-Climax ran away from the field to take both the driver and constructors titles. Lotus-Climax was second, Ferrari third.

D156 F2

256 F1

Dino 156 F1

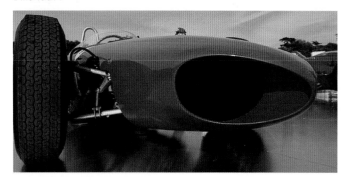

DINO 156 F1
1961-1963

Number made:
65-degree V-6: 6
120-degree V-6: 8
Engine:
65-degree V-6: 1477cc V-6, DOHC,
                180 hp @ 9200 rpm
120-degree V-6: 1477cc V-6, DOHC,
                190-205 hp @ 9500-10,500 rpm
Transmission: 5-speed
Wheelbase:
1961:   91.3 inches / 2320mm
1961-1962:   90.5 inches / 2300mm
1963:   93.6 inches / 2380mm
Weight:
1961-1962:   970 lbs.
1963:   1,060 lbs.

1961-1963
Dino 156 F1

PHIL HILL IS AMERICA'S FIRST WORLD CHAMPION IN ONE OF F1'S ALL-TIME CLASSIC CARS

Ferrari's single victory in the 1960 F1 campaign certainly didn't reflect well on the Scuderia, but actions behind the scenes showed Enzo played the Grand Prix game better than anyone.

When, in October 1958, the FIA announced that starting in 1961 engine capacity would be reduced from 2500cc to 1500cc, the British teams protested loudly and threatened to withdraw. Ferrari simply shrugged his shoulders and had his men make a car to meet the new specifications.

Ferrari chief engineer Carlo Chiti and his crew once again drew on their Formula 2 experience to make their F1 car. The result, the Dino 156 F1, was not unfamiliar in some regards: steel tubular chassis and independent suspension front and rear with double wishbones, coil springs and tubular shocks, and Dunlop disc brakes at each corner. But there was one characteristic somewhat foreign to Ferrari: The engine was in the rear.

Ferrari had actually debuted its first rear-engine F1 car in 1960, at the season's first race in Monaco. It was essentially an experiment, and, driven by Richie Ginther, it finished a distant sixth. The car continued to race the rest of the year as largely a development exercise, then was modified over the winter by Chiti.

He swapped its 65-degree V-6 for a more-powerful 120-degree V-6. That propelled what would become one of the most distinctive of all Ferrari race cars. The Dino 156 F1 had an evocative twin nostril "sharknose" and attractive tail bodywork that enclosed the engine, gearbox, and clutch. The car was beautiful, successful, and historic.

With it, Phil Hill in 1961 became the first American F1 world champion, beating out teammate Wolfgang von Trips by a single point. Their performance helped Ferrari win its first official F1 constructors title.

But the good fortune wouldn't carry into 1962. In November 1961, Maranello was rocked by the infamous Purge, in which Chiti, team manager Romolo Tavoni, and a number of others left the firm. The 1962 F1 season was a disaster, exacerbated by the fact that the British teams were running strong V-8s. Ferrari didn't score a victory and finished tied for fifth in a constructors championship won by BRM.

For 1963, the 156 got a revised body that traded the sharknose for a single-inlet form. New chief engineer Mauro Forghieri did his best to improve the mechanical package with a revised suspension and later, a semimoncoque chassis. Still, Ferrari scored just one victory, a win at Germany's Nurburgring by former motorcycle world champion John Surtees. It finished fourth among eight constructors in a makes championship won by Lotus-Climax.

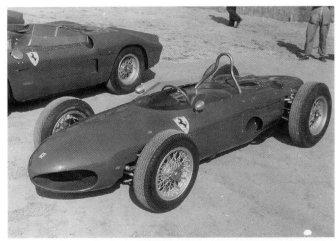

1964-1965
158 F1 & 512 F1

A FIFTH DRIVER'S TITLE, BUT FERRARI'S FOCUS IS OFF F1, AND PROMISE GOES UNFULFILLED

In practice for the 1963 Italian Grand Prix the Scuderia showed it was already looking ahead to the 1964 campaign. Alongside the V-6 Dino models that would actually contest the race, it tested a new car, the 158 F1. The name signified its 1.5-liter 8-cylinder engine, a 90-degree V-powerplant good for 210 horsepower, a more than 10 percent increase in output over the F1 V-6.

The chassis also followed new thinking. Instead of being Ferrari's customary assemblage of tubes, it was a monocoque structure tailor-made for the engine and featured aluminum panels riveted to its framework. The V-8 had an extremely strong crankcase, so it was used a stressed member.

The 158 F1 didn't capture a checkered flag until the '64 season's sixth race, but thereafter, team drivers John Surtees and Lorenzo Bandini were consistent podium finishers. It was enough to give Ferrari the constructors title over BRM, and for Surtees to win the World Driving Championship, the fifth Ferrari driver to do so. Surtees' margin at the end was one point over fellow Englishman Graham Hill in the BRM.

Interestingly, Ferrari's F1 colors for the final two races of the season switched from red to the blue and white of Luigi Chinetti's North American Racing Team—fallout from Enzo's dispute with international racing authorities over the homologation of the 250 LM sports-racer.

The imbroglio did nothing to dim the luster of the season for Surtees. "The best of my years in Italy, as far as motor racing was concerned, was 1964, the year of the F1 world title with the Ferrari 158," the seven-time motorcycle world champion recalled in *Ferrari 1947-1997*.

Though the 158 F1 ran again in 1965, Ferrari's mainstay F1 machine that season was the 512 F1. It had a 225-horsepower 1490cc "flat" 12 instead of the V-8. The car looked good on paper, but no rival was a match for Lotus and Jim Clark; they dominated to take the constructors and driver championships. The best the 512 could muster was two second-place finishes.

It would be 11 years before another Ferrari driver was F1 world champion.

Such technologies as the monocoque structure and the flat-12 demonstrated that Ferrari could welcome fresh ideas in racing. More difficult was dealing with the diverse elements tugging the company this way and that.

"Where Ferrari is concerned, I do have one regret," Surtees noted. "I could have won another three world titles, in 1963, 1965, and 1966, when the cylinder capacity for Formula 1 was increased from 1500cc to 3000cc. But, for one reason or another, we ended up by giving away an incredible number of victories.

"[A]t Ferrari in those years [there were an] incredible number of activities, which led inevitably to energy being expended in different sectors. For example, when cars had to be prepared for Le Mans, Formula 1 was clearly overlooked, although we could compensate in part for our disappointments by the success of the sports prototype cars. I must say the Ferrari 'P' models, from the 250 to 275, P2 and P3, were wonderful cars to drive, very powerful, very well-balanced and a joy to race."

158 F1

158 F1 & 512 F1		
158 F1 1964 512 F1 1965		
Number made:		
158 F1:	2	
512 F1:	3	
Engine:		
158 F1:	1489cc V-8, DOHC, 210 hp @ 11000 rpm	
512 F1:	1490cc flat-12, DOHC, 225 hp @ 11500rpm	
Transmission:	5-speed	
Wheelbase:		
158 F1:	93.6 inches / 2380mm	
512 F1:	94.5 inches / 2400mm	
Weight:		
158 F1:	1,030 lbs.	
512 F1:	1,045 lbs.	

512 F1

312 F1-67

1966-1969
312 F1

**DOWNFORCE AND DOWNBEAT: THE INTRODUCTION OF
AERO AIDS CAN'T LIFT FERRARI TO THE TOP**

For 1966, Formula 1 again changed its engine rules, now allow-ing up to 3.0-liters displacement naturally aspirated or 1.5 supercharged. Ferrari was ready. Chief engineer Mauro Forghieri turned to the company's sports-racing 3.3-liter V-12. He left the bore at 77mm, reduced stroke 5mm to 53.5mm, and came up with a displacement of 2989cc. He increased the compression ratio, fitted twincam heads with two plugs per cylinder, and topped it off with Lucas fuel injection.

The resulting car was called the 312 F1. Though Ferrari's John Surtees started the racing calendar with a win in the noncham-pionship South African Grand Prix in January, he felt the 312 lacked power. During the official F1 season, he and team man-ager Eugenio Dragoni were constantly battling. Surtees would win in Belgium in June, but by September had left the team. Ludovico Scarfiotti's victory in Italy accounted for Ferrari's only other F1 win, as it finished a distant second to Brabham-Repco for the constructors title.

For 1967, the 312 F1 used a revised 36-valve V-12, and the chassis was modified to make it lighter. But the updates were to no avail. Ferrari didn't win an F1 race.

It did win the following year, but just once: Jacky Ickx's victory in France. The 312 F1 now ran four-valve heads that helped make it the first F1 Ferrari with more than 400 horse-power. Perhaps the season's most noteworthy Ferrari moment came in June at the Belgium Grand Prix, where Maranello intro-duced an aerodynamic aid that caught everyone's attention.

A number of cars had experimented with small wings on the nose and rear, but Ferrari mounted an aerofoil on supports high above the gearbox, just behind the cockpit. By September, at Monza, the wing could be controlled by the driver.

The 312 F1 failed to score a victory in 1969. After the Italian Grand Prix, the eighth race of the 11-race season, Ferrari tem-porarily withdrew from F1 to concentrate on development of its new flat-12 engine. Luigi Chinetti's North American Racing Team ran the cars in the final three races, the best finish a fifth by Pedro Rodriguez at Watkins Glen. In all, the 312 won just three races in four F1 seasons.

312 F1	
1966-1969	
Number made:	11
Engine:	
	2989cc V-12, DOHC,
1966:	360-380 hp @ 10,000 rpm
1967:	390 hp @ 10,000 rpm
1968:	410 hp @ 11,000 rpm
1969:	436 hp @ 11,000 rpm
Transmission:	5-speed
Wheelbase:	94.5 inches / 2400mm
Weight:	
1966:	1,205 lbs.
1967-1968:	1,115 lbs.-1,166 lbs.
1969:	1,166 lbs.

312 F1-68

312 F1-69

312 T

1975-1980
312 T Series

**LAUDA 2, SCHECKTER 1, FERRARI 5: A VERY SATISFYING
RUN OF WORLD CHAMPIONSHIPS**

Ferrari's drought in Formula 1 continued well into the 1970s,
relieved only briefly by a second-place showing in the 1970
constructors championship. Its F1 car that season was the innovative 312 B, which had a semistress-bearing flat-12 engine; it
won four races.

A burr under Maranello's saddle that season—since 1967, in
fact—was the Ford DFV V-8. Built by Cosworth and financed
by Ford Motor Company, this stupendous engine won its very
first time out at Zandfoort, in a Lotus, and would soon spread
to most every other team.

In 1974, the tide began to turn. Ferrari withdrew from
endurance sports-car racing to concentrate its resources on
Formula 1. It hired Austrian Niki Lauda, late of BRM, as its No.
1 racing driver. Chief engineer Mauro Forghieri returned after a
one-year absence. And Luca Cordero di Montezemolo became
team manager and was a tremendously equalizing force, eradi-
cating much of the political intrigue that hounded the team.

With the last of the 312 Bs, the 312 B3, Lauda won the

Spanish and Dutch Grands Prix, teammate Clay Regazzoni won in Germany, and Ferrari finished second to McLaren-Ford in the constructors championship

For 1975, Ferrari introduced the 312 T. The "T" stood for *transversale* and indicated that the five-speed gearbox was mounted east-west ahead of the rear axle for a better center of gravity. The suspension was altered front and rear, and Lauda's superb ability as a test driver honed the machine.

The 312 T entered competition in the season's third race, in South Africa. By the sixth race, at Monaco, it and Lauda were in the winner's circle. In all, the 312 T won six of the last 11 races. Lauda was world champion, and Ferrari had its first constructors title since 1964.

Ferrari and Lauda appeared well on their way to a repeat in 1976, with the 312 T2. Underneath, the car was nearly identical to the 312 T. But the body was quite different, with higher side panels and different wings and spoilers. With Lauda and Regazzoni, the 312 T2 won five of the year's first eight races.

Then, in the German Grand Prix at Nurburgring, Lauda had a horrendous, life-threatening crash. He was pulled from his flaming 312 T2 by four fellow drivers and a track marshal; a priest read him the last rites in the hospital.

Miraculously, Lauda recovered, and incredibly, was back in a 312 T2 five weeks later for the Italian Grand Prix. He finished fourth. Ferrari accumulated enough points to repeat as constructor champion. Lauda withdrew from the season's last race, in Japan, because of appalling, monsoonlike conditions, and lost the driver's championship by one point to McLaren-Ford's James Hunt.

The 312 T2 returned in 1977, and Lauda's loss of the driving championship in 1976 seemed a fluke. He and teammate Carlos Reutemann consistently scored points, often placing on the podium. Ferrari handily won the constructors crown, and Lauda had his second driver's title. Nonetheless, the season was dogged with controversy. Animosity between Lauda and the team over a number of incidents during the 1976 campaign caused the World Champion to leave Ferrari at the end of the 1977 season. (Lauda and Enzo Ferrari patched up their disagreements years later.)

Ferrari's mount in 1978 was the 312 T3, which showed

312 T, 312 T2, 312 T3, 312 T4 & 312 T5

312 T 1975-1976
312 T2 1976-1977
312 T3 1978-1979
312 T4 1979
312 T5 1980

Number made:

312 T:	6
312 T2:	7
312 T3:	5
312 T4:	5
312 T5:	6

Engine:

312 T:	2992cc V-12, DOHC, 495 hp @ 12,200 rpm
312 T2:	2992cc V-12, DOHC, 500 hp @ 12,200 rpm
312 T3:	2992cc V-12, DOHC, 510 hp @ 12,200 rpm
312 T4:	2992cc V-12, DOHC, 515 hp @ 12,300 rpm
312 T5:	2992cc V-12, DOHC, 515 hp @ 12,300 rpm

Transmission: 5-speed

Wheelbase:

312 T:	99.1 inches / 2518mm
312 T2:	100.7 inches / 2560mm
312 T3:	100.7-106.3 inches / 2560-2700mm
312 T4:	106.3 inches / 2700mm
312 T5:	106.3 inches / 2700mm

Weight:

312 T & T2:	1,265 lbs.
312 T3:	1,276 lbs.
312 T4:	1,298 lbs.
312 T5:	1,309 lbs.

312 T2

312 T3

important differences from the T2 in aerodynamics and front suspension. It was introduced at the South African Grand Prix, the season's third race. Carlos Reutemann won with it in the fourth race, the U.S. Grand Prix West, at Long Beach, California. He won two more races in the car, and Gilles Villeneuve won one as Ferrari placed second to Lotus-Ford in the constructors championship.

In 1979, Ferrari brought in as its No. 1 driver Jody Scheckter, who had driven for Wolf-Ford the previous season. The South African and the Canadian Villeneuve proved the consummate GP tag team.

"We weren't just teammates," Scheckter recalled in *Ferrari 1947-1997*, "we were friends and wanted to work together to win races, so we made an agreement to share all our technical information."

The arrangement worked quite well, indeed. The duo finished 1-2 in the debut of Ferrari's new car, the 312 T4, in South Africa for the season's third race. The T4 represented Ferrari's

transition from mere areo design to true ground effects, in which the car's structure and shape managed airflow along the sides and underbody to generate maximum adhesion.

Each the winner of three races, Scheckter was World Champion, Villeneuve was runner-up, and Ferrari handily won the makes title, its fourth in five years.

The next season saw the final development of the 312 series, the 312 T5. Bodywork was once again modified, but the rapidly changing science of ground effects had moved beyond what Ferrari could do with its flat-12 engine, a powerplant that was wider and thus more difficult to package in terms of airflow management than the Ford-Cosworth V-8 that powered Alan Jones and his Williams-Ford to the championship.

The 312 T5's best showings were fifth-place finishes at Long Beach, Monaco, and Canada. Ferrari was famous for its 12-cylinder engines, but the close of the 1980 season marked a period of nine years before one of its F1 cars would again be powered by a twelve.

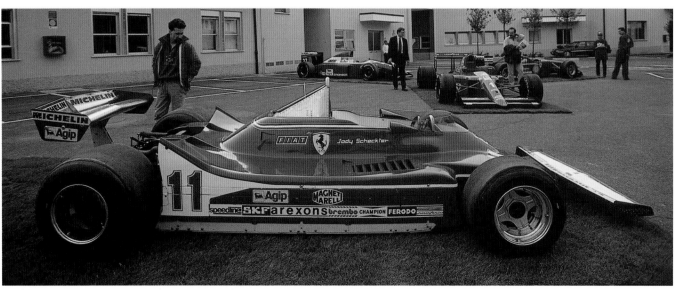

312 T4

312 T5

126 C3

126 C, 126 CK, 126 C2, 126 C3, 126 C4 & 156/85		
126 1980-1984		
156/85 1985		

Number made:
126 C:	2
126 CK:	8
126 C2:	12
126 C3:	4
126 C4:	8
156/85:	6

Engine:
1496cc twin-turbo V-6, DOHC,
126 C:	540 hp @ 11,000 rpm
126 CK:	560 hp @ 11,500 rpm
126 C2:	580 hp @ 11,000 rpm
126 C3:	600 hp @ 10,500 rpm
126 C4:	660 hp @ 11,000 rpm
156/85:	780 hp @ 11,000 rpm

Transmission: 5-speed

Wheelbase:
126 C & CK:	106.9 inches / 2718mm
126 C2:	105.7-112.4 inches / 2658-2856mm
126 C3:	102.3 inches / 2600mm
126 C4:	102.3 inches / 2600mm
156/85:	105.1 inches / 2672mm

Weight:
126 C & CK:	1,342 lbs.
126 C2 & C3:	1,309 lbs.
126 C4:	1,188 lbs.
156/85:	1,207 lbs.

1981-1985
126 C Series & 156/85

THE TURBO ERA NETS FERRARI TWO MAKES TITLES, BUT RACING LOSES GILLES VILLENEUVE

The 312's flat-12 engine had been Ferrari's mainstay F1 power-plant for a decade, but in 1980, the handwriting was on the wall. Even as the team raced with little success that season, Ferrari was hard at work developing a state-of-the-art turbo-charged engine. It was unveiled on the second practice day for the Italian Grand Prix at Imola in September, and it was a half-second faster than the naturally aspirated flat-12 312 T5.

Development continued over the winter for what would be called the 126 C. It reprised Ferrari's tradition of a tube frame overlaid with aluminum sheeting, but was powered by a 1496cc V-6 with two German KKK turbochargers, a pair of intercoolers, and four valves per cylinder. Horsepower was quoted at 540, 25 more than Ferrari's most-powerful flat-12.

Despite its newness, the engine proved remarkably reliable, but the chassis was a handful. Still, on the strength of Gilles Villeneuve's brilliance and the new engine's prodigious power, the 125 C won the Monaco Grand Prix, just its sixth race. The Canadian won again in Spain, but wrecks and chassis problems plagued the team the rest of the year, and Ferrari finished fifth among 11 entries in 1981 constructors points.

To rectify the chassis situation for 1982, Ferrari hired Englishman Harvey Postlehwaite. His 126 C2 chassis of composite materials reinforced by carbon fiber made all the difference, as did an even more-powerful turbo engine.

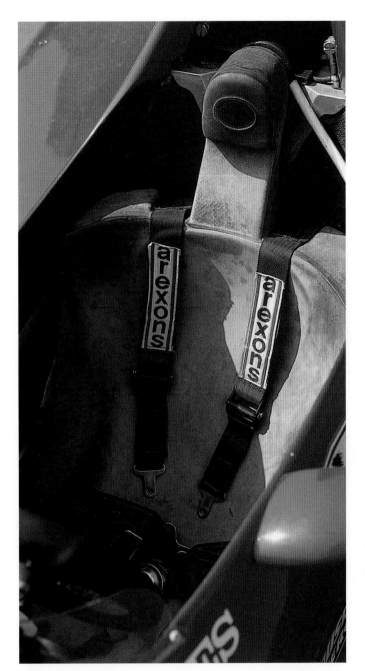

But drivers Villeneuve and Frenchman Didier Pironi were never the team that Jody Scheckter and Villeneuve had been. When Pironi deprived Villeneuve of a victory at Imola against team orders, the two never spoke again.

Then, in May 1982, racing lost one of its stars. In practice for the Grand Prix of Belgium, Villeneuve crashed the Ferrari. He died in the hospital hours later. In June, a crash in Canada sidelined Pironi for the season. Frenchman Patrick Tambay and American Mario Andretti filled in ably, sustaining enough points for Ferrari to win it first constructors championship since 1979.

With ground-effects side skirts banned for 1983, Ferrari's 126 C3 showed completely revised bodywork. Tambay was joined by countryman Rene Arnoux as team drivers and they finished third and fourth, respectively, in points. Arnoux's three victories, Tambay's one, and consistently high finishes were enough to capture for the Scuderia a second consecutive constructors championship.

In 1984, the 126 C4 and the rest of the field were outclassed by McLaren's MP4 and its drivers Niki Lauda and Alain Prost. They won 12 of the season's 16 races, and Ferrari finished a distant second in the constructor chase.

F1's Turbo era lasted through 1988, but Ferrari's only other strong showing came in 1985, with the 156/85. It boasted Maranello's first bodyshell designed completely by computer. Italian Michele Alboreto won twice with it, at Canada and Germany, and the team finished second to McLaren-TAG for the constructors championship.

156/85

F1/89

1989-1990
F1/89 & F1 641

A REVOLUTION IN TRANSMISSION TECHNOLOGY, BUT LITTLE TO CELEBRATE ON THE TRACK

In the second half of the 1980s, Formula 1's turbocharged engines were producing prodigious power—Ferrari's F1/86 and F1/87 delivered almost 1,000 horses in qualifying, and nearly 900 in race trim. In an effort to calm things down, the FIA for 1988 dramatically reduced the allowed turbo boost. For 1989, it banned turbos altogether.

The return to naturally aspirated engines saw Ferrari once again utilize the V-12. The one in its F1/89 displaced 3498cc, had five valves per cylinder (3 intake, 2 exhaust), and produced 600 horsepower at 12,500 rpm.

But the big news the was the F1/89's gearbox. It was an innovation that revolutionized race- and sports-car technology.

Ferrari had developed a seven-speed electro-hydraulic transmission that was, in essence, a manual gearbox that could be upshifted or downshifted automatically by touching a switch on the back of the steering wheel. No longer did the driver have to remove his hands from the steering wheel and reach for a shift lever to change gears. The advantages were impossible to ignore, and soon every F1 rival had a version of Ferrari's inno-

F1/89 & F1 641	
F1/89 1989	
F1 641 1990	
Number made:	
F1/89:	7
F1 641:	8
Engine:	
F1/89:	3498cc V-12, DOHC, 600-660 hp @ 12,500-13,000 rpm
F1 641:	3498cc V-12, DOHC, 665-690 hp @ 13,200-13,600 rpm
Transmission:	7-speed semiautomatic
Wheelbase:	111.3 inches / 2830mm
Weight:	1,111 lbs.

vative gearbox. Within a few years, paddle-shifted manuals would be in many high-performance road cars as well, including several from Ferrari.

The F1/89 came from the drawing board of Ferrari's England based designer, John Barnard, and the car got off to a magnificent start when it won the '89 season's first race, at Brazil, with Brit Nigel Mansell driving. Then electronic gremlins started hounding the car. Mansell won the season's ninth race, in Hungary, and Gerhard Berger won in Portugal. But that was it, and the team finished a distant third in the makes chase.

Ferrari was optimistic about 1990. It had a new car, the F1 641. It had revised bodywork, and the V-12 had a shorter stroke, weighed less, and produced nearly 700 horsepower. Joining Mansell in the cockpit was one of the world's top drivers, Alain Prost. The Frenchman was coming off his third F1 world championship, captured just the year before with McLaren-Honda.

F1 641

The season turned into a dogfight between Ferrari and McLaren, then into one between Prost and Mansell. The intra-team rivalry was much to the detriment of Ferrari.

"If we had been able to cooperate as I had hoped," Prost observed in *Ferrari 1947-1997*, "I am sure Ferrari would have had a world championship to celebrate that year."

Instead, it was as close as Ferrari would come to another makes or driver's title for almost a decade. Prost lost the championship in the season's last race, when archrival Ayrton Senna pushed his Ferrari off the Australian Grand Prix's Adelaide Street Circuit. Senna won the race and the title, in a McLaren-Honda.

412 T1

1994-1995
412 T1, 412 T1B & 412 T2

412 T1, 412 T1B & 412 T2		
412 T1 1994		
412 T1B 1994		
412 T2 1995		
Number made:		
412 T1:	7	
412 T1B:	5	
412 T2:	10	
Engine:		
412 T1:	3498cc V-12, DOHC,	
	780 hp @ 15,000 rpm	
412 T1B:	3498cc V-12, DOHC,	
	over 800 hp @ 15,250 rpm	
412 T2:	2997cc V-12, DOHC,	
	over 600 hp @ 17,000 rpm	
Transmission:	6-speed semiautomatic	
Wheelbase:		
412 T1 & T1B:	116.1 inches / 2950mm	
412 T2:	114.5 inches / 2910mm	
Weight:	1,110 lbs.	

FERRARI CAN'T GET THERE FROM HERE: NEITHER DRIVERS NOR EQUIPMENT ARE QUITE CHAMPIONSHIP CALIBER

After losing the 1990 constructors championship to McLaren-Honda by just 11 points, Ferrari fell into disarray, and the team went three full seasons without a victory. The car that broke the spell was 1994's 412 T1.

The 412 T1 marked two returns. First, Ferrari revived a conventional pushrod suspension system; 1993's F93A had used an electronically controlled active suspension system that was plagued with reliability issues. Second, it welcomed back engineer John Barnard, who had been briefly lured away by Benetton.

With more-efficient airflow management and improved balance, the 412 T1 demonstrated Barnard's talent for original thinking. He substantially redesigned the nose, making it higher than the F93A's. And he moved the air ducts on the side pods, and thus the radiators, further forward.

The car proved relatively reliable, and Ferrari secured podium finishes in the season's first five races. But the engine was starving for air, so the modified 412 T1B made its debut at the French Grand Prix in July, the year's seventh race.

Gerhard Berger finished third with the car, and two races later broke Ferrari's three-plus season drought two races later, with a victory in Germany. Meanwhile, teammate Jean Alesi was also scoring a number of podium finishes, and Ferrari placed third overall in the constructors championship. The Scuderia looked to be regaining its form.

In 1995, a rules change reduced maximum engine capacity to 3.0-liters. Ferrari responded with a new, more-compact V-12 that produced over 600 horsepower at 17,000 rpm. It went into a new car called the 412 T2. Compared to the T1, the T2 was slightly shorter in wheelbase and in overall length—enough to allow the engine to be moved about 3.5 inches (10cm) closer to the platform's center. The 37-gallon (140-liter) fuel tank was similarly relocated, and the T2 proved more balanced and easier to drive than its T-series predecessors.

412 T2

Against the dominating Renault-powered Benetton and Williams cars, however, it was competitive but not top-tier. The Ferrari team had a number of podium finishes, the most memorable Jean Alesi's victory at the Canadian Grand Prix in Montreal. Once the Frenchman took over the lead, he was overcome with joy

"I started to cry in the car," he recalled in *Ferrari 1947-1997*. "I couldn't see the road because when I braked the tears were getting in my visor. It was not the way I expected to react. I told myself to get back to driving and see what happened."

That emotional victory would be the last for a Ferrari V-12 in Formula 1. The following season a new engine and a new driver would come on the scene, laying the foundation for a period of domination unlike any the sport had seen.

F310B

1996-1997
F310 & F310B

SCHUMACHER COMES ABOARD AND FERRARI GETS A TASTE OF A CHAMPION'S TALENT, AND TEMPERAMENT

A revolution was taking shape at Ferrari in the second half of 1995.

After studying several engine types, including V-8s and V-12s, Maranello announced it would use a V-10 in F1 for 1996. It marked the first time the Scuderia had tried a 10-cylinder configuration.

And rumors swirled that Ferrari was actively courting two-time world champion Michael Schumacher, widely recognized as the fastest driver in F1. Schumacher was at the time driving for Benetton-Renault, and two weeks after he won at the Hockenheimring in his German homeland, it was announced he would indeed be with Ferrari in '96. He was signed to a two-year contract worth $24 million.

Ferrari's new F1 car for 1996 was the F310. Among the benefits of its 10-cylinder engine was a compact size that allowed much-improved aerodynamics. The 2998cc unit initially produced 700 horsepower, a figure bumped to 725 later in the season.

As for Schumacher, his importance was obvious to longtime F1 reporter Andrew Frankl.

"Five aspects seem to stand out in an analysis of his talent," Frankl reported in 1996 in *FORZA*, a magazine devoted to Ferrari. "They are: his never-ending commitment to the testing process; his technical ability; his confidence in his own driving ability; his incredible attention to detail, which emanates from a quest for precision and perfection....And last—and not wholly unimportant, his will to win."

Schumacher's teammate was also new to Ferrari. Irishman

F310 & F310B	
F310 1996 F310B 1997	
Number made:	
F310:	6
F310B:	9
Engine:	
F310:	2998cc V-10, DOHC, 700-725 hp @ 16,000-16,500 rpm
F310B:	2998cc V-10, DOHC, 750 hp @ 17,000 rpm
Transmission:	
F310:	6-speed and 7-speed semiautomatic
F310B:	7-speed semiautomatic
Wheelbase:	
F310:	114.1 inches / 2900mm
F310B:	115.5 inches / 2935mm
Weight:	1,110 lbs.

Eddie Irvine had come over from the Jordan team, and he scored the F310's first points with a third-place finish in the season's inaugural race at Australia. Schumacher followed with a third in the next race, at Brazil. He retired in Argentina, then went on a tear.

In the season's final 13 contests, Schumacher scored three victories, three seconds, and a third. He finished third in a driver's championship won by Williams-Renault's Damon Hill. Ferrari was a distant runner-up to Williams-Renault in constructors points.

Ferrari upped the ante in 1997 with the F310B. The aerodynamics were revised, the V-10's output increased to 750 horsepower, the transmission was upgraded, and a new differential was used in an attempt to solve reliability issues. Ferrari was again second to Williams-Renault in the constructors championship, but the points margin was slimmer than in '96. In the driver's chase, Schumacher went into the season's final race, at Jerez in Spain, leading Williams-Renault's Jacques Villeneuve by one point, 78-77.

The race was the setting for one of F1's most controversial moments. On lap 48, Villeneuve's blue-and-white Williams pulled alongside Schumacher's red Ferrari in a corner, and appeared about to pass. Suddenly, Schumacher veered, and his right front tire made contact with Villeneuve's sidepod. Schumacher ended up in a gravel trap, but his rival was able to continue, and finished in third place. Villeneuve ended the season with 81 points. Schumacher accumulated 78, but FIA officials judged his Jerez move an intentional bid to take Villeneuve out, and disqualified the Ferrari driver in the championship standings.

Scuderia Ferrari in the midst of an unprecedented F1 championship run

F399, F1-2000, F2001, F2002, F2003-GA & F2004
F399 1999
F1-2000 2000
F2001 2001
F2002 2002
F2003-GA 2003
F2004 2004

Number made:
F399:	8
F1-2000:	8
F2001:	11
F2002:	9
F2003-GA:	n/a
F2004:	n/a
Engine:	2997cc V-10, DOHC;
F399:	over 750 hp @ n/a
F1-2000:	806 hp @ 17,500 rpm
F2001:	about 813 hp @ 17,900 rpm
F2002:	860 hp @ 17,500 rpm
F2003-GA:	930 hp @ 19,000 rpm
F2004:	n/a
Transmission:	7-speed semiautomatic
Wheelbase:	
F399:	118 inches / 3000mm
F1-2000:	118.5 inches / 3010 mm
F2001:	118.5 inches / 3010 mm
F2002:	120 inches / 3050 mm
F2003-GA:	120 inches / 3050 mm
F2004:	120 inches / 3050 mm
Weight:	1,320 lbs.
F399:	1,100 lbs.

1999-2004

F399, F1-2000, F2001, F2002, F2003-GA & F2004

DYNASTY! SIX MAKES TITLES AND FIVE DRIVER'S WORLD CHAMPIONSHIPS HUMBLE ALL COMERS

By 1998, Ferrari's goal was nothing less than F1 supremacy. It was expected by everyone inside and outside the organization, and by fans around the world.

Michael Schumacher had also grasped the magnitude of the situation, comprehending how his new "home" was indeed different from its competition. "In a way," he observed in *Ferrari 1947-1997*, "I wasn't ready for the 'Ferrari legend.' I observed it from the outside, as a mere spectator, but I had no idea what it meant to be part of it....

"But on that first visit to Maranello [in 1995], I couldn't stop at mere analytical considerations. I began to sense something, like goose pimples. I felt I was in a new atmosphere, which is not easy to define. It was an important moment; I understood that after two world titles at Benetton, I was now embarking on a new stage of my career and even my life."

The final piece of this new reality, one that would shuffle in an era unprecedented in the history of Formula 1, fell into place in 1998, when the influence of two talented men came to the fore. Rory Byrne was a South African designer who had been in

Formula 1 for 15 years. He had masterminded Schumacher's two Benetton world championship cars. He joined Ferrari in late 1996, and his first car for the Scuderia was 1998's F300.

Ross Brawn was Ferrari's Technical Director, and he, like Byrne, had played an integral role in Schumacher's Benetton titles. Not only would Brawn oversee the day-to-day development of the F300 and its successors, he proved a master racing strategist, able to work off preset plans or create them in the heat of battle.

And 1998 was a season-long battle between Ferrari and McLaren-Mercedes. Of the season's first 12 races, McLaren-Mercedes' Mika Hakkinen won six and Schumacher five. The Ferrari driver pulled even in wins with a victory in Italy, the 13th race of the 16-event schedule. But Hakkinen sealed the championship for himself and for McLaren-Mercedes with wins in the final two races.

Ferrari's car for 1999 was the F399. The V-10 was moved forward in the chassis, and aerodynamics were enhanced with a new front wing, side pods, and air intake. Ferrari claimed more than 750 horsepower from 2997cc.

Once again Ferrari's nemesis was McLaren-Mercedes. Ferrari's Eddie Irvine won the first race, Hakkinen the second, Schumacher the third and fourth. And so the fight went until the midway point, the British Grand Prix, when Schumacher had a tremendous crash that sidelined him for the next six races with a broken leg.

Schumacher returned for the inaugural Malaysian Grand Prix,

the season's penultimate race, and was on his way to the win, but let Irvine take the checkered flag. Irvine had upped his game after Michael's crash, with wins in Austria and Germany, and was in fact leading Hakkinen in the driver's championship at the last race in Japan. But the tough Finn won the showdown and took the driver's crown, 76 points to Irvine's 74.

All was not lost for Ferrari, however. Irvine and Schumacher had accounted for six wins overall, helping Ferrari to its first F1 constructors championship since 1983. That wasn't enough to satisfy Maranello, however.

"We've got a great team, both from a human and technical point of view," Brawn said as he introduced the logically named F1-2000 and the team's new No. 2 driver, Rubens Barrichello. "We deserve nothing less than both world titles this year."

Though the F1-2000 looked similar to the F399, it was in design quite different. The first car developed in Ferrari's new wind tunnel, its slimmer nose, reprofiled flanks, and superior undertray airflow improved aerodynamics by 10 percent, a huge number. The V-10 was lighter, produced around 800 horsepower, and its mounting location was adjustable. In all, the F1-2000 was so light that nearly 180 pounds of ballast was needed to bring it up to minimum weight requirements.

Schumacher won the first three races and appeared to be cruising to a championship. Then McLaren and Hakkinen returned to form. With four races left, Hakkinen led. But Schumacher closed the season with a string of victories to become Ferrari's first F1 world champion since 1979. Ferrari

F2002

F2003-GA

also won the constructors crown in an equally hard-fought battle with McLaren-Mercedes.

The wind tunnel again played a key role in designing the F2001. Rule changes stipulated that the front wing be situated two inches higher than the previous year's, so the F2001's nose was lower than the F1-2000's, and the wings curved upward to meet the regulations.

"Testing in the wind tunnel proved that for this car this configuration is best," Byrne said of the team's unique approach. "The first few races will show who was right in their design."

And that they did, as the F2001 dominated the season. Ferrari scored a then-record 179 points for the constructors crown, and Schumacher's 123 points on the way to his second-consecutive world driving championship were almost double those of second-place finisher, McLaren-Mercedes' David Coulthard.

The F2002 sported new sidepods, revised rear suspension, and a lighter, shorter gearbox that delivered even faster shifts. Two-way telematics were now legal, so information and settings could travel between the car and pits.

All that spelled bad news for the competition. The F2002 won 15 of 17 races, with Schumacher taking 11 and Barrichello four. Ferrari set another constructor's record with 221 points (runner-up Williams-BMW had 92) and Schumacher tied Juan Manuel Fangio's record of five driver's world championships.

Ferrari's string of four consecutive F1 constructor championships and Shumacher's run of three straight world titles was in jeopardy for much of 2003.

The team started the season with the F2002, and Schumacher didn't set foot on the podium in the first three

races. As the season neared the halfway point, leading in driver's points was McLaren-Mercedes' new hotshoe, Kimi Raikkonen, and his team was atop the constructors standings.

Then, in the fourth race, at San Marino, Ferrari unleashed its F2003-GA. (GA was a tribute to Fiat's Gianni Agnelli, who died shortly before the car's launch.) Versus the F2002, the GA had better aerodynamics and cooling, a two-inch-shorter wheelbase, and a V-10 that revved to a shrieking 19,000 rpm.

Schumacher won the F2003-GA's debut race in Spain, and the following race in Austria. The season had morphed into an all-out brawl between Williams-BMW and Ferrari. A victory by Schumacher in Canada was sandwiched between Williams-BMW wins by Juan Pablo Montoya at Monoco and by Schumacher's younger brother, Ralf, at Nurburgring. The BMW-powered rivals won again in France and with three races left, Williams-BMW was leading in constructors points. The driver's championship, meanwhile, was a battle royale among Schumacher, Raikkonen, and Montoya.

In Italy, Schumacher fought off a pressuring Montoya for the win, and when the German won the next race, a rainy U.S. Grand Prix at Indianapolis, he was assured of the driver's crown and a record sixth championship. Barrichello's victory at the season finale, in Japan, secured Ferrari's record fifth straight constructors title.

The F2004 may have looked like the F2003-GA, but as Rory Byrne pointed out at its introduction, "Every area of the car has been revised in order to make a further step forward in per-

F2004

formance. So almost every component has been redesigned."
This included the engine, gearbox, chassis, and suspension.

It all led to what may have been the most dominant season
ever in Formula 1. Schumacher won the first five races. An accident in the tunnel at Monaco halted the streak. Then he reeled
off another seven wins in a row. He finished the season with a
record 13 first-place finishes, bringing his record all-time victory
total to 82. With Barrichello's two victories, Ferrari won 15 of
the season's 17 contests.

Schumacher was World Champion for the seventh time (with
a record 148 season points), and the Ferrari team set two more
records—a sixth-straight constructors title and 262 season
points.

Pivotal Figures in the Ferrari Story

Enzo Ferrari didn't do it alone. Here are the others who were indispensable to the creation and growth of the greatest marque in high-performance motoring.

Gianni Agnelli

1921-2003

Role in Ferrari History: Industrialist who orchestrated Fiat purchase of Ferrari

Carlo Felice Bianchi Anderloni

1916-2003

Role in Ferrari History: The designer who gave the Ferrari automobile its first "face"

Gianni Agnelli was the grandson of Giovanni Angelli, a wealthy senator who could be considered the father of Italy's motoring industry as the founder of Fiat. Gianni studied law in college but never practiced it. He served in World War II, then acted as a liaison with the Americans after Italy surrendered in 1943.

His lean build and dashingly handsome looks saw him become known after the war as one of Europe's leading playboys rather than industrialist-in-the-making. He inherited Fiat after his grandfather's death in 1945, and during those years the company was run by Vittorio Valletta, a powerful Fiat executive with a background in economics and banking.

In the 1950s, Agnelli was one of Italy's highest-profile personalities, and he commissioned a number of one-off Ferraris. In the latter years of the decade, he turned his attention to Fiat, and was named the company's managing director in 1963. He became company president in 1966, and was soon expanding Fiat's empire, and thus his, beyond Italy's borders. He opened factories in Poland and in far-flung Russia and South America, and started a number of joint ventures and alliances with companies such as commercial-vehicle giant Iveco. Fiat also began buying up other Italian auto manufacturers, notably Lancia, in the late 1960s.

That was a tumultuous period in the auto industry, and in the gran turismo sector in particular. Labor and social upheaval, and new safety and emissions regulations, had most every GT constructor looking to find a larger company to act as a parent. For Ferrari that partner was Fiat. Enzo Ferrari and Gianni Agnelli completed the transaction in June 1969.

The marriage was timely, for it ensured Ferrari's survival and growth. Four years later, the first oil crisis and resulting worldwide recession spelled the end of a number of GT manufacturers, but not Ferrari. Agnelli stepped down as Fiat's chairman in 1996, but remained a force inside the company up to his death in 2003. Through it all, he was a consistent Ferrari customer, and received a one-off Testarossa convertible in 1985.

Affable and widely respected, Carlo Felice Bianchi Anderloni grew up with automotive design in his blood. The son of Felice Bianchi Anderloni, a principal in and design director of Carrozzeria Touring, young Carlo often accompanied his father to the famed coachbuilding firm during his youth. He also watched his father race successfully, and remembered pouring water on the competition car's brakes to cool them down when, during road races, Felice would stop at the roadside family picnic!

Carlo Anderloni was blessed with a photographic memory, and as a youngster he observed his father's creations from a unique perspective. "As I grew older," he recalled, "my father would come home every day for lunch. From the window of our flat, I would see at least five different cars a week! So early on I became a fan of bodywork."

Those memories, coupled with his own eye, his good taste, and lessons taught by Felice, all but guaranteed his place in automotive history. He graduated from college with a degree in mechanical and coachbuilding engineering. After service in World War II, he went to work at Touring, learning the business at the side of his father. He was thrown in the hot seat when Felice unexpectedly passed away in 1948.

Carlo's first car was Ferrari's seminal 166 Barchetta. "Just imagine if the first Ferrari I did was not a wonderful car," he remembered years later. "Then all the people would have thought that if the design had turned out bad, Touring had finished with the death of my father."

The 166 Barchetta influenced automotive design for more than a decade. Carlo penned a number of other Ferraris, and had clients as diverse as Alfa Romeo, Spain's Pegaso, Britain's Aston Martin, Lamborghini, and Hudson in America.

He remained Touring's design director and a principal until it went under in 1966. The spirited, energetic Anderloni then served as a consultant to Alfa Romeo well into his 70s.

Luigi Chinetti
1901-1994

Role in Ferrari History: Won Le Mans in 1949, Ferrari point man in the United States for decades

The son of a gunsmith, Luigi Chinetti was born in 1901 in Milan, Italy. He demonstrated mechanical aptitude at a young age and began working for Alfa Romeo in 1917. He wound up in Alfa's competition department, where his path crossed Enzo Ferrari's.

Chinetti eventually moved to Paris and became an Alfa salesman. He also proved to be an admirable driver, winning Le Mans in 1932 and '34 in an Alfa 8C 2300. In 1940, he migrated to America, and stayed there when hostilities broke out in Europe. Six years later he became a U.S. citizen.

At Christmastime 1946, he met with Enzo Ferrari in Modena and proposed that he become Ferrari's point man in America. Ferrari could not have picked a better representative. Chinetti's talents were many, as demonstrated in 1948 when he sold the very first 166 Barchetta built off the Turin Auto Show stand to Southern California radio executive Tommy Lee.

Chinetti became Ferrari's official U.S. importer in the early 1950s, a post he kept until 1979. "You never met another man like him," former dealer and racer Bob Grossman remembered in the 1990s. "Everybody tries to dissect Chinetti, to figure him out…[H]e was much shrewder than anybody thought. He reminded me of Gucci. He made the cars so unattainable; [h]e made you want the car. He made you eat out of his hand…."

But there was more to Chinetti's Ferrari story than sales. In 1949, he won Le Mans in a 166 Barchetta. In 1951 he was the riding mechanic in the Ferrari 212 that won the Carrera Panamericana, a victory that brought great publicity to Ferrari in North America and to the Chinetti Motors dealership.

In 1956, he formed N.A.R.T. (North American Racing Team) with backing from wealthy racers George Arents and Jan de Vroom. Chinetti's close relationship with Ferrari ensured a consistent string of competitive cars. N.A.R.T. also acted as a springboard for a number of top drivers such as future world champions Mario Andretti and Phil Hill.

Through the 1960s, N.A.R.T. competed in the world's top races, often winning at venues such as the 24 Hours of Daytona in Florida. In 1965, N.A.R.T.'s 250 LM became the last Ferrari to win the 24 Hours of Le Mans. N.A.R.T raced into the early 1980s, then retired from the sport. Chinetti remained a fixture in the Ferrari world until his passing in August 1994.

Gioachino Colombo
1903-1987

Role in Ferrari History: Gifted engineer who created the first Ferrari V-12

Gioachino Colombo was one of the automotive world's most prolific engineers. Born outside Milan, he began his career at age 14 as a technical draftsman at a noted school of mechanical technology. Work on steam turbines and diesel engines helped him land a job at Alfa Romeo in 1924.

No sooner had he arrived than he was working with the great Vittorio Jano on Alfa's immortal P2, a grand prix car that raced successfully for six years. After four years with Jano, Colombo was appointed head of the technical department where his reach expanded into road cars.

The 1930s saw his name associated with such famed Alfa models as the 2.3 and 2.9, and the radical Touring-bodied 256 berlinettas. He and Enzo Ferrari had been good friends, so in 1937 Colombo was warmly greeted when he moved to Modena to oversee the design of one of Alfa's most famous race cars, the Alfetta 158 single-seater.

Political intrigue surrounded Colombo during and immediately following the war, but that didn't deter Ferrari from calling him in July 1945. Colombo was out of work, and he warmly welcomed the call. "For me," he observed years later, "[the phone call] was something that could obliterate in one stroke those five years of war…."

Colombo designed Ferrari's first V-12 engine, and a great majority of the 125 model, then returned to Alfa Romeo. He worked off-and-on for Ferrari over the next six years, then once again went to Alfa. In 1952-53 he worked at Maserati, designing the 250F and six-cylinder engines.

This was followed by a stint at Bugatti in France, then a collaboration with Abarth on its successful, Fiat-derived twincam engine. He also worked with MV on several engines and its helicopters. Colombo opened his own engineering studio in 1971. At the time of his death in 1987, he could lay claim to approximately 110 different engine designs.

The Competition: Adolfo Orsi, Ferruccio Lamborghini

Adolfo Orsi, 1888-1972

Ferruccio Lamborghini, 1916-1993

Role in Ferrari History: Two competitors that kept Ferrari on its toes.

sile was faster and more radical than anything in Ferrari's road-going stable, and it took the automotive world by storm. Ferrari responded with the Daytona. Lamborghini countered with the Countach. Ferrari replied with the Boxer.

Ferruccio sold his interest in his car company in the 1970s, but his competitive spirit could be seen in the 2000s as the Lamborghini Gallardo sparred with the Ferrari F430 and the Murcielago challenged the 575M.

Mauro Forghieri

1935-

Role in Ferrari History: Last of the great all-around engineers

Adolfo Orsi was born in Modena, the eldest of five children. An impoverished upbringing forced him to leave school at a young age to help his family subsist. This only inspired his entrepreneurial spirit. He became a scrap dealer and soon built his humble beginnings into a flourishing business. By the late 1920s, Orsi employed 2,000 people and owned his own foundries, railway lines, and car dealership.

In 1937, he purchased Maserati from the Maserati brothers in Bologna, and eventually moved the company to Modena. No sooner had it settled into its new surroundings than Maserati was once again creating competition cars. Even though the Maserati brothers left in 1947 to form OSCA, Orsi's leadership skills encouraged most key employees to remain. His business acumen made Maserati a leading producer of prestigious GT cars in the late 1950s and '60s, and Maserati sports-racing and F1 cars were constant thorns in Ferrari's side. In 1957, Juan Manuel Fangio was the F1 championship in a Maserati. Eleven years later, Orsi sold Maserati to Citroën.

Ferruccio Lamborghini appeared on Ferrari's radar screen in the mid 1960s. The industrialist made a fortune manufacturing tractors, heaters, and air conditioners and, as an auto aficionado, decided in the early 1960s another opportunity lay in the production of gran turismos. His first, the 350 GT, was an understated machine that was as fast and more refined than anything Ferrari had at the time.

But, as Lamborghini's former chief engineer Gianpaolo Dallara noted, "It wasn't until we made the Miura that Ferrari took notice." At its debut in 1966, this avant-garde midengine mis-

Mauro Forghieri was born in Modena in 1935, the son of Reclus Forghieri. Reclus was an outstanding toolmaker who worked with Alfa Romeo and Enzo Ferrari prior to World War II. He headed Ferrari's machine department after the war.

Mauro attended the University of Bologna and graduated in 1959 with a degree in engineering. He was eyeing a move to California, hoping to work in aircraft manufacturing and engineering with a firm such as Northrop when Enzo Ferrari called and offered a job. Forghieri accepted and began working for the company in 1960. He started in the engine department, performing calculations on the 1.5-liter engines and acting as liaison between chief engineer Carlo Chiti and the engine testing room.

In fall 1961, Forghieri suddenly found himself in the spotlight when Ferrari promoted him to chief engineer following the infamous Purge.

"There was no way I could have imagined that happening," Forghieri said about the mass firing that led to his promotion. "I was one of the few engineers remaining, so The Old Man offered me to take care of the racing. He made it very clear he was behind me one hundred percent." That gave the green-but-ambitious 20-something engineer the confidence he needed.

Forghieri became one of Ferrari's greatest engineers, the last of a breed that could design an entire car, rather than just a section or component. His résumé included many of the all-time greats, from final development work on the 250 GTO to masterminding Ferrari's midengine movement with the 250 P, 275 P, 330 P, 250 LM, and 330 P3, among others.

He remained at the forefront of the company's F1 efforts, and was involved in a number of world champions. The Dino 158 and 512 from 1964 were his, as was the innovative 312 T series that won four F1 constructors and three driver's titles in the second half of the 1970s. He then successfully guided Ferrari during the early years of the F1 Turbo era, his 126 C2 and C3 winning two constructors championships in the early 1980s.

Forghieri remained with Ferrari until 1987, then joined Lamborghini's fledgling competition department. He stayed for several years before forming his own firm, Oral Engineering.

Girolamo Gardini
1923-1994
Role in Ferrari History: The man who made Ferrari what it was in the marketplace

Ask most any die-hard Ferrari fan about Girolamo Gardini, and at best you'd get a raised eyebrow. But speak with insiders, such as Belgium importer Jacques Swaters and prominent client Count Giovanni Volpi, and they would unhesitatingly declare that it was Gardini who created the mystique around Ferrari by playing the market like a fiddle. Gardini was a master at building desire, orchestrating who would have to wait for a car, who would get it tomorrow, and who wouldn't get one at all.

He was born in 1923 in Modena, the only child of a small shop owner who sold grain. He joined Ferrari's Auto Avio Costruzioni company in 1942, working first in purchasing, then assuming administrative duties. He became the company's sales manager in 1950, keeping the role until his departure 11 years later. Gardini's philosophy on building the Ferrari mystique was simple: "The cars must be 'required,'" he told this author in 1994, "never 'offered.'" In other words, the purchaser went to Ferrari, not the other way around.

That philosophy worked like a charm, and had the era's most prestigious coachbuilders, and some of its most important automotive figures, lined up at Ferrari's door. Gardini recalled milestones such as the importance of the 166 Barchetta and how Henry Ford came calling, desiring one. Word filtered through the market that one of the world's most important industrialists had purchased a Ferrari.

Gardini also marveled at Carrozzeria Vignale's creativity and

its ability to "make a car in 20 days." And by his lights, it was the work of another coachbuilder that truly transformed Ferrari into a "modern" firm. "The true start of the Ferrari factory," he said, "was in 1958 when Pinin Farina built 100 cars that were the same."

Gardini played an instrumental role in the creation of the 250 GTO, but was ousted from Ferrari in 1961's Purge before final development was completed. Gardini was forever loyal to Ferrari, and the respect he had inside the firm caused a number of other managers to also get fired when they tried to convince Enzo to hire him back.

Luca Cordero di Montezemolo
1947-
Role in Ferrari History: F1 manager in 1970s, Ferrari savior in 1990s

If Webster's Dictionary ever needs a new definition for the word "charisma," its editors might simply have the entry read "The Marquis Luca Cordero di Montezemolo." Born in Bologna in 1947, Montezemolo studied law at the University of Rome, then continued at New York's Columbia University, where he specialized in International Commercial Law.

He briefly worked in a Rome-based law firm before being hired by Fiat in 1973. He quickly became Enzo Ferrari's assistant, and in 1975 was named manager of the Formula 1 team, bringing Ferrari its first driver's and constructors championships since 1964. Three more titles followed over the next two years.

In 1977, Montezemolo became the Fiat Group's Senior Vice President of External Relations, a position he held until 1981. After managing Itedi, a Fiat subsidiary that published the widely read *La Stampa* newspaper. The maker of wines and spirits, Cinzano, was his next stop. He also managed Italy's first entry in the America's Cup, and was director of the country's 1990 World Cup-winning soccer team.

Ferrari courted him in 1991 to become its CEO, and Montezemolo recognized what he was up against. As he recalled years later about the 348 model he had recently purchased, "I was utterly disappointed. This was the worst product Ferrari had developed for some time."

No sooner had he arrived than product quality improved dramatically, the 348 becoming an outstanding car. Ferrari went from one winning product to another under Montezemolo, first with the 456 GT, then the F355, and the 550 Maranello. Montezemolo's vision of product pushed boundaries, as the 360 Modena, F430, and the radical Enzo demonstrated.

He was equally active in Ferrari's competition operations. Montezemolo orchestrated the signing of driver Michael Schumacher, and made certain the right team surrounded him. The result was 1999-2004's unprecedented dominance of Formula 1.

His vision didn't stop there. His "Formula Uomo" concept transformed the company and its working environment, making the Ferrari facility into a beautiful, ecologically smart "small town" devoted to constructing cars of the highest technology.

In 2004 he was appointed head of Italy's powerful Confindustria business lobby. That same year he became Chairman of Fiat.

Battista & Sergio Pininfarina

Battista Pininfarina, 1893-1966
Sergio Pininfarina, 1926-
Role in Ferrari History: The design dynasty that gave Ferrari its enduring style

the start, Pinin put his son Sergio in charge of the Ferrari account. Then in his mid 20s, young Sergio had his hands full with a truculent Enzo Ferrari, but won over the great man with his engineering and design acumen, and his good nature, tenacity, and honesty.

Some of the world's most-beautiful and highest-performing automobiles resulted from the relationship between Ferrari and Sergio Pininfarina. But Sergio's role entailed more than handling the Ferrari account. Throughout the 1950s, he became more and more involved in the running of Pininfarina while maintaining a hand in its styling direction. When his father died 1966, Sergio was named the company's president.

In the second half of the 1970s, he was president of the Turin Industrialists' Union, and played an integral role in soothing the city's tumultuous business climate during the period. A worldwide ambassador for Italy, he was also elected to Europe's Parliament, among numerous other honors.

Sergio Scaglietti

1920-
Role in Ferrari History: Championship-winning coachbuilder, Enzo Ferrari confidant

Born Battista Farina, his nickname "Pinin" was local Turinese dialect for smallest of the family. That, however, did nothing to diminish the man's towering influence on the automotive world.

Pinin's career started in his teenage years at his brother Giovanni's coachbuilding firm, Stablimenti Industriali Farina S.A. Pinin's innate design abilities, social graces, and managerial skills saw him rapidly ascend, and by the 1920s he was visiting Ford in America, where he turned down a job offer. That trip taught Pinin much about mass-production techniques.

He left Stablimenti Farina in 1930 to start his own company, Carrozzeria Pinin Farina (the Pininfarina name officially became one word in 1961). The firm grew rapidly through the 1930s, and then especially during the immediate postwar years, with clients as diverse as Cadillac, Alfa Romeo, and Bentley. Pinin is widely regarded as the world's master of elegant automotive shapes, forms, and proportions, as exemplified by his revolutionary berlinetta of 1947, the Cisitalia 202.

That level of design caught the eye of Enzo Ferrari, and in 1952, Carrozzeria Pinin Farina began working with Ferrari. From

Sergio Scaglietti of Modena began his career in the automotive industry at age 13. His father had suddenly passed away, so Sergio's older brother lied about Sergio's age to get him a job at the carrozzeria that employed him. Sergio, who enjoyed working with his hands, became a quick study.

When Sergio was 17, his older brother and another employee formed their own coachbuilding company and took young Sergio with them. They set up shop in downtown Modena across the street from Enzo Ferrari's Scuderia Ferrari, and in a short time they were repairing the Scuderia's cars.

World War II interrupted further development of the relationship. In the years after the war, Ferrari was comfortable enough with Scaglietti's maturing talent that he frequently brought him crashed cars for repair.

Then in the early 1950s, a gentleman racer from Bologna commissioned Sergio to rebody his damaged Touring Barchetta. "Enzo Ferrari saw this and said 'That is not bad,'" Scaglietti remembered. "From this, he entrusted me with a new chassis."

By 1954, Scaglietti was a sanctioned Ferrari coachbuilder who received a number of chassis directly from the factory for coachwork. He designed all his shapes "by the eyes alone," he said, letting his own "good taste, understanding of aerodynamics, style, and function" dictate his designs.

Before long, the Ferraris emanating from the shop would be ranked among the most beautiful and memorable competition cars ever made. The honor roll included such top-flight sports-racing cars as the 500 Mondial and 500 TR and TRC, the classic pontoon-fender 250 Testa Rossa, the winning 290 MM, 315 and 335 S, and the immortal 250 GTO.

In the late 1950s, with Enzo Ferrari setting him up with the banker and cosigning the loan, Scaglietti greatly expanded his enterprise. He began building numerous street Ferraris to designs by Pinin Farina. His business prospered, and Scaglietti enjoyed the rewards and prosperity the expansion brought him.

In the late 1960s, however, with labor troubles a constant, Scaglietti leapt at the opportunity to join Ferrari in a sale of his business to Fiat. Scaglietti continued to manage the carrozzeria until his retirement in the mid 1980s. Ferrari's 612 Scaglietti model, and the Carrozzeria Scaglietti customization program, were named after the humble artisan.

Michael Schumacher

1969-

Role in Ferrari History: Six consecutive F1 constructors championships and five consecutive F1 World Driving Championships with Ferrari

Michael Schumacher was the face of Formula 1 racing as the sport grew to unprecedented worldwide popularity in the 1990s and early 2000s.

Going into the 2004 season, he had amassed more career victories, 82, and more World Championships, 7, than any driver in F1 history. He was by that season 35 years old, the "old man" of the circuit, but he remained its finest-conditioned athlete.

The most dominating driver in the annals of F1 was born near Cologne, Germany, in January 1969. His father managed a local karting track, and hand-built go-karts for Michael, who began competing at age four. Schumacher obtained his first competition license at age 12. As a teenager, he won numerous European karting championships. He graduated to Formula 3,

and won the F3 title at age 21. He was quickly hired by Mercedes-Benz to drive the World Endurance Championship Sauber-Mercedes.

Schumacher's F1 debut came in 1991, for Jordan; he qualified an impressive seventh for his first race, the Belgium Grand Prix, and finished the season 14th among 24 drivers in overall points. Benetton-Ford signed him for 1992. He had one win that year, but finished third in the driver's championship. His first World Championship came for Benetton-Ford in 1994; he repeated in '95. By the end of that season he had been in 31 F1 races, and had finished first 17 times.

Schumacher signed with Ferrari in 1996, finished a close second in driver's points in '97 and '98, and helped bring the constructors title to Maranello in 1999. In 2000, Ferrari and Schumacher began a string of five consecutive constructor and driver's championships.

Schumacher's success didn't come without a controversial "win at all costs" reputation, and he pushed more than one title competitor off the track. Away from F1, Schumacher was intensely private, though the nonracing world took notice in 2004 when he made a $10 million donation to tsunami relief.

Other Cars
with Engines
by Ferrari

The heart of any Cavallino is its engine, but over the years, that magic Maranello beat has thumped under the hood of a few cars that were not Ferraris.

1961-1966
ASA 1000 GT & 1000 GT Spider

In December 1959, Ferrari tantalized the automotive world by displaying an 850cc four-cylinder engine. Using heads quite similar to those found on his V-12s, Ferrari quoted the type 854's horsepower between 64 and 82, depending upon state of tune.

Following a successful series of bench tests, one engine was installed in a slightly modified Fiat 1200. Subsequently dubbed the Ferrarina (little Ferrari) by the press, rumors began flying that Ferrari was going to produce an inexpensive car.

The project met stiff resistance inside Ferrari. Former sales manager Girolamo Gardini recalled the Ferrarina being a nuisance, a product out of character with the company's elite image. Yet, with Enzo Ferrari firmly behind it, it would not die.

Ferrari hit pay dirt in 1961 when he sold the rights to produce and construct the car and engine to the owners of a large chemical-manufacturing concern in Milan. Prominent Ferrari client Oronzio De Nora and his son Niccolo called the company ASA (Autoconstruzioni S.A.), and the production prototype of the car was a far cry from the dowdy Ferrarina proposal.

It made its debut at 1961's Turin show, where it caused a sensation. *Motor* called it an "excellent example of elegance combined with compactness. *Road & Track* said, "The [show's] only headliner was to be found on the Bertone stand. This was the baby Ferrari...its clean shape proclaiming it to be the newest style of businessman's express."

The production version of the ASA 1000 GT went on sale in 1963. Under the clean Bertone coachwork was a tubular chassis, independent front suspension, and the Ferrari-designed 97-horsepower 1032cc four-cylinder engine.

The press loved the car. In a January 1963 *Sports Car Graphic* test, Bernard Cahier saw a top speed of 112 mph and found the "brilliant little car" had "superb road handling."

Despite refinement and impressive performance that belied its 1.0-liter capacity, the 1000 GT languished in the marketplace. It cost approximately 40 percent more in Italy than Alfa's larger-engined Giulia Sprint, and ASA simply couldn't translate good reviews into good revenue. Variations, including a beautiful 1000 GT Spider, didn't change the company's fortunes, and ASA quietly closed its doors in 1966.

ASA 1000 GT & 1000 GT SPIDER		
ASA 1000 GT 1961-1966 ASA 1000 GT SPIDER 1963-1966		
Number made:		
1000 GT:	50 (approx.)	
1000 GT Spider:	10 (approx.)	
Engine:	1032cc inline-4, SOHC, 97 hp @ 7000 rpm	
Transmission:	4-speed	
Wheelbase:	86.6 inches / 2200mm	
Weight:		
1000 GT:	1,719 lbs.	
1000 GT Spider:	1,716 lbs.	

1966-1973
Fiat Dino Spider & Coupe

In late 1964, Enzo Ferrari approached Fiat patriarch Gianni Agnelli about working together on a new engine. Behind the collaboration was a rule change in Formula 2 racing for 1967: To qualify an engine for the series, it had to be used in an automobile with a production run of at least 500 units. That sort of volume would be impossible for Ferrari to accomplish alone.

"A visit by [Fiat managing director Gaudenzio] Bono to Maranello made the contracts official and marked the start of full collaboration," Fiat chief engineer Dante Giacosa recalled in his autobiography, *Forty Years of Design with Fiat*. "[Vittorio] Valletta, Giovanni Agnelli and Bono thought it a good idea to accept Ferrari's proposal and made arrangements for the design of a sports car with the Dino engine."

And so was born Fiat's most prestigious model since the 8V of the 1950s. The first Fiat Dino, a spider designed by Pininfarina, broke cover at Turin in 1966. Several months later, at Geneva, Bertone presented a coupe. Both cars used a front-mounted Ferrari-designed 1987cc V-6 that produced 160 horsepower at 7200 rpm. The Dino's pressed steel chassis had a shorter wheelbase on the spider, an independent suspension up front, and a live axle in the rear. The gearbox was a five-speed, and brakes were discs. Top speed was listed at 130 mph.

Henry Manney was one of the few journalists to test the exclusive model; he drove the Spider. "The Dino is a real sports car," he wrote in *Road & Track*, "with lots of rasp from its... V-6. [It also has] a lovely 5-speed gearbox, supreme comfort for the driver, sleek Italian lines, and instruments for every contingency. Under way [it] felt...Ferrari-like in spite of the Fiat construction...."

An updated version of the car was introduced in 1969. The V-6 now displaced 2418cc and produced 180 horsepower. The five-speed ZF gearbox was new, and an independent suspension replaced the live axle in the rear. Assembly of the cars also moved from Turin to the Ferrari works in Maranello.

Production continued into January 1973, the popular Fiat vastly exceeding the original 500-unit requirement for F2. In total, 7,651 Dinos were made.

FIAT DINO SPIDER & FIAT DINO COUPE

FIAT DINO SPIDER 1966-1973
FIAT DINO COUPE 1967-1973

Number made:
Fiat DIno Spider: 1,583
Fiat Dino: 6,068

Engine: 1987cc V-6, DOHC,
160 hp @ 7200 rpm
2418cc V-6, DOHC,
180 hp @ 6600 rpm

Transmission: 5-speed

Wheelbase:
Fiat DIno Spider: 89.7 inches / 2280mm
Fiat Dino: 100.4 inches / 2550mm

Weight:
Fiat DIno Spider: 3,064-3,328 lbs.
Fiat Dino: 2,881-3,042 lbs.

1971-1975
Lancia Stratos

Fiat's Dino coupe and spider weren't the only cars to use Ferrari's V-6. Lancia's wild Stratos was a completely different animal that broke cover at 1970's Turin Motor Show as a Bertone concept car with a centrally mounted 1.6-liter inline-four.

Surprisingly, the only Lancia person who expressed interest at its raucous debut was the company's competition manager, Cesare Florio. That spark turned into a flame over the next 12 months when Nuccio Bertone drove the prototype to Lancia. Shortly after he parked at the company's factory, it quickly became apparent Lancia was interested in a small-series production, using it as the basis for a rallye car.

The result was the Stratos HF. Introduced at the 1971 Turin show, it was an incredibly compact car with a striking angular body and an overall length some 19 inches shorter than a 246 Dino. Supplementing the stiff steel monocoque center section were tubular steel frames front and rear. Suspension had coil springs and double wishbones up front, and a wishbone and radius arm in the rear. Power came from the centrally mounted 2.4-liter Ferrari V-6.

Incredibly, the Stratos was racing one year after the Turin debut, though it didn't finish either of the first two rallyes it started. Two former Ferrari personnel, engineer Gianpaolo Dallara and driver Mike Parkes were hired to right the situation, and the following year, the Stratos scored two victories. In 1974, it helped Lancia win the World Rallye Championship, a crown it won again in 1975 and 1976.

Production of roadgoing versions began in late 1974. These were among the quickest sports cars of the day, with a 140-mph top speed and capable of 0-60 mph in 6.8 seconds. But they demanded a patient, skilled driver.

"What's it like to drive a car like the Stratos?" asked *Autocar* in a 1975 road test. "The simple answer is that it is exhilaration and frustration at the same time. Exhilarating because the car responds so accurately to whatever input the driver gives, be that acceleration, braking or cornering. Frustrating in that the limits of adhesion are so high that only on a closed course can a newcomer…even begin to explore the outer limits of road-holding."

LANCIA STRATOS
1971-1975

Number made:	492
Engine:	2418cc V-6, DOHC, 192 hp @ 7000 rpm
Transmission:	5-speed
Wheelbase:	85.8 inches / 2180mm
Weight:	2,006 lbs.

1986-1991
Lancia Thema 8.32

Where Lancia's Stratos was a raw sports car born from rallying, its Thema 8.32 was a luxurious sedan. About all they had in common was that each had a Ferrari engine.

The Thema appeared in 1984, the result of a desire for a flagship sedan by four European marques: Lancia, its parent company Fiat, Alfa Romeo, and Saab. They pooled their resources to make a new platform that could be shared and adapted by each company.

The result was the Fiat Croma, Alfa 164, Saab 9000, and the Thema. The Thema marked Lancia's return to a more-exclusive market segment. As such, it had proper luxury amenities such as a full leather interior, heated seats, sunroof, and air conditioning. Power initially came from a variety of naturally aspirated, turbo, and diesel Lancia-speced engines.

With two oil crises and the economic and political strife of the late 1970s and early 1980s receding from Europe's collective memory, speed and ever-greater luxury came once again to the fore. Lancia's response was the Thema 8.32. Introduced in 1986, the model name referred to its use of the 2926cc V-8 (8-cylinders, 32 valves) from the Ferrari's midengine 308 quattrovalvole and Mondial.

Because the Thema was front-wheel drive, the transversely mounted V-8 slipped nicely into the sedan's engine compartment. The engine used a two-plane crank for better and smoother low speed performance. Though horsepower decreased to 215, from 240 in the Ferraris, torque remained 209 pound-feet at 4500 rpm. (Later "Series II" Themas had catalytic converters that dropped power output 10 hp.) Other mechanical changes included a beefed-up suspension with electronically controlled dampers, improved brakes, and a new ZF steering system.

The Thema 8.32 was distinguished from other Themas only by badging, a different grille, alloy wheels, and a trunklid spoiler that raised automatically when speed exceeded 80 mph. The interior had the finest woods on the dashboard, and finer leather than the standard models.

The 8.32 was a wolf in sheep's clothing, running 0-60 mph in the mid-7-second range, the quarter-mile in the mid 15s, and topping out just shy of 150 mph.

LANCIA THEMA 8.32		
1986-1991		
Number made:		
Series I:	2,370	
Series II:	1,167	
Engine:		
Series I:	2926cc V-8, DOHC,	
	215 hp @ 6750 rpm	
Series II:	2926cc V-8, DOHC,	
	205 hp @ 6750 rpm	
Transmission:	5-speed	
Wheelbase:	104.6 inches / 2660mm	
Weight:	3,100 lbs. (factory)	

Other Ferrari Models

Among the scores of different Ferraris produced over the years are these obscure or limited-volume road and sports-racing models.

1950 195 SPORT A Touring-bodied berlinetta that was the only one to use a 2431cc V-12; looks identical to the 166 MM touring-bodied berlinettas.

1950 275 SPORT As with the 195 Sport, this was also a special touring-bodied model that used a 3322cc V-12; two were made.

1952 225 EXPORT A unique 212 Export that used a 2715cc V-12 in place of the standard 2562cc engine; one made.

1953 625 TF Ferrari's first four-cylinder car was a Series II 166 MM that used a Lampredi-designed 2.5-liter grand prix engine; three were made, all with Vignale coachwork.

1953 735 SPORT Two were made, Lampredi's four-cylinder engine enlarged to 3.0-liters

1955 857 SPORT The precursor to the 860 Monza, the Scaglietti-bodied 857 S used a 3432cc inline-four that derived from the 750 Monza; three were made and they raced with some success in 1955-56.

1956 625 LM This 2.5-liter 500 TR-derived machine used a 3.5-liter inline-four and was the last Ferrari to use Carrozzeria Touring coachwork. The lines were similar to those done by Scaglietti, and just three were made.

1958 412 MI Similar in appearance to the TR58, the 412 MI used an experimental one-off four-cam 4.0-liter V-12. Just one was made.

1959 196 SPORT DINO A front-engine V-6 endurance-racer with Farntuzzi coachwork that looked similar to the enclosed TR 59. Engine was 1984cc; just one was made.

1959-1960 246 SPORT DINO This front-engine sports-racer used a 2417cc V-6 and looked like a TR 60. Two were made, one placing second overall at 1960's Targa Florio.

1975-1982 208 Because of the high price of gas and Italian taxation on cars with engines larger than 2.0-liters, Ferrari built a series of 308s with a 1991cc V-8. They are almost identical in appearance to their 3.0-liter brethren, and production numbers were 840 GT4, 160 GTB, 140 GTS.

1978-1985 308 GTB MICHELOTTO In the late 1970s and first half of the 1980s, talented mechanic and prototype builder Giuliano Michelotto of Padova had close factory cooperation while building a series of 15 308 GTBs for competition—11 for Group 4, four for Group B rallying.

1980 PININ This factory-sanctioned Ferrari sedan was made by Pininfarina to commemorate the coachbuilder's 50th anniversary. It used a 5.0-liter flat-12 engine, and to Sergio Pininfarina's disappointment, the model remained a one-off.

1982-1985 208 TURBO The 208 GTB & GTS Turbo used a turbocharged version of the 1991cc V-8 with a claimed 220 horsepower. GTB production was 437, GTS production 250.

1985-1986 308 GT/M That last of the Michelotto 308s was the radical 370 horsepower GT/M. Its coachwork looked quite similar to the 288 GTO Evoluzione; three were made.

1985/1986 328 SPIDER Sergio Scaglietti made this one-off as a proposal for a completely open 328. It was one of the last two Ferraris done by the great coachbuilder.

1986-1989 GTB & GTS TURBO These two models continued Ferrari's use of the 1991cc V-8 in the 328 series. The engine produced a quoted 254 horsepower, and production was 308 GTB, 828 GTS.

1988 3.2 PPG PACE CAR This Mondial-based one-off had styling by the IDEA Institute in Turin, and used a longitudinally mounted V-8, as seen in the Mondial t and 348. PPG was a sponsor of Indy Car racing, and planned to use it as a pace car for the series.

1988 408 Made in conjunction with Alcan Automotive Structures of Montreal, the four-wheel-drive midengine 408 used that company's Aluminum Structured Vehicle Technology (AVST) that featured advanced technologies, such as an adhesively bonded folded-aluminum box-section structure. Two were made.

1991-1992 348 ZAGATO In the early 1990s, Carrozzeria Zagato modified the coachwork of the 348 for a client and in many ways predicted the look of the 355. According to Zagato, fewer than 10 were built.

1995-1996 456 "VENICE" SERIES In the mid-1990s the Brunei royal family commissioned a large number of unique cars, including several Ferrari models. The "Venice" series started with the 456, then Pininfarina received factory sanctioning to modify them into a cabriolet, sedan, and four-door station wagon. All were superb in finish, engineering, and design, each variant made in a series of just six.

1996 FX Brunei's royal family also commissioned a radical redo of the F512M. The result was the FX, which featured carbon-fiber coachwork, paddle-shift technology prior to its introduction in the 355, and a startling shape. A series of six was built.

1996-1997 550 MARANELLO SPIDER The last Ferrari Brunei's royal family commissioned was the lovely 550 Spider. Unlike the 550 Barchetta, the 550 Spider had a proper windscreen and retractable top that folded into the trunk as seen on Mercedes' SL. Only one was made.

1996-1997 F50 GT Based on the F50, the F50 GT weighed less than 2,000 pounds and was built to compete at Le Mans. It complied with all FIA regulations, but at the last minute, Ferrari halted production. Subcontractor Gian Paolo Dallara built only three.

Index